S0-CDR-385

Toy Trains

Trains at Skinner Christmas 1989 Toys & Dolls Auction: Bing HO gauge engines, left, foreground, $275; Fleischmann boxed wind-up set, 1950s, HO, $130; Hornby boxed TS 401 clockwork set(4), $176; Carlisle & Fitch painted tin and wood set, 1905, fly-wheel driven, $660. (Photo courtesy of Skinner Auctions)

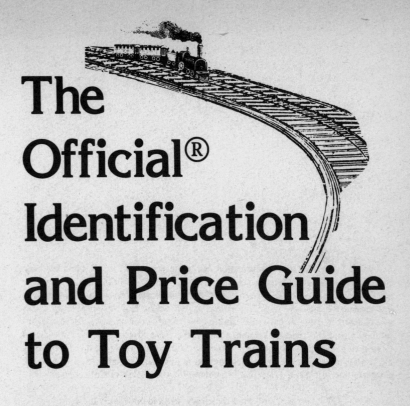

The Official® Identification and Price Guide to Toy Trains

RICHARD FRIZ

FIRST EDITION

HOUSE OF COLLECTIBLES · NEW YORK

Important Notice. All of the information, including valuations, in this book has been compiled from the most reliable sources, and every effort has been made to eliminate errors and questionable data. Nevertheless, the possibility of error, in a work of such immense scope, always exists. The publisher will not be held responsible for losses which may occur in the purchase, sale, or other transaction of items because of information contained herein. Readers who feel they have discovered errors are invited to *write* and inform us, so they may be corrected in subsequent editions. Those seeking further information on the topics covered in this book are advised to refer to the complete line of *Official Price Guides* published by the House of Collectibles.

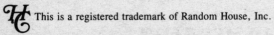 This is a registered trademark of Random House, Inc.

© 1990 by Richard Friz

All rights reserved under International and Pan-American Copyright Conventions.

Published by: The House of Collectibles
201 East 50th Street
New York, New York 10022

Distributed by Ballantine Books, a division of Random House, Inc., New York, and simultaneously in Canada by Random House of Canada Limited, Toronto.

Manufactured in the United States of America

ISBN: 0-876-37804-1

First Edition: October 1990

10 9 8 7 6 5 4 3 2 1

*To my wife Madaline,
who takes pictures with a caring "eye"
despite being a noncollector.*

Table of Contents

Acknowledgments

For their invaluable assistance, I would like to extend my gratitude and appreciation to the following for availing themselves of their auction and sales catalogs: Dana Hawkes, Collectibles Department, Sotheby's, New York; Lloyd Ralston Toys, Fairfield, Connecticut; Ted Maurer, Pottstown, Pennsylvania; Dr. Bruce Greenberg of Greenberg's Auctions, Sykesville, Maryland; Rich Opfer, Timonium, Maryland; Phillips, New York City, New York; Skinner Auctions, Bolton, Massachusetts; Christie's East, New York; and Alex Acevedo of Alexander Gallery, New York City. Many of these auction houses also provided us with photographs and other background material. For allowing us to photograph examples from his vast prewar collection, a special thanks to Carl Wiley of Peterborough, New Hampshire. To Dick Christianson, editor of *Classic Toy Trains*, we'd like to acknowledge his cooperation in helping us with photographs and good solid information from that excellent fledgling magazine. And above all, thanks to my wife Madaline who handled much of the on-site photography, and son Josh, lighting man extraordinaire.

On
Track

The Prices in This Book

Values in this guide are based on prices gleaned from a number of major train meets over the past few years, in addition to mail-order prices and prices at retail outlets.

Although the train market tends to be more stable and less volatile than the toys, dolls, and games market, there is always the possibility that prices for certain high-end items may be quickly outdated. Let us state categorically, here and now, that in buying *or* selling, particularly with items normally ranging in four figures and higher, make certain you consult with fellow collectors or an acknowledged authority on trains before you make the transaction.

In *selling* an item to a dealer, keep in mind that he has to factor in his overhead. This means you can expect guided prices listed in these pages to shrink by up to 50%.

We also have included recent prices at auction. Unfortunately these prices do not always reflect such variables as condition of the train, rarity, the prestige of having come from a major collection or even the phase of the moon. Coupled with price estimates, however, we feel it will give you a more accurate assessment of the value of a given item.

Unlike certain guides which have graduated value ratings of examples in good, very good, and sometimes even mint condition, we offer a price *range* that a train in mint condition might bring. This allows for such variables as to whether the piece may be sold at shows and meets vs. at auction. These prices will, in all probability, reflect values that are somewhat higher than in other price guides for trains.

How to Use This Guide

All trains and accessories are grouped alphabetically beginning with *Electric Trains*. In this largest classification, the groupings are further broken down alphabetically by manufacturer, beginning with "American Flyer" and continuing through "Marx Trains." The next classification, *Specialty Trains*, begins with "Cartoon/Character Novelty Train Sets and Hand Cars" and ends with "Wooden Lithographed and Painted Floor Trains."

As there are so many variables that combine to determine price, including condition, rarity, and desirability, we're allowing ourselves some latitude by giving a generous range on each specific listing. As often as possible, in the *Electric Trains* section, we will include a manufacturer's catalog number and actual production date. Keep in mind that this is probably the most specialized of all collecting pursuits, and our attempt is to provide a comprehensive overview. For those who seek in-depth information on various manufacturers, we recommend a number of excellent publications and books which are listed at the end of this guide.

Grading Model Trains

Whether one collects baseball cards, vintage automobiles, guns, fine art, or model trains, there is always one common denominator that profoundly affects the value of those objects—*condition*. It has become increasingly obvious in auctions, shows, and swap meets that dealers and collectors alike are becoming more and more discriminating; rigid grading standards are being set by various collecting organizations.

The following is a grading scale that should prove helpful in future transactions.

Mint—In "as new" condition; virtually unmarred; complete and fully operable; in original box. (10 points)

Like New—Between excellent and mint; may have minor paint or lithograph wear; but 98%-plus is as near as most train sets get. (8–9 points)

Fine—Barely perceptible scratches or nicks; no dents, rust or fading. 90% intact. (6–8 points)

Good—Average condition with 70% of all requisite finish. (4–6 points)

Fair—Well worn; possibly dented; paint fading; rust; with approximately 50% paint coverage. (2–4 points)

Poor—Example has less than 30% paint; past redemption. (0–2 points)

Any train example in only *fair* or *poor* condition we recommend passing up, unless it is an extreme rarity or perhaps even unique.

The hobby also has another grading classification and that is *Restored*. This can be defined as any example professionally refinished with a color that approximates the original train and has been brought back into an operable stage.

We must point out that there are passive train collectors who are not remotely concerned about operating their trains but emphasize displayability and are sticklers for flawless appearance.

Conversely, many model train operators are not as fussy about aesthetics as long as their train sets stay fine-tuned in working condition. There is far less of a stigma over repaints and modified examples in the train operator's roundhouse than in other toy categories such as mechanical banks, games, or dolls.

The value of the train set or individual car being accompanied by its original box, however, carries equal weight in this hobby as with other toy classifications. We've noted that examples *with* the box command a premium of at least 20% or higher.

Model Railway
Market Overview

When Citibank Center in New York City opened its first annual Christmas holiday model railway exhibition to the public last year, they anticipated perhaps 25,000 to 30,000 visitors. By the time the remarkable panorama of mid-Manhattan, the Hudson River Valley, and the old New York Central terminal in Weehawken, New Jersey, along with vintage Lionels and American Flyers, was closed to the public four weeks later, nearly 125,000 enthusiasts had passed through the 32-ft.-high Victorian structure called Citibank Station.

There's no question about it, the bloom is back on the romance of model railroading. Sidetracked by several generations of slot cars, video games, and other electronic gadgetry, an entire subculture of railroading fanatics has resurfaced in the 1980s. In the United States alone, trains have become serious business for several hundred thousand hobbyists (some observers estimate as high as a half million). Sales of model trains are now running in the millions; Lionel alone boasts annual sales of a million sets and climbing!

To get some feel as to the intensity and fervor of those who ride the rails, one can attend any of a number of regional swap meets and shows or the semiannual national T.C.A. (Train Collectors of America) conventions at York, Pennsylvania. Here at York over

Lionel New Haven R.R. streamliner diesel with array of oversize Pullmans and observation cars at Greenberg Train Show.

7,000 attendees in four cavernous state fair buildings buy and sell at 1,600 tables chock-a-block with engines, rolling stock, model kits, accessories, "how-to" books, and videotapes.

While there is considerable crossover between various subcategories in the hobby, a natural division exists between the collectors and the scale modelers. A collector may prefer his prizes mint in their original box and never so much as take them off the shelf. A collector may also be a scale modeler but rarely vice versa. Modelers are more inclined to create their own miniature replicas from scratch or from model kits. They might spend years perfecting elaborate layouts and then immersing themselves in the complexities of operating their railway. Their bible is *Model Railroader*, a magazine with a circulation of nearly 200,000, or *Railroad Model Craftsman* (see "Train Collector Publications" in the *Resources* section of this book).

The Greenberg Great Train, Dollhouse, and Toy Show at the Philadelphia Civic Center hosts hundreds of exhibitors, and at least 90% specialized in post–World War II or current production trains (primarily low-priced plastic models and kits).

There were books and videotapes dedicated to just about every major U.S. train manufacturer. When a dealer in trains of the more vintage variety was asked if there was anything available from European makers, such as Märklin, Bing, Fleischmann, etc., she replied that her husband tended to become confused by German names and terminology and consequently did not stock them. One of the hobby's head honchos, publisher/promotor Bruce Greenberg, however, indicated that there is considerable interest in overseas manufacturers. *Greenberg's Guide to LGB Trains, Fleischmann HO, Märklin HO*, and *Z Train Guides* have all recently been published.

While collectors with pronounced preferences for vintage and/or prewar examples (anything from the late 19th century to World War II) are vastly outnumbered by modelers, *they* are the "highrollers" who have sent prices into orbit in recent years.* The following train categories reflect the most intensified activity among dealers and collectors at major auctions, shows, and exhibitions.

Vintage Steamers

High on the list among vintage train enthusiasts, as well as crossover collectors of scientific toys, are the brass steam trains that hark back to the mid-1840s. These earliest versions, almost always minus a cab, were by far the most advanced and most expensive toys of their day. The firm of Eugene Beggs of Patterson, New Jersey, for example, offered sets with price tags from $10 to $30 at a time when $1 was a pretty fair day's wage. For nearly 30 years, the Beggs sets and later sets by Garlick, a former Beggs associate, typified the best available in U.S. toy trains. Unfortunately, not many Beggs and Garlick steamers have survived; when an example surfaces, it is likely to go in the $2,000 to $3,000 range. Beginning in 1888, William Weeden of New Bedford, Massachusetts, introduced a lower priced version, the "Dart." This 2-in.-gauge beauty is avidly pursued by collectors, as it represents

---

*In 1987, *Classic Toy Trains*, a new magazine focusing on this more esoteric adjunct, sold out all 35,000 copies of its premier issue. A year later, the magazine had already surpassed 45,000 circulation and switched from a quarterly to a bi-monthly.

perhaps the finest example from the 19th century in terms of accuracy of scale and detail down to the last rivet. Although thousands of the popular "Dart" were produced, a fine specimen today commands four-figure prices.

Of lesser interest to U.S. train buffs, but more highly prized on the Continent, are steamers from the French maker Radiguet & Massiot of Paris (which show less detail but have an undeniable charm); also the countless German designs from the 1880s, first by Schönner and Plank and soon followed by Bing, Doll, Carette, and Märklin.

In Great Britain, the birthplace of the railway, the major producers of steamers were Stevens Model Dockyard, Whitneys', Newton & Co., John Theobald, Lucas & Davies (all of London), plus Clyde Model Dockyard of Glasgow and Jones & Co., Manchester. Many British makers produced steamers up through the 1920s; prolific but also prosaic, they appeared reluctant to model anything but those based on prototypes that had been running for 40 or 50 years. Rarely did the engine come with a tender. A sterling exception, the Newton 2-2-2, ca. 1890s, is known to bring $4,000–$5,000 on today's market.

Other favorites include the Gebruder Bing 4-2-0 storkleg engine, "No. 17528" (Bing was the first to number its trains), ca. 1885, in the elusive gauge 4.* This example appeared in a popular 1970 movie, *The Railway Children*, and blew up in grand style. The fact that blowing up was also a real-life possibility may account for the "17528's" ultimate rarity and five-figure price tag. A ca. 1875 Schönner live steamer train set sold at $6,050 at Sotheby's in June 1989.

Not all the more coveted steamers bear 19th-century lineages, however. Eminent New York City toy impresario Alex Acevedo featured a superb Aster "Big Boy" in $1/32$ scale, produced in the early 1940s, in his Christmas catalog last year. At $10,500, this finely articulated miniature ranks among the most expensive stocking stuffers of any Yule season.

---

*Another Bing gem, which Acevedo acquired from a Paris collector, a mint 1905 set of two coaches, three freight cars, a steam locomotive pinstriped in gray, and a tender; sold recently for $18,000.

Collectors seeking a viable alternative to technically precise, but "cold," scale models in vogue today could well find it in the period charm of 19th-century live steam fantasies.

Painted Tin Clockwork Trains

As with the early live steam floor trains, painted and stencilled clockwork tin trains from the 1860s to 1890s featured exaggerated smokestacks, cowcatchers, bells, and cabs. Any resemblance to real-life prototypes was strictly accidental.

Stencilled eagles, garlands, and other filigree appeared in gilt along with patriotic and allegorical names (i.e., "America," "Excelsior," "Pegasus," "Comet," "Vulcan," "Gen. Grant," "Venus," and "Union"). They were crafted by the Connecticut clock-making firms of Ives, George Brown, Stevens & Brown, Merriam, and Hull & Stafford, and by two Philadelphia makers, Fallows and Francis Field & Francis.

Painted tin clockwork trains are often disparaged by modelers as being mere dalliances. You're less likely to find prime examples at train meets as opposed to toy and folk art shows and exhibitions.

These whimsical fragile specimens are not prone to surface every day. When they do appear, as was the case with the Atlanta Toy Museum Auction in 1986 and the Perelman Museum Sale in 1988, sparks usually fly.

At the Perelman "Great Grab of '88" in Philadelphia, for example, a George Brown "Excelsior" sold at $16,500; an "America" by James Fallows, $3,000; an "Omnibus" clockwork railroad, $20,000; a "Whistler" by Ives, $18,500; and the Fallows oversized train set "Warrior," $15,000.

Among vintage tin train specialists, the real coup is to "fill out" a given set, such as the Althof Bergman "Union" locomotive, for instance. When many firms introduced a new train in their catalog, as did George Brown in the 1870s, they would soon follow suit with other sizes of the same model, should it prove popular. Thus, a medium size (the first introduced) often inspired a medium fine, large fine, and small spinoff. Just as in poker, "four of a kind" go for high stakes indeed.

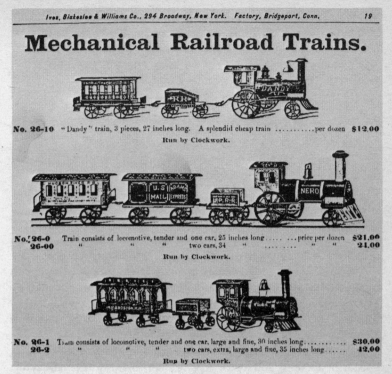

Mechanical Railroad Trains.

No. 26-10 "Dandy" train, 3 pieces, 27 inches long. A splendid cheap train ....per dozen **$12.00**

Run by Clockwork.

No. 26-0 Train consists of locomotive, tender and one car, 25 inches long ....price per dozen **$21.00**
26-00 " " " two cars, 34 " .... " " **21.00**

Run by Clockwork.

No. 26-1 Train consists of locomotive, tender and one car, large and fine, 30 inches long........... **$30.00**
26-2 " " " two cars, extra, large and fine, 35 inches long...... **42.00**

Run by Clockwork.

Ives painted tin clockwork train sets, 1890s, $1,500–$2,000.

In charting auction prices of 19th-century tin trains, there are all kinds of fluctuations. Invariably, this is due to the condition of the specimen: flaking paint or a missing stack or bell can mean a drastic reduction in price, more so than with any *other* train collecting category. Also worth noting: despite the fact that European makers (i.e., Emile Favre and Charles Rossignol in France, Märklin, Bing, and Carette in Germany) all produced superb tin clockwork trains, collectors on these shores remain staunchly pro-American.

According to Jack Herbert in an article titled "Trackless Toy Trains,"* George Brown's toy designer had had just a "wee taste"

*Antique Toy World, October 1989.

before he sat down at his drafting board to create the 1870's tinplate "Red Bird," as everything appears "enchantingly out of proportion." Selling at $2,000 at the Perelman Museum Sale in 1988, here's another example of a classic train commanding a price that sends collectors reeling as we move into the '90s.

Cast-Iron Floor Trains

Ives, Blakeslee & Williams, one of the first and foremost cast-iron train makers, patented their maiden locomotive with a clockwork mechanism in 1884. Cast-iron versions were mass produced by countless toy manufacturers, almost exclusively American, with the English firm of Wallworks being an exception. The trains covered a vast spectrum in quality and design from the 1880s through the 1930s. The 19th century is clearly where the action is.

At least several dozen major manufacturers produced cast-iron trains. Collectors are particularly enamored with those created by Secor, Ives, Hubley (with its single- and double-track "Elevated Railway" variations), Carpenter, Pratt & Letchworth, and Wilkins.

This market is intensely specialized and ultimate rarities seldom appear in auctions and sales. A Hawaiian cast-iron train collector, perhaps the most dominant in the hobby, is planning a definitive book on the subject.

Assembling an all-star lineup of cast-iron classics, ultimate rarities aside, may still be accomplished without too steep a bankroll, but prices around the bend in the 1990s are destined to accelerate.

Lithographed Paper-on-Wood Floor Trains

Conceivably the most aesthetically appealing of all vintage floor trains is the relatively small but selective category of lithographed paper-on-wood. Here you'll find intense crossover activity from far afield which may be completely unrelated to any fascination with railroads.

An example: the R. Bliss "Lincoln Park Railroad" ($1,200–$1,500) commemorates a specific event, the World's Columbian

Exposition of 1893, thus bringing expo specialists into the chase. Similarly, circus collectors covet the Bliss "Barnum Circus" train set, ca. 1895. The Bliss "Brownie Picnic Train" has allure for Palmer Cox fans as well as those who choose to document the golden age of chromlithography with examples by leading illustrators of the period.

Wooden models of legendary prototype trains of yesteryear (i.e., Atlantic & Pacific R.R. "Hercules," ca. 1895, by Milton Bradley or W.S. Reed's "America" locomotive and Palace Car, ca. 1877) are particularly desirable. They command upwards of four figures on those rare occasions when examples surface in pristine condition.

R. Bliss, Milton Bradley, McLoughlin Brothers, W.S. Reed Toy Co., and Morton Converse not only manufactured lithographed paper-on-wood or pasteboard floor trains, but train puzzles, building blocks (which often were included with the train sets and stored flat in the coaches), and train board games in handsome lithographed boxes as well. Such items have belatedly gained newfound respectability. The popularity of litho-on-wood floor trains into the 1990s will be tempered only by the scarcity or survival rate of these fragile playthings.

Electric Trains

Electric trains, after you exclude scale models fashioned from kits and scratch-builts, both of which are another ball game, are considered to have the greatest collectible potential by the largest segment of rail fans. This market tends to be less volatile than 19th-century tin, lithographed wood, or cast-iron categories, however, and you seldom see dramatic upswings in prices at auctions or swap meets.

By the same token, more post–World War II model trains command four-figure prices today than any other contemporary toy category; only a handful of 1950s battery-operated robots and space toys have escalated in value in so short a time.

The old adage "what goes around, comes around" certainly applies to electric trains. On one extreme, the oversized muscular Standard-gauge trains of the 1920s and 1930s, which many regard as "the golden era," were upstaged following the Depression by smaller, less expensive, starkly realistic O-gauge models. In the post–World War II decade, miniaturization made even deeper inroads in popularity as first HO (or OO), then Märklin's Z gauge and Arnold's N gauge entered the picture. In the 1980s, while there was still a tremendous market for smaller scale, we saw harbingers of a renewal of big train enthusiasm—most notably with Lehmann Gross Bahn's contemporary G scale, known as "Big Trains." There is also a strong market for such oversized classics from the 1920s and 1930s as American Flyer's 1928 "President's Special," Ives long cab "Olympian" set, and Lionel's "Blue Comet" Model 390E (the first version, which emerged in 1930, boasted a 3-ft.-long locomotive!).

Collectors on these shores show a marked preference for the big four among U.S. train manufacturers: American Flyer, Ives, Marx, and Lionel. Although its train-making days were short lived, we should also add Dorfan, with its powerful die-cast locomotives. These sets are not known to have a high survival rate; examples still found in good condition bring premium prices.

A fierce but friendly rivalry exists among specialists in any of the above manufacturing categories. Political columnist George Will, an avid American Flyer collector, once joked that those who enjoyed his favorite line "were precocious and discerning . . . while children who embraced Lionelism had dark pasts and dangerous futures."*

While European makers (i.e., Märklin, Bing, Carette, Fischer, Rossignol, and Burnett) have been known to produce exquisite, precisely detailed trains over the years, U.S. rail fans remain fiercely loyal to their own.

In addition to the obvious success story of Lehmann Gross Bahn's G-model trains in the United States, there are other signs at auctions and exhibitions that our once frigid reception to imports is beginning to thaw. This is particularly true of crossover collectors, many with strong preferences for Carette, Bing, and Märklin, whether the collection be toy boats, automobiles, train sets, or any transportation specialty.

*From "Trains/Railroading For Grown-up Boys" by Don Fernandez, *The Encyclopedia of Collectibles*, Time-Life Books, 1980.

AUCTION PREVIEW
Sotheby Parke Bernet
London, May 29, 1984

Antique Toy World *ad for record-breaking Märklin "Rocket" with Märklin catalog listing from 1909–1912. Ultimate rarity sold for £28,050, approximately $39,000.*

The record at this writing for a toy train at auction goes to a Märklin tinplated model of a 19th-century steam-fired "Stevenson's Rocket," produced as a set in 1909, which includes a locomotive, tender, open passenger coach, and luggage car. It happened at Sotheby's London in 1984 with New York dealer Alex Acevedo as top bidder at $39,270. Subsequently, Acevedo resold this star offering at $60,000.

Another Märklin ultimate rarity, a rather awkward-appearing oddity, is the "Armored Train" set from 1904. It was inspired by a prototype used in the Boer War. This six-car set, which is said to have been produced in very limited quantity in gauge O, I, II, and possibly III, was rated in the $3,000-plus range in 1986. Today's asking price is more likely to hover between $50,000 to $60,000. At least that is what one might expect to pay at such leading emporiums as Alex Acevedo's Alexander Gallery in Manhattan or Jeffrey Levitt's Mint & Boxed in London.

To dispel any notion that train collecting is strictly a hobby for millionaire playboys, we hasten to add that many prewar Marx and Lionel cars, and even sets, are often available for well under $100 (many sell today for little more than their original outlay). Miniature 4-6-4 steam engines still crop up in the $100 range, with

Märklin "Armored Train," 1904; an open car for Boer War soldiers and a cannon car (not shown) make up complete set. Priced today in the $50,000-plus bracket.

some 2-4-2's priced as nominally as $50. Superb brass HO locomotives from Japan and other Far Eastern imports offer still another alternative for the budget-conscious rail fan. One of the attractions of train collecting is the fact that it can be approached from many different levels.

We feel it is stimulating to mention and illustrate, when possible, some of the classic beauties that have set the standards in collectibility over the years. Many, of course, have reached prices beyond our comprehension or ability to afford. The important thing to remember is that most train collections are made up primarily of good strong examples of considerable appeal, yet modestly priced.

A growing number of collectors contend that rarity alone, or the fact that a particular model proved to be so oddball or unpopular when introduced that the manufacturer hastily withdrew it from production, qualify that example for one prize list only—the booby prize. Ultimately, the valued model trains as we enter a new decade will be those that meet the *true* test in performance, precise detail, aesthetics, construction, and size.

David Lander, in the December 1988 *Popular Mechanics*,* points out that it's a good bet Digital HO models recently produced by Märklin already are collectors' items. In "Trains/Railroading for Grown-up Boys,"** Don Fernandez states that age is not directly indicative of value, adding that because there are more col-

*From "Treasure Trains."

**The Encyclopedia of Collectibles, Time-Life Books, 1980.

lectors who want a plastic engine such as the (Lionel) 1959 "Great Northern No. 58 Snowplow," it is worth perhaps 10 cast-iron electric engines made by Gebruder Bing in the 1920s.

Top Trains on the Value Scale

In canvassing a number of train authorities, the following is a consensus pick of the elite classics of bygone years which will continue to command rarefied prices into the 1990s.

- 1901 Baltimore & Ohio No. 5, Lionel's first electric locomotive; also the first to be modeled after a real-life engine.
- Chicago, Milwaukee, St. Paul & Pacific "Olympian" long cab design by Ives, produced by American Flyer and Lionel in the 1930s after Ives went into bankruptcy. The 381E Olympian was one of the most elaborate locomotives Lionel ever produced.
- 1928 "President's Special" by American Flyer; handsomely detailed down to a figural wingspread eagle fronting the observation car; sparkling blue, red, and gold finish.
- Lionel "State" set, Standard gauge, 1930s; pairs any one of three different engines with four passenger cars named after the states of New York, Illinois, Colorado, and California. This combination has topped-off as high as $8,000 at auction.
- "Hiawatha" Milwaukee Road, by American Flyer, 1936; the snazziest of their advanced die-cast short steel streamliners. The last great gasp by American Flyer before its mid-'30s demise. ($1,200–$1,500)
- "Hudson" New York Central by Lionel, 1937; Lionel's first O fine scale model locomotive with matching freight cars in 4-6-4 configuration. A "Hudson" in unassembled kit form from 1938 is even more highly esteemed. In 1987, Lionel Trains, Inc., as a daring marketing strategy, offered a reproduction "Hudson" set including eight Standard O freight cars via direct mail. Very few collectors responded at the time, but the limited-run set now rates as one of the "hottest" of the postwar collectibles.

- Lehmann Gross Bahn's "100th Anniversary Set," 1981; this brawny G-scale version has appreciated 10–15 times in value since the day it was introduced.
- "Blue Comet" Model 390E, 1930, by Lionel; desired for its size, copper and brass trim, and distinctive blue color, a cheerful departure from the standard black. Largest steam locomotive Lionel ever made.
- "Lady Lionel" pink set from the late 1950s; featured white and gold transformer and rainbow-hued coaches, but the concept fizzled. Brief production run helped propel it to $600–$800 range.
- Lionel "Boy's Set," 1955; limited number of sets were produced (only four known); each car finished in color that sets it apart from any known Lionel production model. An example from the Vendetti collection brought $23,000 at Greenberg's November 12, 1988, auction.
- Dorfan No. 3930 locomotive with five freight cars, late 1920s, large Standard gauge; a set sold recently at a Ted Maurer Auction in Pottstown, Pennsylvania, for $1,000.
- "Commodore Vanderbilt" New York Central engine and tender, Märklin, 1938; matte black and streamline design (only eight were made); from the Count Antonio Giansanti Coluzzi collection; was offered at $50,000 in 1987 by New York dealer Alex Acevedo.
- Ives No. 3243 locomotive with buffet, parlor car, and observation cars. Special edition "White Set" was produced between 1922 and 1927 and limited to a few hundred examples. Offered in dealer Alex Acevedo's Christmas 1988 catalog at $9,500.
- Lionel No. 2625 "Irvington" O-gauge passenger car (1946–1949) in a highly uncommon green finish variant; can go for thousands of dollars, but almost never surfaces in a public sale. (An Irvington car in the common tuscan color is valued in the $100–$150 range.)
- "Transcontinental Limited" No. 3273 locomotive with 187, 188, 189 brass plate cars by Ives, 1920s. Brought $3,000 at March 1989 Ted Maurer Auction.

- Gilbert's American Flyer GP7 "Geep" No. 370, 1950–1954. One of American Flyer's S-gauge post–World War II successes. Modeled after one of the most important locomotive prototypes in recent railroad history. Originally in silver, blue, and yellow, but a later GP7 favorite had a black and "swamp holly orange" color scheme (a Texas and Pacific beauty).
- Ives No. 3240 electric, 1912; its first gauge-1 electrified set, with magnificent cast-iron locomotive. ($2,000–$3,000)
- "Pocahontas" American Flyer set, 1928; with wide-gauge bi-polar locomotive; generous-sized coaches. ($1,000–$1,500)
- Ives "Circus Train" set with No. 1134 locomotive and six cars including wild animal car and performers' Pullman; early 1930s; colorful set brought $5,750 at Ted Maurer Auction recently.
- "Santa Fe" twin diesel streamliner by Lionel, 1953; not uncommon, but eagerly pursued, this was a Lionel all-time best seller; in attractive bright silver and red finish.
- "Lionel 381 E," 1928; an underpowered 12-wheeled behemoth, hurriedly withdrawn for a twin engine Model 402. At one time, the 381 E brought big bucks, but an excellent Williams reproduction has downscaled value.
- "City of Portland" Union Pacific streamliner by Lionel, 1941–1943; first model released after Lionel's design office had been transferred from Italy back to the United States; its sales success moved Lionel back into solvency. Affectionately dubbed the "Banana" because of yellow finish.
- "Joy Line 350" by Marx, 1927–1930; along with "351" tender; one of the last of Marx's keywinds, with red and blue body and lithographed engineer; was one of the most popular of low-end value sets.
- Ives "Prosperity Special," 1929; No. 1134 R steam-type locomotive with 241-242-243 passenger cars, finished in copper and nickel; intended to celebrate the close of a golden decade, but had only a brief production run. An example sold at $12,000 in Ted Maurer's March 24, 1989, auction.

Collecting Train Catalogs: A Diverting Spinoff

The structured, often muddled world of model train production brings with it the need for a substantial backlog of explanatory literature.

Since the hobby relies so heavily on identification through catalog numbers, the catalog itself proves to be one of the most reliable sources of tracking down all known model/sets and subvarieties, and bridging gaps among major collections.

Train catalogs typically offer an elaborate colorful portrayal of merchandise in which descriptions, artwork and/or photographs, salient features, and a manual of layout suggestions are combined.

In recent years, the classic catalogs of yore have become highly collectible in their own right, particularly among ephemerists who tend to prefer style and aesthetic impact over content. (Ephemerists are those who collect printed or handwritten paper items produced for short-term use that were generally intended to be discarded. They might collect topically, by era, by lithographer, or illustrator.)

One of the most skilled practitioners in the art of cataloging was Ives, Blakeslee of Bridgeport, Connecticut. Ives produced catalogs for their line of clockwork tin and cast-iron trains beginning in the 1880s.

It was in 1909, however, that Ives originated a new concept in train catalogs; rather than targeting their message to the wholesaler or to retail toy stores, Ives addressed itself to an imaginary 12-year-old boy. A personal letter penned by Harry Ives addressed the boy as "Division Manager" for the Ives miniature railway system and indicated that the venture's success depended on the boy as manager, and his parents as "advisory board." Although it might sound simplistic by today's hard-sell standards, this personal approach, mixed with exciting railway atmosphere, was heady stuff for the early 1900s. It certainly helped build a cult of Ives loyalists that still exists today, long after the firm's demise. In the ensuing decade, Lionel, American Flyer, Märklin, Carette, and others would emulate, and perhaps surpass Ives in developing colorful and informative catalogs. But at the time, the merchandising wizardry of Ives helped stave off the invasion of German

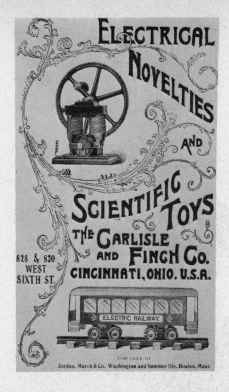

One of the rare early toy train catalogs, by Carlisle & Finch, 1898.

imports, as well as the challenge of less expensive American Flyer trains.

Another catalog innovator was the English firm, Bassett-Lowke, which issued its first modest edition in 1899, complete with photographs of its models tipped-in by hand. So enthusiastic was the response that by 1904 the Bassett-Lowke entry had expanded to a 250-page tome; in the ensuing few years its catalog had grown so unwieldy that Bassett-Lowke published it in sections, including one printed in French.

In 1925 Frank Hornby, the Liverpool, England, train manufacturer, issued its first *Hornby Book of Trains*. Richard Lines, writing in *The Art of Hornby* (see Bibliography) points out that "the descriptive commentary need not be taken too seriously." This inspired sales tool, however, was packed with information

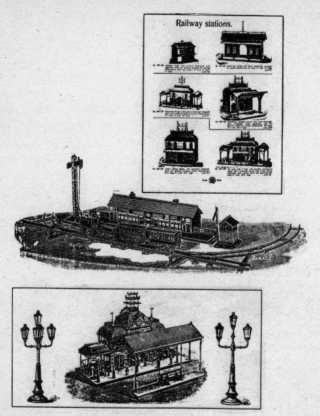

Early 1900s pages from catalogs by Bing (top); *Carette line in Gamage catalog* (middle); *Märklin accessories* (bottom). *Ornately designed and often in full color, these are highly prized by rail fans and ephemerists alike.*

about real-life trains, and its evocative, full-color cover renderings (many of which bore no relevance to the train models being offered inside), place Hornby in high esteem among collectors today.

Lionel produced its first train catalog in 1902, referring to the entries as "Miniature Electric Cars," and including them with other toys under the heading "Holiday Gifts." Window displays and other merchandising ideas were included for the retailers and it was not until Lionel's founder, Joshua Lionel Cowen, introduced

Standard gauge in 1906 that catalogs took the firm's message directly to the consumer.

All Lionel catalogs are highly prized, with some of the finest examples represented from 1949–1955 when more than one million were printed annually. As Ron Hollander writes in *All Aboard:** "It was required reading, its forty-four pages demanding Solomon-like choices among engines and accessories . . . only the Sears and Montgomery Ward catalogs were better known." "The Happy Lionel Boy" appearing on numerous catalog covers as well as train set box covers, flyers, and store counter and window displays was none other than owner Joshua Lionel Cowen's son, Lawrence.

A number of classic vintage catalogs by Ives, Gamage, Bassett-Lowke, Hornby, Märklin, and Lionel are currently available as reprints, faithfully reproduced from the originals by certain enterprising publishers (see Bibliography) and collecting organizations, including the T.T.O. and T.C.A. Although it is common for original catalogs of the early rarer variety to command upwards of several hundred dollars at auction, the availability of reproductions has tended to "cool down" collecting fervor and some rather torrid prices.

Look for catalog values to stabilize in the 1990s, save for those exceptional specimens admired more for their aesthetic presentation than the information they convey.

*Workman Publishing Co., New York, 1981.

History of Toy
and Model Trains

Toy trains constitute one of the oldest and most widely collected single classification in the hobby. There are toy trains constructed in whole or in part of tinplate, brass, wood, paper, pressed steel, cast iron, rubber, Bakelite, and other plastics. They may be powered by clockwork, friction, steam, electricity or simply pushed or pulled along the floor by youngsters on their own imaginary routes.

22   *Ives, Blakeslee & Williams Co., 294 Broadway, New York. Factory, Bridgeport, Conn.*

MECHANICAL LOCOMOTIVES.

The " ROCKET."
PATENTED.

The " ROCKET."
PATENTED.

BEFORE THE EXPLOSION.

No. 19   12½ in. long......Price per dozen, **$36.00**

Wind the Engine up and place a harmless paper cap in the receptacle prepared for it; when barely run down the cap "goes off" and the explosion occurs.

AFTER THE EXPLOSION.

No. 19   12½ inches long.

Exploding locomotive patent was issued to William D. Hardin and Joseph P. White in 1886; marketed by Ives through the 1890s.

Tin Pull Toy Trains: 1830s–Early 1900s

Trains preceded other popular motive-powered transportation toys
by almost a half century, making their appearance on the scene
almost simultaneously with the advent of the first real railroads in
the 1830s and 1840s. These earliest examples tended to be highly
stylized and imaginative with exaggerated cabs, smokestacks, and
bells. The first American maker to introduce tin clockwork trains
is reputed to be George Brown & Co. of Forestville, Connecticut.
Other early makers included James Fallows and Francis, Field &
Francis of Philadelphia, Union Manufacturing Co., Hull & Stafford of Clinton, Connecticut, Merriam Manufacturing, Durham,
Connecticut, and Althof, Bergmann & Co., New York City.

Cast-Iron Toy Trains: 1880s–1930s

Almost an exclusively American phenomenon (the possible exception being Wallwork, a Manchester, England-based iron foundry
which produced a small number of cast-iron trains in 1892), cast-
iron pull toy trains dominated the toy train market in the late 19th
century. Usually trackless, this category was known for its adherence to detail, authenticity, and attempt to capture the "feel" of
the genuine article. Two major cast-iron train innovators were Ives,
Blakeslee & Co., Bridgeport, Connecticut, and Francis W. Carpenter, Port Chester, New York. They were soon followed by Wilkins Toy Co., Keene, New Hampshire; Hubley Manufacturing,
Lancaster, Pennsylvania; Jerome Secor, Bridgeport, Connecticut;
Dent Hardware Co., Fullerton, Pennsylvania; Kenton Hardware,
Kenton, Ohio; J.&L. Stevens, Cromwell, Connecticut; and Harris

*Ives catalog from 1892 features the No.
19-9, one of its earliest clockwork cast-
iron locomotives.*

Toy Co., Toledo, Ohio. Some makers, such as Pratt & Letchworth, Buffalo, New York, also produced parts for real railroad trains. Although most of these cast-iron versions relied almost exclusively on child power, there are examples powered by clockwork mechanisms.

Toy Train Diplomacy

Time and again, a gift of a model train has served as an instrument of friendship. On one such memorable occasion in 1852, President Millard Fillmore dispatched a letter, transmitted through Japan's ruler Kanagawa Shogun, to the Emperor, encouraging that country, long isolated from the rest of the world, to open its doors to Western trade.

Fillmore's courier, Commodore Mathew C. Perry, also bore gifts for the Emperor, including a miniature steam engine, tender, passenger coach, and track. The Japanese were delighted, and undoubtedly the gift helped to create a favorable impression. A pact was signed between the two nations, even as certain Japanese warlords were advocating that all foreigners within their borders be killed. Judging from the flood of model trains and other toys that Japan has exported to this country over the years, Commodore Perry's presentation train has come back, so to speak, a million times over.

Wood and Lithograph Paper-on-Wood Toy Trains: 1850–Early 1900s

Wooden toys are the earliest mass-produced playthings made in this country, dating back to 1855. Many early toy trains were unadorned. Later they were stencilled and painted by hand. Since the 1880s, the most popular toy train versions were embellished with brightly colored lithographic paper glued to the wood surface. Two of the earliest wooden toy makers were the Tower Guild of South Hingham, Massachusetts, and Ellis, Britton & Eaton, Springfield, Vermont, both of which were operating by the mid-19th century. The leaders among the litho-on-wood playthings were Milton Bradley, Springfield, Massachusetts, Morton E. Converse, Winchendon, Massachusetts, W.S. Reed of nearby Leominster, and R. Bliss Manufacturing of Pawtucket, Rhode Island.

Live Steam Trains: 1880s–Early 1900s

Live steam trains usually comprised a firebox with a kerosene or alcohol lamp, a boiler, plus a steam chest for power storage. A pulley system or similar apparatus hooked to the power system would drive the wheels. Early steam train makers in the United States included Buckman Manufacturing of New York City, Weeden Manufacturing of New Bedford, Massachusetts, and Eugene Beggs of Patterson, New Jersey. While potentially dangerous and not easy to operate, their great appeal lay in their realism, as they operated almost as identically as full-size steam trains.

The British went for several decades leading into the 20th century with outmoded train designs incorporating steam power. Steam trains, or "dribblers" as they were known in England, were produced by Newton & Co., London, Steven's Model Dockyard, London, Clyde Model Dockyard, Glasgow, Whitneys', London, and J. Bateman & Co., London and Manchester, among others.

A major French firm which joined the British in continued production of brass "dribblers" was Radiguet & Massiot of Paris, examples of which appeared in British train catalogs from 1880 to late 1890.

Electric Toy Trains: 1884 to Present

In Louis Hertz's *Riding the Tinplate Rails*, a Carlisle & Finch advertisement from 1897 illustrates what many considered to be the first American electric train. According to an 1892 Horsman catalog, however, an electric "Elevated Railway" is depicted; it is possibly an outgrowth of a patent granted to a Murray Bacon and assigned to the Novelty Electric Co. of Philadelphia in 1884. Other U.S. pioneers in electric trains (often hailed as the "gauge-II aristocracy") were Howard of New York, Knapp Elec-

ELECTRIC TROLLEY CAR AND RAILWAY

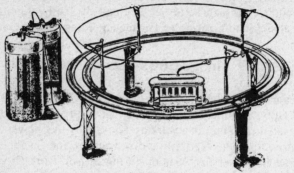

No. 11.

Single Track Elevated Railway with Trolley Wire and Poles.

Equipment—One Model Electric Street Car, with motor in car, trolley on roof of car running on trolley wire, electric current taken from trolley wire and track, same as present street car system. One charge of battery will run car 60 hours.

The design and construction of this toy is entirely original it is an exact model of the Standard Electric Street Railway of to-day. This toy requires a motor of special design which we have perfected. It is positively without dead centre and the speed can be regulated as desired by means of a rheostat adjusted to one of the columns. It can be run by any battery now on the market, but we furnish with the toy the well-known Edison-Lalande battery, which we find to be the most perfect and durable battery for electric toys. This equipment is finished in black japan, yellow carmine and gold. Sample by express on receipt of $30.00. Express charges paid to any point east of the Mississippi.

First electric toy train illustration from 1892 Horsman Catalogue is one assigned to Novelty Electric Co., Philadelphia, in 1884.

tric & Novelty Co. of New York City, and Voltcamp Electric Manufacturing of Baltimore, Maryland. Meanwhile Ives, which had a heavy stake in clockwork trains (they would continue to manufacture them over the ensuing 15 years), made their first electric train entry in 1910.

Electric-powered toy trains were not widely available in the United States until this period, when Bing and Lionel joined Ives in popularizing these units. Ives' leaders proved to be the eight-wheeled versions in gauge I, patterned after the New York Central's "S-class" electrics. Bing countered with a close copy of the Ives locomotive, with improved under-frame castings. Lionel produced still another Ives copy in four-, six-, and eight-wheeled versions. Their 2½-in. track size gave Lionel a crude, rather cumbersome, but imposing appearance.

European Manufacturers of Electric Trains

A progression of leading German toy makers sprang up in the last half of the 19th century. They included Karl Bub, 1851; Märklin, 1859; Issmayer, 1861; Bing, 1865; Plank, 1866; Schönner, 1875; Gunthermann, 1877; Lehmann, 1881; Fleischmann, 1887; Falk & Doll, 1898; and Distler, 1899. All of these firms produced painted or lithographed tin trains; all hailed from Nuremberg, the toy mecca of Europe, with the exception of Märklin, located in Goppingen, and Lehmann in Brandenburg. A large portion of their toy train production was designed for export to the American market.

Gebruder Märklin became the first of the German makers to introduce an electric drive for steam outline locomotives. The renaissance in toy trains really came in 1891 when Märklin introduced a figure-eight exhibit at the Leipzig Toy Fair. Included with the unique layout were miniature stations, grand terminuses, trestles, bridges, signals, and even refreshment carts for the miniature passengers. Thus was born a new concept that a toy train was part of a total system and not a separate entity.

By 1895, gauges I, II, III, and V had become standard among German train makers. The "O" gauge was added in 1900.

French Toy Trains

As mentioned earlier, Radiguet & Massiot of Paris produced live steam trains in the last quarter of the 19th century. Engines tended to be larger and more distinctively French than their English or American cousins.

Toy trains enjoyed greater popularity in France during the 1880s than in either England or Germany. Among the "initial-happy" French firms producing trains were F.V. (Emile Favre et E.F. Fevre Successeurs), C.R. (Charles Rossignol, Paris), D.S. (Dessin), G.P. (Georges Parent), and J.C. (J. Caron). Rossignol and Favre led the field, with elaborate lithography, gadgetry, and offbeat designs that bore little relevance to the real thing.

One of the major French distributors, Heller & Coudray, had special designs created for them by the German maker Schönner, while Märklin still dominated the high end of the French toy train market.

The U.S. Big Four (Plus One)

After all is said and done, American toy train collectors tend to concentrate most heavily on the "Big Four" U.S. firms of American Flyer, Chicago, Illinois; Lionel, New York City; Ives, Bridgeport, Connecticut; and Louis Marx, New York City. One other manufacturer, Dorfan, is frequently overlooked. This Newark, New Jersey, firm produced some of the finest train sets and led the industry with innovations such as die-cast locomotives and remote control uncouplers. Dorfan produced trains for only 10 years, from 1924–1933, before fading into history.

Marx trains spanned almost a half century, leading off with the "Joy Line" series (actually produced by Girard Toy Works under a commission sales agreement). Marx's golden era was from the 1930s up to World War II, living up to their motto of "selling trains that ran better than they should for the price."

Ives evolved from clockwork power to become the first of the group to electrify trains. They were the only American firm to adopt the European No. 1 gauge. The finest examples from Ives shops were produced from 1904–1920. On the eve of the Depression, with Ives in financial difficulties, American Flyer and Lionel seized the opportunity to buy them out.

Early Period of Standard Gauge: 1906–1923

In 1906, a maverick named Joshua Lionel Cowen made one of the boldest, most brilliant marketing moves in the annals of the hobby. He recognized that the typical American toy train purchaser was not as concerned about attention to scale or accuracy of livery as their British and German counterparts. What *did* impress the American buyer was size, price, and technical innovation. Cowen's firm, Lionel of New York City, introduced a 2⅛-in. nonstandard gauge as opposed to the typical 2⅞-in. gauge, thus rendering all other gauges "nonstandard" by definition from that time on. The strategy proved overwhelmingly successful. By 1912, Lionel had served notice to American and European competitors alike as one to be taken seriously.

Meanwhile, American Flyer of Chicago, Illinois (originally known as "Chicago Flyer"), also joined the ranks of electric train producers. American Flyer locomotives had been closely patterned after the Ives line—all cast-iron steam outline 0-4-0s, clockwork-powered—but priced lower to appeal to the mass market.

World War I Ends German Dominance

The Great War proved to be the undoing of the German toy train industry. A number of major firms were diverted into the manufacturing of munitions. The economic chaos that ensued following the war was equally a disaster and many German makers never fully recovered. Carette, for example, closed its doors forever in 1917. Plans for Märklin's projected gauge III sets destined for the U.S., French, and German markets had to be abandoned, undoubtedly a great loss to the toy train world. German firms were hit by protectionist tariffs, particularly in the U.S. market.

After a five-year hiatus from the toy train scene imposed by the war, the Germans faced formidable competition from British firms, including Brimtoy, Whitanco, Wells, Chad Valley, and, most notably, Hornby. In the United States, Ives, Lionel, American Flyer, and Dorfan had clearly strengthened their positions. Another more

The snow plough (this one by Hornby of Liverpool, England, 1930s) rates high on the desireability list, along with crane cars, $200–$225.

subtle deterrent to post–World War I growth among the Germans was that the glory days of expensive toy railroads for the advanced enthusiasts were over.

In the 1920s, Märklin would retrench and drastically cut back on its rather unwieldly prewar range of trains and specialize in O gauge and gauge 1 only. Renewed emphasis was placed on realism and scale models patterned after prototypes operating on the Reichsbahn and the Swiss lines.

The 1920s Boom in Standard Gauge

In the 1920s, Ives, American Flyer, Dorfan, and a newcomer, Boucher, a New York model boat firm that had taken over Voltramp, all moved to compete on Lionel's turf in Standard gauge. Since Lionel had a copyright on the phrase "Standard gauge," its rivals adopted "Wide gauge" as their nomenclature.

Ives' sleek new line was better proportioned, showed superior workmanship, and had a heavy enamel finish while still following Lionel styling. American Flyer, after dallying in the low-end market to compete with the low-priced Bing and Ives cast-iron windups, emerged in 1925 with a Wide-gauge line that was larger and less expensive than Lionel's. (American Flyer actually bought its passenger coaches from Lionel, and painted and lettered them with their own logo.)

Dorfan was known for its die-castings and the superior power of its locomotives. By 1926, Dorfan engines could outperform the field, but the die-castings soon showed signs of suffering from metal fatigue and became a major "headache." In the late 1920s, Dorfan added a small array of very appealing O-gauge trains.

Boucher, the newcomer, could come up with but one new design, the "Blue Comet," an updated Voltamp 4-6-2 "Pacific" with three large, nicely proportioned coaches in tow. The coaches were constructed of wood and steel and lacked interior detail.

Lionel did not take this latest Standard-gauge incursion lightly. They again got a jump on the competition by introducing the "402," an impressive, handsome, and powerful eight-wheeled electric based on the New York Central's "S-class." Die work and design was relegated to La Precisa, a firm in Naples, Italy. Replacing Lionel's customary maroons, olives, and drab blacks were an attractive brown, brilliant blue, red, tan, and light green—a rainbow of colors completely foreign to full-sized American trains. The epitome of American toy train production may well be the Lionel "381," a brawny, 12-wheeled bi-polar electric, pulling four "State" Pullmans, each 21½ in. long, rolling on 12 wheels, and complete with full interiors, lights, and brass fittings. This 1928 entry's one drawback was that it could not deliver enough power with one engine, so a "402"-type twin motor had to be hastily substituted.

The Wall Street Crash to Pre–World War II Recovery: 1930–1945

The uncertainty of the 1930s following the Depression in the United States helped bring the long parade of deluxe toy trains to a screeching halt, a calamity which many firms could not survive.

The first victim was Ives, although this firm's finances had been shaky for some time. In 1928 Ives declared bankruptcy, but with financing from Lionel and American Flyer the firm managed to continue, producing what many collectors deem to be Ives' all-time greatest—the copper-plated beauty ironically named "Prosperity Special," powered by a huge, die-cast steam outline 4-4-2 engine. First American Flyer and then, two years later, Lionel, withdrew their support and Ives went to raildom's Valhalla in 1932. By the mid-1930s, Dorfan had closed its doors, American Flyer was at the brink of extinction, and Boucher, perhaps wisely, elected to abandon its trains and concentrate on its original line of model ships.

Lionel also was in trouble, with "too many Standard gauge trains chasing too few dollars."* After four years of red ink, Lionel was in receivership in 1935.

*From *Toy Trains: A History*, Harper & Row, New York, 1986, by Pierce Carlson. *Toy Trains* is recommended as offering the most comprehensive account of the strategies of major toy train makers through the years of any book to our knowledge.

Die-Cast Streamliners and
the Late 1930s Rejuvenation

Riding the wave of a new sense of optimism in the mid-1930s were a new series of ultra-sleek streamliners—real-life trains that even surpassed the burgeoning airways as the most chic and luxurious way to travel.

A number of leading toy train makers, with Lionel in the forefront, rushed to cash in on this unexpected resurgence with replications of the new streamliners. Lionel's first venture was a nice "Torpedo"* model of the Union Pacific "City of Portland." Standard gauge was hastily abandoned in favor of the radically smaller gauge O. Lionel's very smallest, called the O-27, had a track radius of only 27 in., with the largest being 74 in.

A.C. Gilbert of New Haven, Connecticut, had, in the meantime, stepped in to bail out American Flyer. An entirely new line of trains was introduced in gauge O and these were even more miniscule than Lionel's O-27s, with superbly detailed die-castings. American Flyer sales quickly took off.

Lionel soon recognized the feasibility of employing die-castings to shave manufacturing costs off their steam outline locomotives. Availing themselves of the resources of a leading Swedish-American tool and die firm, Lionel came up with a gauge-O, semiscale, nicely detailed die-cast model of the New York Central 4-6-4 "Hudson," with matching freight cars, soon followed by an 0-6-0 "Pennsylvania" engine. Not only did Lionel recover its tooling costs in the first year, they achieved a standard of realism that has rarely been equalled to this day.

Märklin Responds with Its Own O-Gauge Refinement

Märklin was the last holdout still manufacturing and updating a gauge-I range at the time of the dramatic O gauge entry in the

---

*Whether it was coined by Lionel or the Pennsylvania R.R. is unclear, but the term "Torpedo" for this type of locomotive captured the imagination of train set buyers. (See "Lionel's Streamlined Torpedo" in the Fall 1989 issue of *Classic Toy Trains*.)

high-end market. Märklin made a switch to gauge O and added a distinctively international flavor to its range with the following: a 4-6-4 "Hudson" streamliner; the "Commodore Vanderbilt"; an uncataloged nonstreamlined "Hudson" with matching Pullmans; an "Etat" 4-8-2 Mountain (French); L.N.E.R. 2-8-4 "Cock of the North" (English); "Borsig" (German); a 4-6-2 "Pacific"; plus a huge (Swiss) "Crocodile." A matched set of these prototypes in this incomparable series ranks as probably the most expensive of all sets to complete.

Faced with the ever-increasing demand for scale and realism among collectors, Märklin's solution was a still further reduction in scale. In 1935 the firm introduced gauge OO, a size half that of gauge O, in which trains were scaled 3.5 mm to the foot and ran on 16.5 mm-gauge track. Later, this new gauge and scale combination was to be designated HO. Trix, a new German firm founded by Stefan Bing, quickly followed suit with an OO gauge—a 16.5 mm version but slightly tinier in scale: 1:90 vs. 1:87.

Always one to cash in on a good thing, Lionel simply reduced its scale O 4-6-4 "Hudson" to 1:76 size and added a few die-cast freight car copies (from a Scalcraft design) with a 19 mm track gauge.

As the storm clouds gathered for the outbreak of World War II, few realized it would spell the end for gauge O, whose remarkable and timely entry in the 1930s saved many a toy train firm from extinction.

Post–World War II Transition: 1945–1955

While the end of World War II marked a slow recovery period for firms such as Märklin and Hornby, the top two U.S. producers, Lionel and American Flyer, were quick off the launching pad with new lines.

American Flyer was fortunate to be stocked with a completely redesigned series from 1938–1940, a nicely precisioned scale smaller than normal gauge O 1:43. Following the war, American Flyer christened an "S" gauge by reducing the distance to 24 mm between tracks, so that the gauge was in better proportion to scale.

Lionel resumed its gauge O pursuits, adding new gadgetry including trains that whistled and puffed smoke, magnetic couplers, enhanced traction, and an entire railway lit by electric lights.

Headlining Lionel's new array of locomotives was a large 6-8-6 "Pennsylvania" steam turbine with 25 wheels, plus the "Pennsylvania GG1," 4-6-6-4 electric, with the futuristic look inherent in the Raymond Lowey design of the prototype.

In the ensuing 10 years of postwar prosperity for Lionel and American Flyer, both giants were caught napping as other firms quietly converted to miniature scale. As Jim Doherty phrased it in the *Smithsonian*,*

> Scale modeling had taken off like the Twentieth Century Limited. Thousands of returning servicemen got interested in it. Hundreds of new hobby shops and specialty manufacturers appeared all over the country. But when HO and other ready-made miniature models came along, together with superb brass locomotives manufactured in Japan, many hobbyists began shifting their attention from equipment to scenery and structures. Smaller trains meant that more track and scaled-down scenery could be laid out in a limited amount of space. It was the beginning of a transition beyond purely mechanical concerns to an appreciation of the worlds within which railroads operated.

Failure to capitalize on what Doherty terms "a mania for miniaturized minutia" cost Lionel dearly. American Flyer ceased production in 1966, with Lionel purchasing the remnants. The days were numbered for Lionel as well. In 1955, the Lionel Corporation was ranked as the largest toy company in the world. In 1969, when Lionel was diminished to become a small, loss-generating subsidiary of monolith General Mills, all that remained of a once mighty empire was stocked inventory and a handful of O-27 train sets.

The 1980s: End of An Era

The era of the traditional toy train that children and their fathers cherished and with which no Yuletide season was complete without

*"Modelers, too, work on the railroad all the livelong day," Smithsonian Publishing Co., December 1988.

survived innumerable incarnations for over a century. However, as Pierce Carlson concluded rather pessimistically in *Toy Trains: A History* in 1986:

> The cheerful, brightly colored, imaginative and rugged toy train has been transformed into the technically perfect, cold and delicate scale model that would never run on any child's dream railway.

Epilogue

It has been an upgrade battle for the entire model train industry, but as we round the bend into the 1990s we see signs of a true resurgence. Märklin, the sole survivor of the early German model train makers, along with firms such as Lehmann Gross Bahn and the revitalized Lionel Trains, Inc., are harking back to the hobby's heydays. As covered in greater detail in this guide's "Market Overview," enthusiasts are flocking back to the hobby by the hundreds of thousands. Once again, it's full steam ahead!

Who Collects Model Trains?

Kings and maharajahs, clergymen, medical men, porters, signalmen, schoolboys, titans of business and industry—every type of person from every walk of life is represented in the worldwide brotherhood of railway modeling.

Among the celebrity collectors from past and present: ex-Harvard President James Conant; stripper Gypsy Rose Lee; Arthur Godfrey and TV star Gary Coleman; singers Frank Sinatra (who has a layout reminiscent of his boyhood home in Hoboken, New Jersey) and Mel Torme; baseball greats Joe Dimaggio, Gil McDougald, and Roy Campanella; P.G.A. golfer Ed Dougherity; former Secretary of State John Foster Dulles; King George VI and King Edward II; King Ananda of Siam; and Walt Disney, who was a modeler along with his two-time Academy Award-winning animation supervisor Ward Kimball. Real estate mogul Richard Kughn augmented *his* vast personal train collection by purchasing the Lionel Corporation in 1985.

Abbreviations of Real-Life Railroads

Occasionally, there may be slight deviations as to major train model makers' use of abbreviations appearing on locomotives, tenders, and rolling stock.

North America

AA Ann Arbor Railroad
ACL Atlantic Coast Line
ADN Ashley, Drew & Northern
AL Algoma Central
ALKA Alaska Railroad
AM Amtrak
AP Atlantic & Union Pacific
ASA Atlantic & St. Andrews
AT & SF Atchison, Topeka & Santa Fe Railway (Santa Fe)
AWP Atlanta & West Point Railroad
B & A Bangor & Aroostock

B & LE Bessemer & Lake Erie
B & M Boston & Maine Railroad
B & O Baltimore & Ohio Railroad
BN Burlington Northern
C & NW Chicago & Northwestern
C & O Chesapeake & Ohio
C & P Clarendon & Pittsford
C & S Colorado & Southern
CANP Canadian Pacific (Canada)
CB Cotton Belt

CBQ Chicago, Burlington, Quincy Railroad (Burlington Route)

CH Chattanooga Traction

CIM Chicago & Illinois Midland

CNA Canadian National (Canada)

CNJ Central Railroad of New Jersey (Jersey Central Lines)

CNW Chicago & Northwestern

COB Chicago Outer Belt

CON Conrail

CPR Canadian Pacific Railways

CR Clinchfield Railroad

CRI & P Chicago, Rock Island & Pacific

D & H Delaware & Hudson Railroad Corp.

DLW Delaware, Lackawanna & Western

DSSA Deluth South Shore & Atlantic

DTI Detroit, Toledo & Ironton

EL Erie & Lackawanna

ERIE Erie Railroad

FEC Florida East Coast

FGEX Fruit Growers Express

FR Frisco (St. Louis & San Francisco)

G & W Genessee & Wyoming

GAEX General American Express

GMO Gulf, Mobile & Ohio

GN Great Northern Railway

GTW Grand Trunk Western Railway System

IC Illinois Central Railroad

IT Illinois Terminal Railroad

KCS Kansas City Southern

L & N Louisville & Nashville

LNA Lewisville, New Albany & Corydon

LNE Lehigh & New England

LV Lehigh Valley

M & P Maryland & Pennsylvania

MC Maine Central

MILW Milwaukee Road (Chicago, Milwaukee, St. Paul & Pacific)

MKT Missouri-Kansas-Texas Railroad Co. (Katy Railroad)

MP Missouri Pacific Railroad

MSL Minneapolis & St. Louis

MTW Marinette, Tomahawk & Western

N & W Norfolk & Western Railroad

NH New Haven (New York, New Haven, & Hartford Railroad)

NKP New York, Chicago & St. Louis Railroad (nickel plate)

NP Northern Pacific

NYC New York Central System

ON Oregon & Northwestern

ONNO Ontario Northland (Canada)

OPE Oregon, Pacific & Eastern

PAEL Pacific Electric

PC Penn Central

PE Pittsburg & Lake Erie

PEAB Peabody Short Line

PFE Pacific Fruit Express
PHD Port Huron & Detroit
PRR Pennsylvania Railroad
PSR Petaluma & Santa Rosa Railroad
RDG Reading Railroad
RFP Richmond, Fredericksburg & Potomac
RI Rock Island (Chicago, Rock Island & Pacific Railroad)
RIO Rio Grande (Denver & Rio Grande Western Railroad)
RUT Rutland Railroad
RV Rahway Valley Railroad
SAL Seaboard Air Lines
SCL Seaboard Coast Lines
SDRX Sinclair
SIR Sierra Railroad
SOO Minneapolis, St. Paul & Sault Ste. Marie (SOO Line)
SOU Southern Railroad
SP Southern Pacific
SPI Spokane International Railway
SPS Spokane, Portland & Seattle
SR Southern Railway System
SRN Sabine River & Northern
SSW St. Louis, Southwestern
SUS Susquehanna
T & P Texas & Pacific (also designated as TEXP)

THB Toronto, Hamilton & Buffalo (Canada)
TPW Toledo, Peoria & Western (Rocket)
UP Union Pacific Railroad Co.
USRA United States Railroad Administration
UTLX Union Tank Leasing Co.
VMC Vermont Central
VR Virginian Railway
VT Virginia & Truckee Railway
W & A Western & Atlantic
WAB Wabash Railroad
WM Western Maryland Railway
WP Western Pacific

Foreign

England

CLU Central London Underground Railway
GE Great Eastern
GN Great Northern
L & N London & Northeastern
L & SW London & Southwestern
MLD Midland Railway

France

MD Midi
PLM Paris-Lyon Mediterranee
PO Paris-Orleans
SNCF Societe Nationale des Chemins de Fer Francais (private French railways were nationalized in 1938 under this name)

Germany

DB Deutsche Bundesbahn Lines in West Germany adopted this designation in the late 1940s
DR The DRG designation disappeared in World War II, but the East German government retained the DR, for Deutsche Reichsbahn
DRG Deutsche Reichsbahn Gessellschaft (government railway system set up in the 1920s)

Gaining Greater Satisfaction from Train Collecting

The fascination of model railroading—the urge to build and operate a miniature railroad system—is typically American. Each individual has the opportunity to inject his own personality into his work, to create a railroad system unlike any other one in the world.

—*Joshua Lionel Cowen,*
late Chairman of the Board,
the Lionel Corp.*

Pray for me. My husband's a train collector.

—*Bumper sticker caption*

Part of the romance of model railroading is that it can take you over any route your heart desires.

- You can be an armchair railroader and immerse yourself in the lore of real-life trains.
- Or buy or make from scratch or from model kits realistic versions in scale of any train you fancy, including "live steamers" that operate outdoors.

*From foreword to *Model Railroading*, Bantam Books, Inc., 1951.

- Or develop your own sophisticated sound systems and incorporate computerized commands into your electronic control system.
- Or concentrate solely on creating mountains, rivers, entire cities, and other scenic details as a backdrop for your model trains.
- Or enjoy wiring up your own layouts and concentrate on keeping your trains rolling.
- Or specialize in models that are identified with real-life railroads companies that conjure up fond memories, such as the Baltimore & Ohio and the Lackawanna.
- Or collect by material such as vibrant, lithographed paper-on-wood examples, rugged, distinctively American cast iron, delicate painted and stencilled tinplate, or copper or brass steamers.
- Or document an era such as the Classic Period, 1923–1940, vs. the 1980s or Contemporary Period—a choice that may often be dictated by budget.
- Or collect by type; complete sets vs. individual examples (locomotives vs. tenders, trolley cars, cabooses).
- Or by size (scale), from the bold, brawny Standard gauge to the finely precisioned Z gauge.
- Or by specific manufacturer or country of origin—there is plenty to go around to suit every taste and price range.
- Or as a purist collector you might be more concerned about the aesthetic appeal of a toy train and whether it comes with its original box; you are content to admire it on the shelf vs. making its loops around a track. (Often this group is dismissed by other modelers as ''speculators'' who deal in cash, not true railroading.)

While it may sound simplistic, it is essential to collect what *you* like and resist the urge to switch to certain categories that may be in vogue at a given time. Buy the best example you can afford. One superb toy train is worth five lackluster models.

Do your homework. Read every book on the subject you can get your hands on; consult old toy train catalogs, flyers, and price lists. Join a club or organization (see listing in back of this guide) that conducts seminars and museum tours, reprints old catalogs, and serves as a conduit of information on anything relating to model railroading. Also, seek out only the more knowledgeable experienced dealers whose integrity and judgment are respected within the hobby.

Despite all the articles and books these days about ''Collecting for Fun and Profit,'' we feel this may be a contradiction in terms. There's no denying that train collectors or modelers should have a thorough comprehension of the value of engines and rolling stock they own.

Anyone deciding on the investment route had better have deep pockets and accept the fact that there may be days when you'll experience the financial equivalent of a derailment. This may prove stressful and anything but relaxing. And isn't *that* what it's all about? Forgetting the cares of the world for a while . . . relaxing and having fun!

Wolfgang Richter, manager director of Lehmann Gross Bahn, summed it up this way in an interview in the Fall 1989 issue of *Classic Toy Trains*: ''It's a friendly hobby and a friendly business, and it should stay that way.''

Creating a Complete Model Railway System

If you are a newcomer to railway modeling or even if you've been around the track a few times, the whole subject of hooking up a complete compatible system seems fraught with confusion, considering all the mumbo-jumbo dished forth by various manufacturers over the last hundred years. Hopefully, the following information will help put things in proper perspective.

Gauge and Scale

First, *gauge* and *scale*, which you might think are one and the same, actually impart different meanings. All true models are miniaturized replicas of full-sized originals, known in the hobby as prototypes. As an example, the exact reduction is expressed mathematically as 1:87 or $1/87$ for HO gauge. This is the *scale*.

Gauge is simply the distance between the inside of each rail. In HO gauge, the most common now used by modelers, the track *gauge* or width is 16.5 mm or $5/8$ in.

Other Popular Gauges and Their Eras

- $2^7/8$ = $2^7/8$ in. (1901–1905)
- Standard Gauge = $2^1/8$ (1906–1939)

- OO Gauge = ¾ in. (1938–1945; introduced by Märklin. For a number of years, European makers labeled *anything* smaller than O gauge as OO.)
- HO gauge = 16.5 in. (1945–to date)
- S Gauge = ⅞ in. (1945–1960s)

Modelers Go Metric

Note that the metric system is used extensively, particularly among European train manufacturers. This accounts for certain discrepancies that may be noted on the chart. A meter, of course, equals 39.37 in.; an inch equals 25.400 mm. To change millimeters to inches, either multiply by 0.03937 or divide by 25.4. The mixup occurs when certain makers turn affectionately to the nearest equivalent, rounding it out in terms of an inch. Since scale is related to gauge, we see large variations among makers as to scales compatible with each gauge.

Whyte System

This method of describing locomotive type by wheel arrangement or trucks is standard throughout the hobby. In the number reference 0-4-0 or 4-6-6-4, for example, the first number refers to the lead trucks; the second, and sometimes the third, denotes the sets of drive wheels; the final to trailing trucks. The driving wheels are always smaller than the lead or trailing wheels. The locomotive in the latter instance above is referred to as a six-coupled engine.

Some of the more widely copied modeler wheel or truck configurations include the 4-4-2 "Atlantic"; the 2-2-2 British "Planets" series ("Mars," etc.); the 0-40 "Bury"; the 6-8-6 "Pennsylvania"; and the 4-6-4 New York Central "Hudson."

Wheels

In the United States, virtually all major manufacturers and those importers supplying that market use wheels that conform to a profile called *RP25*, which was adopted some years ago by the National Model Railroad Association. The *RP25* standard not only shows well, but it will also run on fine-scale track, which is more shallow than the Code 100 track standard in HO train sets.

Couplers

This could pose a problem if you try to mix rolling stock of a maker from one country with that of another. Since one major manufacturer is often identified with certain gauges (i.e., Märklin for Z gauge, Arnold for N gauge), there are no problems. The biggest bugaboo is with HO gauge, where numerous model variations of couplers exist. HO models produced for the United States have their own distinctive coupler called the *horn hook,* which has been standardized since the early 1950s. Realistic *Kadee magnetic couplers* are an alternative but must be purchased separately for HO or O gauge.

In Great Britain, the *tension-lock* or *hook-and-bar* coupler has now become standard. Other European models may have a *Fleishmann tension lock-type coupler,* a *Roco close-coupler*, or an *NEM Class A*, often called the *Märklin* after its primary user. Generally, it is prudent to decide at the offset to standardize on either of the above three and alter other stock correspondingly to be compatible if you are operating a system with HOs of mixed national origin and makers. The greatest number of makers, including those whose couplings are difficult to alter, fit the *Märklin (NEM Class A) hook-with-loop coupler*.

Controls

Movement is what a model railway layout is all about. The manner in which the models operate depends on the system incorporated by the manufacturer. All the different locomotives can't normally be mixed on the one layout.

Most models today are powered by electric motors and controlled through the tracks, with the current supplied to the tracks varied by a controller. This regulates the speed at which the motor revolves. Gears in the motor assure you that the locomotive travels at a reasonably realistic speed.

In every instance, the current is stepped down to a safe level through the transformer. Most motors function at 12V DC, although there *are* exceptions. Voltage varies: 110–120V AC in the United States; 240V AC in Great Britain; 220V AC in Germany. Power plants also vary, so be cautious about mixing those from various manufacturers of different countries of origin without double-checking first.

Except for the early days of electric model railways, in which trains ran on a three-rail track, most layouts include the two-rail 12V DC system (the notable exception being Märklin, which uses a 16V AC system). Most train sets come complete with at least an adequate unit (you can also purchase controllers separately), and all but the very simplest also are equipped with AC/DC outputs for operating equipment.

One important caveat regarding the two-rail system: reversing loops (when a train is in a turning triangle) or return loops (where

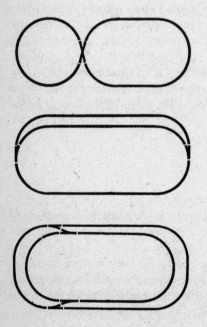

Three of the most common track layouts: (top) *simple use of diamond crossing;* (middle) *oval and half oval, two turnouts;* (bottom) *two ovals with two crossovers.*

a train changes direction on the same track) will not function unless special changeover or polarity reversing switches are installed in the track circuit. Track turning on itself sets up opposite polarity, resulting in a short circuit.

Command Control

Computer technology now encompasses a chip being wired into the locomotive so that the system can run several trains simultaneously without all the complex wiring and sectionalizing complexity typical of big layouts. Scores of catalogs and flyers are available to help you select your command control. Or better still, avail yourself of *Walthers, Inc.*, an annual modeler's bible which lists over 50,000 railroad accessories by more than 300 firms.

Lionel's Railscope

Early in 1989, Lionel introduced Railscope, available in G, O, S, and HO models. This fascinating breakthrough consists of a black-and-white TV camera powered by a 9V DC alkaline battery and mounted in the front end of a locomotive. A TV signal is transmitted via the rails back to the TV set to provide an "engineer's-eye view" of what lies ahead on the track. The one major glitch is that it uses up more batteries than a youngster's remote control racer at Christmastime (battery life runs from 30 to 45 minutes). The enterprising modeler, with a will, finds a way. We have already seen several different remedies expounded, including using track power to extend battery life.

High-Tech Railroading

If you're really into high tech and you're looking into the closest approximation of real railroading there is, consider the layout of Bruce Chubb, a Grand Rapids, Michigan, electrical engineer who's been at it for 35 years. His Sunset Valley Railroad operates with a computer that coordinates signals, keeps 16 trains running simultaneously, and prints out car-switching lists while monitoring individual train and car movements. Chubb, sitting at his five-ft.-long control panel, supervises his crews assisted by a computer, an electronic map, and telephone hookups.

We hope you're now on track and ready to go highballing down the line!

Digital Electronics

The German innovator Märklin led the way in introducing digital electronics to the hobby. Its digital system has the capacity for operating up to 80 HO trains and 256 switches and/or signals on a single layout. It can also be programmed through your personal computer. Märklin's most recent catalog contains several digital engine models and engines that, with the simple retrofitting of a chip, can be converted to digital operation.

Manufacturers' Listing

Althof Bergman, New York City, New York
1867–1880
Founders: Three Bergman brothers, New York City jobbers, merged with another jobber, L. Althof
Specialty: Tinplate clockwork toy jobbers (in addition they may have done some manufacturing and assembling). One of the first U.S. toy outlets to offer carpet-running tinplate trains.

American Flyer (See "American Flyer" in *Electric Trains* section)

American Miniature Railway Co., Bridgeport, Connecticut
1907–1912
Founders: Ex-Ives employees
Specialty: Almost exact duplication of Ives gauge O locomotives. Firm's meager production lasted just five years before folding due to financial difficulties.

Arcade Manufacturing Co., Freeport, Illinois
1868–1946 (Originally operated as Novelty Iron Works)
Specialty: Mass producer of cast-iron transportation toys, including trains.
Slogan: "They Look Real," adopted in 1920.

Arnold Co., Nuremberg, Germany
1906–to present day
Founder: K. Arnold
Specialty: Stationary steam accessories including nautical toys and trains. Introduced "Rapido" gauge N model railroad sets in 1960s.

Bassett-Lowke, Northampton, England
1899–to present day
Founder: Wenman J. Bassett-Lowke
Specialty: First distributor to recognize and carry model trains by leading German manufacturers in Great Britain (i.e., Märklin, Bing, Carette, Issmayer). Bassett-Lowke commissioned specific British train designs.

Eugene Beggs, Patterson, New Jersey
1872–early 1900s
Specialty: Produced well-designed toy steam locomotives based on 4-4-0 American type. For 30 years Beggs represented the best available American trains.

Biaggi, Rome, Italy
1946–to present day
Specialty: Made primarily locomotives, similar to prewar Märklin offerings; produced gauges O and 1; also limited run of rolling stock.

Gebruder Bing, Nuremberg, Germany
1866–1933
Founders: Brothers Ignatius and Adolph Bing
Specialty: Wide range of clockwork transportation toys. Initiated a line of trains in 1882 that was successfully imported to the United States, Great Britain, and France. Bing closed doors during the Depression in 1933. Karl Bub acquired the train division and Fleishmann, the toy boats.

R. Bliss Manufacturing Co., Pawtucket, Rhode Island
1832–1914 (Sold to Mason and Parker, Winchendon, Massachusetts)
Founder: Rufus Bliss
Specialty: Pioneered in development of lithographed paper-on-wood toys, including trains, boats, building blocks, and doll houses.

Boucher, New York City, New York
Early 1920s–1929 (Bought out Voltamp)
Specialty: Changed Voltamp's line to Standard gauge, but faithfully adhered to old designs, except for a "Blue Comet." Boucher elected to drop its train line in 1929 and return to its original ship modeling pursuits.

Bowman Co., Norwich, England
1920s–?
Specialty: Steam-powered O-gauge locomotives which were actually closer to gauge I in scale. Freight cars were crude wood affairs; the handpainted "Goods Wagons" are especially scarce and desirable.

Milton Bradley, Springfield, Massachusetts
1861–to present day
Founder: Milton Bradley
Specialty: Known for board games, books, educational games; produced a small range of lithographed paper-on-wood toys, including trains.

George W. Brown & Co., Forestville, Connecticut
1856–1880
Founders: George Brown and Chauncey Goodrich
Specialty: First toy maker to use clockwork mechanisms. Also the first to produce clockwork tin trains, beginning in 1856. Merged with J. & E. Stevens in 1868.

Karl Bub, Nuremberg, Germany
1851–1966
Founder: Karl Bub
Specialty: Nicely enameled, and later lithographed, clockwork tin transportation toys, including trains; distributed in the United States through F. A. O. Schwarz, New York City, during 1920s and 1930s. Acquired Bing's train division in 1933.

Buddy "L," Salem, Massachusetts
1910–to present day
Founder: Fred Lundahl
Specialty: Went through many corporate name changes beginning with Moline Press Steel (1910–1913). Buddy "L" line was introduced in 1921 and named after Lundahl's son. Buddy "L" sheet steel trains, typically 21–24 in. or more in length, were produced until 1931.

Georges Carette, Nuremberg, Germany
1886–1917
Founder: Georges Carette (with Gebruder Bing's financial backing)
Specialty: Tin clockwork cars, boats, and trains, mostly lithographed. Best known for quality, nicely detailed, electric street-cars and model trains. Carette, a French citizen, was deported from Germany in 1917, thus closing the firm.

Carlisle & Finch Co., Cincinnati, Ohio
1895–1915 (Toy line dates; firm continues as marine lighting manufacturer)
Specialty: Produced one of the first successful electrically run trains in the United States in 1897. Later expanded line to include steam outline locomotives and rolling stock. Also served as a distributor, handling the Knapp Electric first toy automobile in 1900.

Francis W. Carpenter, Port Chester, New York
1880–1890 (Sold patent rights and toy inventory to Pratt and Letchworth)
Specialty: Cast-iron horse-drawn toys as well as trains.

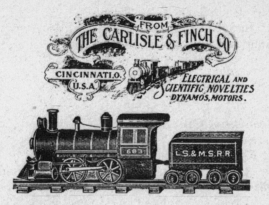

D.P. Clark, Dayton, Ohio
1898–1909 (Renamed Schieble Toy and Novelty Co. in 1909)
Founder: David P. Clark
Specialty: Sheet steel novelty transportation toys, including trains
with friction/flywheel mechanisms.

Morton E. Converse Co., Winchendon, Massachusetts
1878–1934 (Mason & Converse until 1883)
Founder: Morton Converse
Specialty: "Toytown Complex" was once recognized as largest
wood toy factory in the world; also produced metal transportation toys, including floor-runner trolleys. Made the first trolley
bodies for Lionel in 1902, including the famous "City Hall
Park."

Dayton Friction Toy Works, Dayton, Ohio
1909–1935
Founder: D.P. Clark (see also D.P. Clark)
Specialty: Pressed steel friction cars and trains with patented flywheel (1926) under trade name "Gyro." Produced child riders
up to 24 in. long, known as SON-NY line.

Doll et Cie (& Co.), Nuremberg, Germany
1868–1946
Founders: Peter Doll and J. Sondheim
Specialty: Inexpensive steam engines and accessories; novelty
   trains and cars, both steam and clockwork.

Dorfan (See "Dorfan" in *Electric Trains* section)

Dowst (Tootsietoy), Chicago, Illinois
1876–to present day
Founders: Charles and Samuel Dowst
Specialty: Miniature cast-metal transportation toys, primarily automobiles. In 1921, produced its first train set. Of the approximately 50 versions produced, most range in the $5–$10 area.
   Note: Tootsietoy trade name was in honor of a Dowst grand-
   daughter named Toots.

J. Falk, Nuremberg, Germany
1898–1940
Founder: J. Falk
Specialty: Stationary steam engines, optical projectors; steam-
   propelled boats and trains. Inexpensive but unimaginative line.

James Fallows & Sons, Philadelphia, Pennsylvania
1874–late 1890s
Founder: James Fallows (a continuation of Francis Field & Francis, of which Fallows was head designer and inventor). Firm
   began carrying his name in 1880. In 1894, name was changed
   to Frederick & Henry Fallows Toys.
Specialty: Painted and stencilled horse-drawn tin toys, boats, and
   trains. One of few early makers to identify their toys ("IXL,"
   supposedly based on wordplay "I excel"). Fallows' demise
   closely coincided with advent of lithographed tin toys in the
   1880s.

H. Fischer & Co., Nuremberg, Germany
1908–early 1930s
Founder: H. Fischer
Specialty: Produced erratic-action tin toys and O-gauge trains, distributed in the United States by George Borgfeldt.

Gebruder Fleischmann, Nuremberg, Germany
1887–to present day
Founder: J. Fleischmann
Specialty: Quality tinplate boats, automobiles, trains. Took over Doll et Cie just before World War II and concentrates on model railroads to this day.

Francis Field & Francis, Philadelphia, Pennsylvania
1838–1870
Founders: Henry and Thomas Francis. Originally went by name of Philadelphia Tin Toys (into the 1840s). James Fallows entered firm in 1870 and in 1880 name became Fallows.
Specialty: Tinplate clockwork toys and trains.

Fulgurex (Elettren), Lausanne, Switzerland
1947–to present day
Founders: Originally by Elettren, an Italian maker, but today produces under Fulgurex name
Specialty: Elettren made only two locomotives, both larger than the normal O scale; the elaborately detailed coaches of Elettren are considered by many to be the finest ever produced.

A.W. Gamage, London, England
1890s–late 1920s
Founder: A.W. Gamage
Specialty: Leading London department store specializing in toys; also ran a huge mail-order business throughout Great Britain. Gamage placed large train orders with Bing, Märklin, Carette, and Issmayer—by 1906 most trains in their catalog were British outline and Bing and Märklin were primary suppliers.

J. Garlick Co., Paterson, New Jersey
1888–1890s
Founder: Jehu Garlick
Specialty: Small manufacturer of quality steam toys, 1-gauge trains. From 1882–1888, Garlick worked with Eugene Beggs. A distinctive feature of certain Garlick locomotives is a patented reversing valve attached to the cylinder.

A.C. Gilbert Co., New Haven, Connecticut
1908–1966
Founder: Albert C. Gilbert
Specialty: Boxed magic sets. Introduced Erector Sets in 1913, an instant success; 30 million would be sold over the next 40 years. Bought out Richter Anchor Blocks and an American affiliate of Meccano in 1914. Pressed steel autos and trucks were added that same year, plus a variety of scientific toys. Purchased American Flyer in 1938 (see ''American Flyer'') and retained only the name for its line of electric trains. Gilbert subsequently had financial woes of its own and sold its toy train inventory to Lionel in 1966.

Girard Manufacturing Co., Girard, Pennsylvania
1908–1966
Founder: Frank E. Wood. Also went by name of Girard Model Works, Inc. (1922–1935) and The Toy Works (1919–1922).
Specialty: Produced toys and toy trains for Louis Marx under the Marx label back in the early 1920s. Girard also made toys under their own label, which bore the slogan ''Making Childhood's Hour Happier.'' Otherwise, the Marx and Girard toys are, for all intents, indistinguishable. Girard declared bankruptcy in 1934, although toy production continued until 1975. Quaker Oats bought out Marx's interest in Girard when they took over Marx's American and English toy division in 1972.

S.G. Gunthermann, Nuremberg, Germany
1877–1965 (Acquired by Seimens Co. in 1965)
Founder: Sigfried Gunthermann, who died in 1890. His widow
married Adolph Weigel, who ran the company until his death in
1919.
Specialty: Tinplate mechanical cars and trains as well as comic
character windups.

Harris Toy Co., Toledo, Ohio
Ca. 1887–1913
Specialty: Cast-iron transportation toys, including trains. Harris
also acted as jobber for Dent Hardware, Hubley, and Wilkins.
Harris was closed down in 1913 due to financial difficulties.

J.L. Hess, Nuremberg, Germany
1826–mid-1930s
Founder: Mathias Hess
Specialty: Tinplate pull-along trains and various other parlor toys;
autos bore "Hessmobil" trademark. Hess and Issmayer led the
way in developing strong miniature clockwork mechanisms for
locomotives in the 1870s.

Hornby, Liverpool, England
1920s–to present day (produces trains today as Hornby Hobbies,
Ltd.)
Founder: Frank Hornby
Specialty: Produced toy trains beginning in 1920s with its Meccano "Mechanics Made Easy" trademark and slogan. Märklin
marketed the Meccano system under license in Germany, and,
in return, supplied Hornby with accessories such as steam engines. Hornby's elaborate leather-like boxes and colorful yearly
catalog, *The Hornby Book of Trains,* were frequently more impressive than the train sets. Hornby's experiment with train kits
proved unsuccessful. One of their premier ready-built offerings
was a 0-4-0 "Metropolitan Railway" electric outline engine in
1925 with gleaming brass detail. Hornby targeted their markets
in England and France, with only a few attempts to crash the
American scene.

Hubley Manufacturing Co., Lancaster, Pennsylvania
1894–to present day
Founder: John E. Hubley
Specialty: Originally produced cast-iron electric toy train equipment and parts. Hubley's finest cast-iron transportation toy was the "Double-Track Elevated Railway" from 1893. Toy automobiles became Hubley's headliners in the 1930s. They avoided Depression woes by converting to lower priced toys. Iron shortages during World War II, plus wartime contract commitments, eventually led to the demise of Hubley's toy division in 1942. Later, the name was changed to Gabriel Industries, which still exists today as a division of CBS.

Hull & Stafford, Clinton, Connecticut
1860s–1880s (Established as Hull and Wright; acquired Union Manufacturing Co. in 1869)
Specialty: Enameled clockwork tin toys, including trains and boats.

Issmayer, Nuremberg, Germany
1861–1930s
Specialty: Produced lithographed tinplate American outline trains of the novelty type in the 1880s. Its specialty by the turn of the century was small 30 mm gauge (not quite true O gauge) plus 1 gauge. Firm also supplied entire Carette line of clockwork trains and several sets for Schönner during this period.

Ives (See "Ives" in *Electric Trains* section)

J. E. P. (Jouets en Paris), Paris, France
1899–1965 (Known originally as the Societe Industriel de Ferblanteriel, the firm conveniently changed to J. de P. in 1928, then J. E. P. in 1932)
Specialty: Lithographed tin clockwork trains, toy automobiles, and other transportation miniatures. After World War II, J. E. P. was producing France's finest O-gauge trains, typified by the 12-wheeled "Mistral" electric locomotive and P.L.M. 2-8-2 steam-type with twin motors. Factory closed down in 1965.

Keystone Manufacturing Co., Boston, Massachusetts
1920s–date unknown
Specialty: Toy motion picture machines; pressed steel transportation toys including "Siren Riding Toys" and "Ride-Em Trains." In post–World War II, most of Keystone's toy output was based on output from Kingsbury's defunct toy division.

Kingsbury Manufacturing Co., Keene, New Hampshire
1919–1942 (See also Wilkins Toy Co.)
Founder: Harry T. Kingsbury
Specialty: Kingsbury bought out Wilkins in 1895 and combined it with Clipper Machine Works, specializing in farm equipment. Introduced toy automobiles and trains in early 1900. Wilkins name was dropped following World War I in lieu of Kingsbury. The toy line was discontinued in 1942, but the company still exists as Kingsbury Machine Tool.

Knapp Electric Novelty Co., New York City, New York
1852–to present day
Specialty: One of the earliest manufacturers of wet cell-powered trains and other transportation toys. Carlisle & Finch distributed Knapp's line.

Lehmann Gross Bahn, Nuremberg, Germany
1881–to present day (Originally Earnest Lehmann Co., Brandenberg; reorganized in 1951 in Nuremberg as LGB)
Founder: Earnest P. Lehmann
Specialty: Produces trains as well as toys. Began producing large G-scale electric trains in 1968.

Le Rapide, Paris, France
1920s–1954
Founder: Louis Rouissy
Specialty: Electric and clockwork O-gauge model trains, toy racers on oval tracks. In the 1930s, Le Rapide excelled with smartly styled die-cast O-gauge trains, touted as "the fastest in the world" (attributed to their weight and low center of gravity).

Lionel (See "Lionel" in *Electric Trains* section)

Lutz, Nuremberg, Germany
Mid–19th century–1891
Specialty: Lutz produced nicely enameled clockwork and steam-driven floor trains in the 1890s, including the heralded American 4-4-0. At the dawn of the new era of German toy trains, in 1891, Lutz was absorbed by Märklin.

Gebruder Märklin, Goppingen, Germany
1859–to present day
Founders: Theodor and Caroline Märklin. Founders' sons took over firm in 1888 and name was changed to Gebruder (Brothers) Märklin.
Specialty: Originally a maker of tinplate kitchenware (doll-size), Märklin expanded its line to enameled tinplate boats, aeronautical toys, and trains. Unsurpassed in production of clockwork, steam, and electric trains from the 1890s to World War I, Märklin introduced the first standardized tinplate tracks in 1891. The firm was also the first with the concept of train sets as part of an entire railway system including accessories, toy figures, and scenery. In the postwar (World War II) era, Märklin has been closely identified with the miniature N-gauge trains.

Marx (See "Marx" in *Electric Trains* section)

Paya, Alicante, Spain
Early 1900s–1960s
Specialty: Made O-gauge clockwork trains beginning in 1918; electric in 1927; locomotives were primarily 4-4-4s and coaches were long, attractive lithographed examples. Paya appeared to concentrate its line in Spain and France.

Ernst Plank, Nuremberg, Germany
1866–1930s
Founder: Ernst Plank
Specialty: Tinplate trains, airplanes, boats, and automobiles. Plank originally copied the British steam engine designs and exported

them back to Great Britain. The Plank "Vulkan" from 1895, spidery and upright, fashioned in brass, is typical of their styling. Somehow, a faltering Plank company survived the 1920s with their ancient turn-of-the-century locomotives, but by the end of the decade they closed their doors.

Pratt & Letchworth, Buffalo, New York
1880–1900
Founders: Pascal Pratt and William Letchworth
Specialty: Cast-iron toy trains, horse-drawn hansom cabs, and pumpers. Originally operated as Buffalo Malleable Iron Works. Carpenter's stock and patent rights were acquired by Pratt & Letchworth in 1890.

Pride Lines Ltd., Lindenhurst, New York
1980s–to present day
Specialty: Reproductions of Walt Disney Collectors Series novelty hand cars, including Mickey and Minnie, Donald and Pluto; also replicates numerous Märklin accessories such as street lamps, signals, etc.

Radiguet & Massiot, Paris, France
1872–unknown
Founder: R. Radiguet
Specialty: Scientific and educational instruments. In 1889, in partnership with Massiot, Radiguet produced parts for numerous British train makers, as well as its own large steam locomotives. The sole significant model locomotive manufacturer in France up through the early 1900s.

W.S. Reed Toy Co., Leominster, Massachusetts
1875–1897
Founder: Whitney S. Reed
Specialty: Lithographed paper-on-wood naval toys and trains, as well as doll houses and construction sets.

William Rissman Co. (RI-CO), Nuremberg, Germany
1907–unknown
Founder: William Rissman
Specialty: Toy trains and mechanical motor toys. Often confused
  with Rico, the Spanish train maker. Look for additional word,
  ''Germany,'' to identify as Rissman.

Rock & Graner, Nuremberg, Germany
1850–1904
Specialty: Old-line toy maker from mid-19th century added clockwork tin floor trains and accessories in 1896. Folded in the early
  1900s because it couldn't achieve volume production and keep
  up with Bing and Märklin.

Charles Rossignol, Paris, France
1868–1962
Founder: Charles Rossignol
Specialty: Painted and lithographed tin clockwork vehicles, including toy trains. Introduced electric trains in their line in 1919.
  By the late 1950s, Rossignol's train production was in decline;
  its main interest focused on clockwork buses and cars.

Sakai, Tokyo, Japan
1930s–unknown
Specialty: In the 1930s and then following World War II, Sakai
  produced a line of Japanese, electric outline steam locomotives
  and rolling stock that combined the best features of Märklin and
  Lionel.

Schönner, Nuremberg, Germany
1875–1910
Specialty: Brass steam locomotives in American outline, featuring
  cowcatchers of pierced tin. Produced the outstanding floor runner of the 1900–1910 era, a giant, tightly detailed American
  4-4-0. The balance of the line, however, proved unsuccessful
  and by 1910 Schönner had closed its doors.

Jerome Secor Manufacturing, Bridgeport, Connecticut
1872–mid-1880s
Founder: Jerome Secor
Specialty: Clockwork tin toys, including some of the hobby's rarest platform toys and mechanical banks. Secor manufactured the first cast-iron clockwork-powered locomotive in 1880, besting Carpenter in a patent dispute. Secor sold its business to Ives in the 1880s but continued to design and manufacture clockwork toys through Ives.

Stevens & Brown, New York City, New York
1869–1880
Founders: Elisha Stevens and George Brown
Specialty: Painted clockwork tin toys, including trains. Also distributed toys for various manufacturers.

J. & E. Stevens, Cromwell, Connecticut
1843–1930s
Founders: John and Elisha Stevens
Specialty: Cast-iron mechanical banks and transportation toys, including trains.

Stevens Model Dockyards, London, England
1843–unknown
Specialty: A craft guild specializing in manufacturing and distributing toys and toy trains. Produced a number of hefty floor-running steam engines, including the ''Thunderer'' and ''Greater Britain.'' Stevens' cars (or wagons as they were called), are rare and seldom found intact.

Structo Manufacturing Co., Freeport, Illinois
1908–to present day
Founders: Louis and Edward Strohacker, C. C. Thompson
Specialty: Line of stamped steel push toys and trains. In the 1920s, A. C. Gilbert distributed the line. Structo was then partnered with American Flyer. In 1935, Strohackers sold most of the business to J. G. Gokey. F. Ertel of Dyersville, Iowa, another toy maker, acquired Structo in 1975.

Trix, Mangold, Nuremberg, Germany
1930s–to present day
Specialty: OO-gauge locomotives and railway accessories under "TRR" trademark. Bassett-Lowke served as Trix's agent for its British subsidiary.

Unique Art Manufacturing, Newark, New Jersey
1916–1952
Specialty: Comic/character tin mechanicals; their first clockwork trains were produced in 1949. Tried unsuccessfully to compete with Marx in electric train sets in 1950s.

Voltamp Electric Manufacturing Co., Baltimore, Maryland
1879–early 1920s
Founder: Manes E. Fuld
Specialty: By 1903, Voltamp was producing electric trains of the highest order. Their 4-6-0 and 4-6-2 Pacific locomotives with large eight-wheel tenders were hailed as the finest produced by any U.S. maker before World War I. Aimed at the high-end market, Voltamp's production was always limited. In the early 1920s, Boucher, the model boat firm, bought out Voltamp, continuing the old designs and appealing to a small, select, and highly affluent clientele.

Wallwork, Manchester, England
1890s–early 1900s
Specialty: The only British manufacturer to produce cast-iron floor-runner trains (sans mechanisms).

Weeden Manufacturing Co., New Bedford, Massachusetts
1883–1939
Founder: William N. Weeden
Specialty: Produced working steam engine in 1884; also live steamboats, trains, and automobiles. Sold to Pairpoint Co. in the 1930s.

Wells Brimtoy, Hollyhead, Wales and London, England
1920–to present day
Specialty: Tinplate automotive toys and trains. Acquired Brimtoy
  in 1922.

Wilkins Toy Co., Medford, Massachusetts
1890–1919 (See also Kingsbury)
Founder: James S. Wilkins
Specialty: Early manufacturer of cast-iron automobiles and trains.
  Wilkins' trains achieved incredible standards of realism. Kings-
  bury bought out Wilkins in 1895.

Williams Electric Trains, Columbia, Maryland
1950s–to present day
Specialty: Classic O-scale electric train reproductions of some of
  the most popular examples of bygone years. Quality and workmanship are such that Williams' models have become highly
  valued in their own right.

Model and Toy Train Gauges

Gauge is the distance between the inside edge of each rail (initially, the gauge or track width was measured from rail center to rail center; hence the adoption of a more accurate system).

Major Train Manufacturers	Train Gauges (Millimeters in Parentheses)
American Flyer (U.S.)	HO(16.5); S(24); O(35); W(57)
Bassett-Lowke (U.K.)	HO(16.5); OO(16.5); O(35); I(48); II(54); III(67); IV(75)
Biaggi (It.)	O(35); I(48)
Bing (Ger.)	OO(16.5); OO(25); OO(28); O(35); I(48); II(54); U(57); III(67); IV(75)
Bub (Ger.)	OO(16.5); S/OO(24); O(35); I(48)
Carette (Ger.)	U(24); OO(25); OO(28); U(30); O(35); I(48); II(54); III(65); III(67)
Carlisle & Finch (U.S.)	2 in.(51)
Distler (Ger.)	U(16.5); OO(28); O(35)
Dorfan (U.S.)	O(35); W(57)
Gamages (U.K.)	OO(16.5); 1 in.(25); 1 1/8 in. (28); O(35)

Hornby (U.K.)	OO(16.5); O(35)
Issmayer (Ger.)	U(25); U(28); U(30); O(35); I(48)
Ives (U.S.)	O(35); I(48); W(57)
J.E.P. (Fr.)	U(18); S(24); U(28); O(35)
Lionel (U.S.)	OO(19); O(35); ST(57); 2⅞ in. (75)
L.G.B. (Ger.)	G
Märklin (Ger.)	OO/HO(16.5); OO(26); O(35); I(48); II(54); U(57); III(75); U(120); Z(6.5)
Marx (U.S.)	HO(16.5); ST(57); O(35)
Plank (Ger.)	O(35); I(48); VIII(65)
Schönner (Ger.)	OOO(25); OO(28); O(35); I(48); II(54); IIA(67); III(75); IV(85); U(90); U(115)
Trix (Ger.)	OO(16.5)
Voltamp (U.S.)	2 in. (51)

Key:

U =   Undesignated.

W =   Wide gauge. The "W" designation was adopted by Ives, Dorfan, and American Flyer when Lionel had a copyright on the phrase "Standard gauge." All gauges were adapted from manufacturers' catalogs, flyers, etc., as means of identification. They may not always prove accurate.

ST =   Standard gauge.

OO =   Designation by European manufacturers over period of years for anything smaller than O gauge.

S =   Gauge that was originally called H1 (half gauge 1).

Z =   Smallest commercially produced gauge. Märklin is, at this writing, the only major manufacturer of this minute gauge which could run around the brim of a hat!

The Three Rs: Coping with Reproductions, Repaints, and Restorations

Unlike the rest of the toy world, where reproductions, repaints, and repairs are not only frowned upon but rigidly policed, collectors of model trains tend to be more flexible in accepting examples found in these altered states.

Reproductions

From their very inception, model train makers have been notorious "copy cats" or cloners. To begin with, most classic models were closely patterned after a real-life prototype train. Patent protection for models often proved tenuous and easy to circumvent. Even when certain manufacturers were able to patent certain innovative features (i.e., a special coupler, truck design or power system), they were prone to be lax and let the patents expire.

Another factor is that a large segment of the hobby—the modelers—often modify their *own* equipment to achieve greater authenticity and aren't satisfied until their trains and layouts attain perfection. Modelers dismiss those purists who insist on owning vintage mint originals in their original boxes as behaving like stamp collectors.

Actually, in terms of quality and workmanship, many contemporary train reproductions can hold their own, and, in some cases, surpass the genuine article. Such current replicators as Williams, Varney & Sirus, Pride Lines, Ltd., McCoy, and Classic Mike's Train House all have produced excellent repro ready-mades as well as model kits. This poses a threat to the investor dealer/collector who may have paid dearly in years past for a scarce original, only to see its value eroded by a darn good reproduction. A recent Williams copy of the classic Lionel No. 381E from 1928 is a case in point.

Most reproductions today are, in most cases, by companies that are not out for the fast buck or any intent to deceive with out-and-out ripoffs. There is also some validity in their claim that a modestly priced look-alike helps open up the hobby to those who might otherwise find market prices too rarefied when it comes to the more elusive and endangered species of classic models.

It is only at some unspecified time in the future, when a given reproduction or altered train is *resold*, that the ethical dilemma rears its head. Entry-level collectors and even more seasoned modelers could possibly be fooled by a supposedly rare variation faked by clever craftsmanship or misrepresented by unscrupulous sellers.

Imitation . . . The Sincerest Form of Flattery

In the early 1900s, Ives seemed content to produce almost exact copies of its German rivals, Issmayer and Märklin. Ives' tiny O-gauge tinplate locomotive of 1901 featured a cone smokestack and arched cab windows that were the spitting image of an Issmayer version. Ives' wedge-shaped spoke on their wheels was copied from Märklin, but even more obvious was their adoption of the Märklin shield-shaped logo. Ives continued to use the symbol until 1905, when it was finally removed following Märklin's strenuous objections.

For those collectors who prefer *only* the genuine article, there are certain guidelines to observe to avoid being stung.

1. There is no substitute for knowledge and experience. Attend shows and exhibitions, check and re-check catalogs and flyers, pore over books that illustrate and describe models in every detail; keep posted through publications which regularly deal with the subject and often issue "repro alerts." Knowing your area of specialization backwards and forwards is the best way to avoid the repro trap.
2. Deal only with those people in the hobby who you can trust and who will guarantee the train's authenticity.
3. If even the slightest doubt persists, never hesitate to seek a second opinion from a trusted fellow collector or anyone whose astuteness you respect.
4. Watch price. Any variation that is offered far below its market value may appeal to your baser instincts, but at the same time should raise some doubt as to its pedigree.
5. Never be shy about questioning the seller as to *his* knowledge of the item.
6. Carefully examine every facet of the model, including the materials used in its makeup. Are the parts indigenous to the time frame in which they were allegedly produced? Obviously a molded plastic boiler or a cowcatcher affixed to a 1930s vintage known to be of cast-metal construction would be highly suspect.
7. Rely on your second sense or "third eye" to determine if the model train is right. This comes with time and experience in handling trains. Once you gain confidence, there should be no fears.

Repaints

Whether it's a new "creation" or a conversion of a less desirable model to one that is difficult to locate in original condition, repaints require more careful scrutiny than reproductions. Here, there is far more cosmetic trickery than meets the eye. Old or original paint has the following characteristics:

1. Often shows its age by crazing (minute hairline cracks).
2. Evidence of wear and tear in normal wear areas (i.e., next to keywind or switch; around moving parts).

3. Has a harder finish than new paint and will not scratch easily.
4. Will appear a different color than new paint under black light testing: original red will appear olive green under UV light; newer red comes out as bright orange.

New paint may be detected as follows:

1. Often betrays its presence by odor.
2. Easily scratches because of softness of paint.
3. Parts of same color match up and change color uniformly under black light.
4. Using a cotton swab applied with xylene or acetone agents to a less visible part of the model, new paint quickly dissolves while old paint remains unaffected.
5. Watch for decorative details such as striping, lettering, and logo details that are *too* solid or crisp to be true. Older original versions tend to have a nicked, worn, and chalky look about them.
6. Eventually, it is vital that you do some research on areas of production on your own. Learning about frames, overspraying, shells, stress marks, and other features all provide clues as to repainting.

Restoration (Replaced Parts)

There exists a whole universe of mini-junkyards offering missing spare wheels, trucks, frames, bells, and headlights for model trains. For years, Approved Lionel Service Stations, for example, provided a service to collectors who wanted their trains repaired. Customers requested and paid willingly for converting, revitalizing or reoutfitting their trains with reproduction components and body shells. This led further to repainting and retouching. Here again, the majority of purchases were intended to transform the train whole again, to make it presentable in the layout or display case. Only a small percentage were added with intent to pass them off as unadulterated originals. The watchword here again, as with all-out reproductions, is to educate ourselves as to the differences between the real and the bogus. We must remain constantly on the alert to protect our investment.

Mix and Match in the Train World

One of the most frequently found mutants (those models with replaced parts from another manufacturer entirely) in the hobby are the Dorfan issues from 1928 through 1930. Dorfan's die-cast trucks on their freight cars were prone to buckle and fall apart due to some imperfection in the metal. With Dorfan's demise, collectors with defective trucks resorted to using Lionel 200 or 500 series replacement trucks purchased at their local repair or hobby shops.

It was not unusual for one train maker to produce interchangeable components for another maker. When American Flyer, for example, entered the Standard-gauge sweepstakes in 1925, they bought all their passenger coaches from Lionel and then painted and lettered them as their own. In 1928, following Ives' bankruptcy, the firm struggled for two more years under the joint auspices of American Flyer and Lionel. The Ives line became a complex hodgepodge of Ives, American Flyer, and Lionel components.

Pros and Cons of Custom Refinishing

Peter Riddle, writing in the Summer 1989 issue of *Classic Toy Trains* (''The Case For Custom Refinishing'')*, believes that some old trains may be customized without reducing their intrinsic value. He applies certain guidelines:

- Only common pieces should be customized. True rarities should remain unaltered. Relatively scarce examples in a condition that has diminished value should be restored in original colors.
- Only items in need of restoration should be customized. Don't touch examples that grade very good or higher.

*From *Classic Toy Trains*, Kalmbach Publishing Co., 1989.

- A custom finish should make sense aesthetically and historically. Matching a caboose to a locomotive is one instance. Redecorating a passenger set to a more attractive livery than the original is another.

While we can find no fault with Mr. Riddle's customizing guidelines, it would behoove all of us to obey the rules set forth by Congress under Public Law 93-167, the Hobby Protection Act, which requires that imitations of various kinds of Americana be clearly marked "Reproduction" (or "Repaint") in a prominent place on the item and in a nonremovable manner. Unfortunately, most manufacturers and entrepreneurs are either unaware of the law or choose to ignore it.

Buying and Selling At Auction

Buying At Auction

Buying at a train auction tends to be a bit more complicated than buying at any other type of toy or doll auction. The procedure is usually quite similar to auctions of antiquarian books; for example, entries of a certain maker or category may be lotted as one and the value and condition of each item may vary drastically. Also, train auctioneers move along at a much faster cadence or tempo and sometimes the information on each lot is sketchy. (In our opinion, Greenberg Auctions, Inc. of Timonium, Maryland, gives probably the most precise and complete catalog description of each auction item as any we've seen in the hobby.) It therefore behooves you to be on site for the auction preview so that each item can be examined carefully, unless of course you are very familiar with a given estate consignment and you know precisely what you intend to bid on, well in advance.

There may be occasions, however, when you simply can't attend the preview or the auction itself. If you still know the merchandise in question, many auction houses allow you to participate as a phone bidder or absentee mail bidder. When sending in a mail bid, some auction houses require a deposit. Another alternative is to appoint a proxy, preferably someone you know well who has a knowledge of trains, who would be willing to bid from the floor on your behalf. The best way for absentee bidders to enhance their chances of winning a desired lot is to post a ceiling bid that is clearly on the high side. This by no means implies that you'll ultimately pay that amount. It only enhances your chances of winning your prize train model. Most house rules dictate that should you actually wind up with a top bid, it will not exceed that of the next highest bidder by 10% or at the most, 20%. Even so, you should prepare yourself for the contingency that someone out there may be even more determined to own the item than you are.

When a major auction house holds a train auction, particularly an estate auction, it invariably issues a lavishly illustrated catalog (some even include color plates) that is available for $15–$25. These catalogs usually prove to be well worth the investment as: 1) they help you determine if it's worth your time and energy to attend; 2) they normally give presale estimates as a guideline; and 3) they serve, along with the after-sale prices realized sheet provided by the auction house, as a handy reference for buying and selling at future auctions and shows.

When a specific entry is *not* pictured in the catalog, many auction houses will provide you with a colored Polaroid for a nominal fee. Also, don't be hesitant about calling and clarifying any doubts you might have as to provenance or condition. It could save you a lot of grief later.

The following suggestions may also prove helpful in buying model trains at auction:

- Always get to the preview as early as possible so that you can give any entrees of interest a thorough inspection without being rushed or distracted by the crowd. If you have any question regarding condition and provenance, or if you wish to have the item put up at a certain time (providing it is not a cataloged sale), you will have time to discuss it with the auction manager.
- Be sure to find a seat or a place to stand where you can be readily spotted by the auctioneer. Make positive bidding motions. Some bidders we know go through all manner of method-acting machinations such as eye twitchings, shoulder tics, and head scratchings to indicate a bid (as if to disguise their identity from others while bidding). What generally hap-

pens is that the auctioneer is the one who misses your bid and you may be ''out'' a very desirable artifact.

- Try to contain your excitement by taking a few deep breaths between bids and don't raise your own bid. Most auctioneers are charitable about this, but we do know of a few who will have you up there well beyond what you should be paying. If you are not certain who has the high bid, don't be shy about asking the auctioneer.

- This advice is easier to give than to follow, but decide *beforehand* the very maximum you'd be willing to pay, and hold to it.

- Above all, don't be intimidated by any bidding ''pool'' that may be working in the audience. Remember, those involved in the pool are usually dealers who have yet to hold their little ''side auction''; ultimately, they must resell the item at a profit. As long as they are in there bidding with you, in all probability the price of the lot remains within the realm of reason.

Selling At Auction

The consignor's role in an auction is often clouded in mystique and most auction goers find it more difficult to comprehend than the buyer's role. Usually this is because the seller is the silent partner in the auction process. Once the would-be seller has consigned his property to the auction house, his participation ends. Usually, unless a single item is of significant value, an auction house elects not to accept it, preferring, of course, sizable lots of items. The latter balances things out; an item might go disappointingly low, but the law of averages dictates that other items will correspondingly top off beyond expectations.

The first consideration in selecting an auction house to handle your consignment of model trains is that house's ''track record.'' In this highly specialized field, it is important that they *know* trains and how to promote and sell them. Auction houses such as Greenberg Auctions, Inc., Ted Maurer, Lloyd Ralston, Rick Opfer, and Sotheby's (particularly on high-end upscale German and French imports) all have mounted impressive estate train auctions in recent years. Bruce Greenberg and Lloyd Ralston are themselves collectors and have been active in the T.C.A. for years.

Auction houses charge varying rates to consignors and for different services, including transportation, insurance, photography, advertising, and repairs. There is also a seller's commission to be exacted. Rates vary from house to house, according to how the contract is negotiated. You pay the house a fee ranging from 10% to 21%, depending on whether the house has a buyer's premium. There have been, of course, auction houses who have accepted extremely coveted properties without charging a seller's fee.

Before choosing an auction house, it pays to check out their commission arrangement thoroughly. Also, most houses assume complete responsibility as to how the consignments are described in the catalog or advertisements. Be sure to touch bases with your auction house to make certain that the item will be described accurately. Resolve any differences before committing yourself to anything.

To protect your investment, you may also want to discuss selling your consignment subject to reserve. This price is usually determined by the seller and ranges from 50% to 80% of the low estimate. On items of higher value, the reserve is usually mid-range between the low and high estimate. If perchance your consignment fails to meet reserves, you still may be money-out-of-pocket. At many big auction houses, the contract stipulates that the consignor authorize the house to act as exclusive agent for 60 days following the auction to sell the property privately for the previously agreed reserve price.

Preserving, Displaying, Housing, and Operating Your Model Trains

How a train collection should be housed and showcased is strictly a matter of individual taste, personality, imagination, and creative flair.

There are those collectors who stash their treasures away in crates and boxes for some indeterminate rainy day. There are others, meanwhile, who "live" their hobby, turning their quarters into one giant roundhouse with mazes of track leading from room to room. More than one modeler has purchased a particular home because it featured a "railroad" attic, game room, or basement with plenty of wide open space for benchwork, layouts, and trains.

Lionel president Richard Kughn houses one of the nation's most imposing private train collections in a remodeled bowling alley in Detroit. The Count Antonio Giansanti Coluzzi collection of Lausanne, Switzerland, features a track that meanders all around his estate; a small steam railroad of amusement park-size takes visitors on a tour of the premises. Inside the mansion, over a dozen rooms and hallways are lined with bookshelves filled from floor to ceiling with gems from the Coluzzi collection.

P.G.A. golfer Ed Dougherity from Philadelphia had a two-car garage structure redesigned for his superb collection of postwar

Lionels. He even keeps some of his silver cars such as the F3s swathed in silk sheets for protection against dust, something he doesn't even have on his own bed.

Those collectors less endowed with the luxury of space can always consider the popular HO gauge or the even more miniscule Z-gauge train sets. The latter could easily be operated on the brim of someone's hat.

As Jim Doherty writes in the December 1988 *Smithsonian,* "When it comes to building equipment and scenery, the little things don't just mean a lot; they mean everything." Doherty profiles such zealous modelers as Bruce Williams Zaccagnio of Three Bridges, New Jersey, who puts in 14 to 15 hours a day on what he calls "The World's Largest Model Railroad," with over 2.5 miles of track, more than 1,000 switches and 400 bridges, and over 37 tons of plastic rock! Then there is Bruce Chubb of Grand Rapids, Michigan, who has spent more than 34 years perfecting his Sunset Valley Railroad layout with a computer that coordinates signals to keep 16 trains running simultaneously.

By contrast, there are still untold numbers of more passive modelers who are content to follow the time-honored family ritual of running the train under the Yule tree once each year.

The most important requisite is to put your trains, accessories, scenery, track layout, and wiring together following a unifying concept or theme—one that conveys not just convincing realism but a feeling of nostalgia for a certain time and place. For technical guidance in assembling the ideal layout in your home there are scores of "How-To" books and tapes available today through your local train dealer or hobby shop, and which can be ordered from the pages of publications such as *Model Railroader* and *Classic Toy Trains*. A video tape that many modelers swear by is "The Basics of Model Railroading" with Wayne Wesolowski, produced by Kalmbach Video in 1984.

Storing Trains

One of the preferred methods of storing lighter-weight rolling stock is to enfold each unit in a slightly larger cloth bag, allowing enough bag to overlap and protect the car's ends. Heavier locomotives and cars with fragile extensions such as pantographs, ladders, and lights can be wrapped in sections of soft, flexible packing foam. Stack bagged cars in sturdy cardboard or wooden boxes up to three layers deep with the heavier cars at the bottom, of course. Second- and third-tiered cars are best turned on their sides to prevent wheels and other extensions from digging into the cars beneath them.

Displaying Trains

There are so many advantages to exposing one's prized trains to daily scrutiny in open display areas that it is easy to overlook its drawbacks—dust, humidity, and direct sunlight—all of which can exact their toll.

To avoid overexposure to these harmful side effects, many modelers wisely rotate their train displays, keeping those not on view well protected in boxes and bags, as described above, or in special climate-controlled drawers and vaults.

To reduce the amount of contact with dust and dirt, many collectors opt for glass- or plexiglass-enclosed shelves and bookcases. To avoid the harmful glare of ultraviolet light, low-wattage mini shelf lights arranged in tandem are recommended. They show off trains to best advantage without distorting colors and tones. Fluorescent lighting is another option, but it tends to give a different cast to an object. Treated plexiglass is another way to block out UV rays, which can inevitably lead to fading. It is also advisable to set up your displays in a part of the room where daily exposure to direct sunlight is minimal.

Other little hints include:

- Make a periodic cleaning schedule for your trains and stick to it.
- Field strip and inspect cars from your entire collection thoroughly at least once a year to determine any signs of trouble, then take immediate remedial steps.
- Try to eliminate as much handling as possible. A single fingerprint has been known to etch metal, and oil from the skin can smudge vintage finishes.

It's Show Time

In displaying a collection of locomotives and rolling stock, it is important to use shelves that are not so thick as to overwhelm the cars themselves. To keep the cars from rolling off the smooth boards, they can be placed diagonally, but they appear less than life-like in this manner. There are several possible solutions.

We know of one collector who lines his shelves with straight sections of track he's been able to pick up at junk shops, enabling the cars to be viewed side-on. Eric Sayer Patterson, writing in the Summer 1989 issue of *Classic Toy Trains*,* finds another remedy in an old familiar building material. He recommends prefabricated tongue-and-groove boards used for wall paneling, known by such names as "wainscotting," "4-in. beadboard" or "beaded ceiling." Patterson removes the tongue section with a jigsaw, then rounds off the board's edge with a Stanley Surform woodworking tool. He cuts the boards to lengths, sands the backs, then removes the groove, thus allowing the support blocks to be recessed from the leading edge of the shelf sides. Because the shelving is so narrow, it should be anchored to the wall with angle brackets. The trains can now be shown to best advantage with the wheels set into one of the two grooves running down the center of the board. What's more, they'll remain in perfect alignment.

*From "Beadboard Shelves for Your Collection," *Classic Toy Trains*, Kalmbach Publishing Co., 1989.

Cleaning and Oiling

Cast-iron and other cast-metal cars should not be cleaned with soap, detergent solutions or water, even on paint that has been permanently bonded. Instead, apply a cloth dipped in a few drops of light machine oil and exert very little pressure when cleaning the object. Plastic cars and parts are sometimes adversely affected by certain machine oils so always check first about the proper lubricant with your local dealer or hobby shop owner. Lithographed tin trains can normally be cleaned safely with water and a mild detergent such as Murphy's Oil Soap Household Cleaner. If there is any doubt about the material being cleaned, dip a cotton swab in the cleaning mixture and test the botton area of the car first, before cleaning the entire item. It is always advisable to periodically apply a light machine oil to all moving parts to keep your cars running quietly and smoothly.

Above all, *know what you don't know* and never hesitate about asking for outside guidance. Professionals at shows, museums, conservation centers, and hobby shops are willing to give you the benefit of their experience.

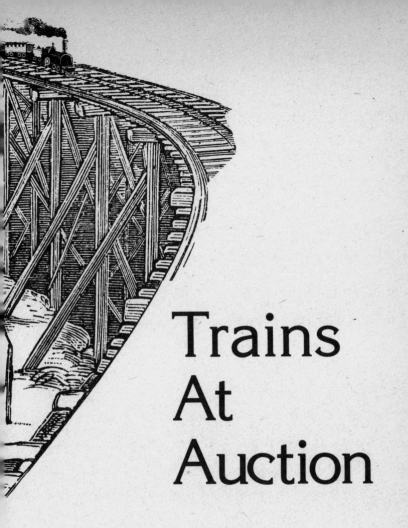

Trains
At
Auction

Ted Maurer Auction

The following pages list trains sold at the March 24 and 25, 1989, Ted Maurer Auction in Pottstown, Pennsylvania. The two-day event featured a number of rarities, including the American Flyer "President's Special," the Ives "White Train Set," the Ives "Prosperity Special," the American Flyer "Mayflower" four-car passenger set, the Lionel "Blue Comet" passenger train set, and the Lionel 408E "State" set.

American Flyer

Train Sets and Locomotives

AF No. 4019 Locomotive, 4040 "America," "Pleasant View," maroon passenger set. $700

AF No. 4644 Locomotive, with three lithographed "Statesmen" passenger cars, green. $7,000

AF No. 4692 Locomotive, with 4671 tender. $700

AF No. 4644 Locomotive, maroon, with 4341-4341-4342 "Hamiltonian" cars. $800

AF No. 4692X Locomotive, with 4693 tender, 4331-4331-4332 passenger cars, "The Iron Monarch."   *$1,150*

AF No. 4692 Locomotive, with "Vanderbilt" tender in original box.   *$775*

AF No. 4694 "Adams" Locomotive, with red plate 4694 "Vandy" tender in original box, 4-4-2 configuration.   *$725*

AF 4-4-2 (Simple Valve Gear) Locomotive, with 4671 coal tender.
    $400

AF 4-4-2 (Triangle Valve Gear) Locomotive, with 4671 coal tender.
    $500

AF No. 4670 Cast-iron Locomotive, with 4671 coal tender.
    $625

AF No. 4683 Electric 0-4-0 Locomotive, red.   *$400*

AF No. 4684 "Statesman" Locomotive, with 4151-4151-4152, original box and set box.   *$1,200*

AF No. 4689 "President's Special" Locomotive, with 4390-4391-4392-4393 passenger cars.   *$7,500*

AF No. 4694 Locomotive, 4-4-2 and tender (to restore).   *$400*

AF No. 4695 Deluxe Locomotive, with tender.   *$775*

Rolling Stock

AF Rigid Truck Lumber Car, NN, with "American Flyer Lines" decal.   *$125*

AF Rigid Truck No. 4017 Gondola, "8 Million."   *$70*

AF Rigid Truck No. 4018 Box Car, "8 Million."   *$175*

AF Flex Truck No. 4018 Box Car.   *$125*

AF No. 4020 Stock Car, "6 Million."   *$225*

AF Rigid Truck No. 4021 Caboose, "8 Million."   *$90*

AF Rigid Truck No. 4022 Lumber Car, "8 Million."   *$70*

AF Rigid Truck No. 4010 Tank Car, yellow.   *$900*

AF Rigid Truck No. 4023 Lumber Car.   *$120*

AF No. 4000-4040-4041-4042 Passenger Set, green.   *$700*

AF No. 4017 Sand Car, with rigid trucks, "8 Million."   *$90*

AF No. 4018 Box Car, with rigid trucks, "8 Million."   *$130*

AF No. 4020 Stock Car, with rigid trucks, minus "Million" plate.
                                                                           $220

AF No. 4018 Box Car, "8 Million."   *$140*

AF No. 4006 Hopper, "7 Million," flex truck, red.   *$600*

AF No. 4017 Sand Car, "6 Million," with flex truck, original box,
green.   *$350*

AF No. 4018 Box Car, "6 Million," with flex truck, original box,
tan/blue.   *$325*

AF No. 4020 Stock Car, "6 Million," with flex truck, blue/green,
original box.   *$350*

AF No. 4011 Caboose, with flex truck, red.   *$200*

AF No. 4684 "*Bunker Hill,*" three-car passenger set.   *$600*

AF No. 4689 "*Mayflower,*" four-car passenger set.   *$4,750*

AF No. 4687, three-car "President's Special," 1927, blue lithographed. $2,800

AF No. 4039, three-car "President's Special," tan. $2,000

AF No. 4637-4010-4011-4017-4018-4022 Freight Set, original box plus set box. $1,600

AF No. 4643 "America," with "Pleasant View" passenger set, green. $270

AF No. 4678-4340-4341-4342 "Hamiltonian," passenger set, maroon. $700

AF No. 4006 Hopper and No. 4017 Sand Car, illuminated caboose with rigid truck, "6 Million Cars." $725

AF No. 4637-4340-4341-4342-4343 "Pocahontas," passenger set. $1,900

AF No. 4683-4350-4351-4352 "Stadium," passenger set, blue/red. $2,300

AF No. 4686 "Flying Colonel," three-car passenger set, dark blue. $6,000

Reproductions by Miscellaneous Manufacturers

Varney-Sirus AF "President's Special," four-car set, enameled. $3,500

Varney-Sirus AF No. 4380-81-81-81-82 "Flying Colonel," passenger cars, tan/green. $1,500

Accessories/Lineside Equipment

AF No. 4684 Train Controlling Semaphore, in original box. $370

AF Gate and Tower Unit, plus bell signal.   *$250*

AF No. 2116 Bell Signal, with original box.   *$55*

AF Small Lithographed Station, plus pair of switches.   *$65*

AF Crossing Gate and Bell Tower, on base.   *$175*

AF Street Lamps (Two), Semaphore, Three Gates.   *$60*

Ives

Train Sets and Locomotives

IV No. 1132 "Gray Ghost" Locomotive, with 184-185-186 brass plate cars, 1928.   *$475*

IV No. 1134R "Prosperity Special" Locomotive, steam-type with 241-242-243 passenger cars in copper and nickel finish, cataloged only in 1929.   *$12,000*

IV No. 1132 Locomotive and Tender, with 184-185-186 passenger set, tan finish.   *$1,250*

IV No. 1134 "President Washington" 4-4-0 Locomotive With No. 40 Tender, 187-188-189 passenger cars, green locomotive and cars.
$2,200

IV No. 1132 With New York Central & HR Tender, cast-iron locomotive.   *$675*

IV No. 1132 Black Locomotive, No. 40 tender (incomplete). *$450*

IV No. 1134 Locomotive and Tender, red (repainted).   *$600*

IV No. 1134 Locomotive With No. 20-192-195-198 Freight Cars, comprise "Merchants Fast Freight Set," with original box, 1929, sold separately at $800 but, combined with freight cars, lot bought.
$1,425

IV No. 1134 Locomotive and Tender.   *$850*

IV No. 1134 Locomotive and Tender, center headlight on locomotive.   *$600*

IV "Black Diamond Express Senior" With 1134 Locomotive and Tender, American Flyer/Ives black/red 24-242-243 passenger cars, 1929.   *$5,000*

IV No. 1134 Locomotive and Tender, missing rear truck.   *$500*

IV "Circus Set," including No. 1134 locomotive, wild animal car/equipment car, three flat cars, and performers' Pullman car.
                                                            $5,750

IV No. 3235 Locomotive, with 171-173 passenger cars, sold as Set No. 690, in original box.   *$350*

IV No. 3235 Locomotive, brass plate with rubber-stamped "170" buffet and "173" observation cars.   *$200*

IV No. 3241 Locomotive, brass plate with maroon 184-185-186 rubber-stamped passenger cars.   *$550*

IV No. 3241 Locomotive, rubber stamped, maroon, with 184-185-186 passenger cars.   *$350*

IV No. 3242 Locomotive, "Gray Ghost" with 184-185-186 brass-plate passenger cars.   *$475*

IV No. 3242 Locomotive, brown, rubber stamped.   *$350*

IV No. 3242 Locomotive, maroon, with 187-188-189 passenger cars in original box.   *$275*

IV No. 3241 Locomotive, with 184-186 passenger cars, Set 700, original box.   *$475*

IV No. 3241 Locomotive, maroon, rubber-stamped.   *$300*

IV No. 3237R Locomotive, brass plate.   *$600*

IV No. 3243 Locomotive, green, with eight-wheel rubber-stamped cars.   *$900*

IV No. 3245 Locomotive, black/orange with Lionel/Ives 247-248-249 passenger cars.   *$3,700*

IV No. 3243 Locomotive, white with white 187-1, 188-1, and 189-1 passenger cars, 1922.   *$5,100*

IV No. 3237R "Transcontinental Limited" Locomotive, with 187-188-189 passenger cars and brass "Southern Pacific" plates, blue finish.   *$3,500*

IV No. 3273 "Transcontinental Limited" Locomotive, green with 187-188-189 brass plate cars in original box.   *$3,000*

IV No. 3245 Locomotive, blue/green.   *$1,025*

IV No. 3237R "Transcontinental Limited" Locomotive, with 187-188-189 cars, cadet blue.   *$3,000*

Reproductions by Miscellaneous Manufacturers

M. & V. Enterprises No. 3245R, black short cab locomotive with motor.   *$300*

Varney-Sirus "Olympian," five-car passenger set, powered.
                                                          $1,700

Varney-Sirus No. 3245R, orange/black with motor.   *$365*

Rolling Stock

IV No. 170-171-172 Passenger Cars, tan, rubber-stamped.   *$350*

IV No. 184-185-185-186 Passenger Set, brass plates, black and red, for No. 3242R. $600

IV No. 187-188-189 Passenger Set, maroon, with original box, for No. 3243. $1,225

IV No. 190 Texas Oil Tank Car. $190

IV No. 190 Texas Oil Tank Car, orange. $300

IV No. 191 Pennsylvania R.R. Coke Car. $275

IV No. 192 Santa Fe Reefer. $275

IV No. 193 Pennsylvania R.R. Stock Car. $225

IV No. 193 Stock Car, brass journals. $120

IV No. 194 Pennsylvania R.R. Hopper Car. $225

IV No. 194 Pennsylvania R.R. Coal Car, gray. $210

IV No. 195 Caboose. $425

IV No. 196 Flat Car. $275

IV No. 196 Flat Car, green. $110

IV No. 197 Lumber Car, brass journals. $280

IV No. 198 Gondola. $200

IV No. 199 Crane. $350

IV No. 246-247-248-249 Passenger Cars, restored. $800

Reproductions by Miscellaneous Manufacturers

Varney-Sirus No. 241-242-243 Passenger Cars, green. $950

Varney-Sirus "Black Diamond" 241-242-243 Passenger Cars.
$1,050

Varney-Sirus No. 241-242-243 "Prosperity" Cars, copper/nickel.
$700

Wanamaker No. 187-3, 188-3, 189-3 Passenger Cars, maroon.
$4,700

Ossisek Reproduction Ives Circus Cars, two flat cars, equipment car, stock car, and six wagons. $550

Accessories/Lineside Equipment

IV No. 89 Water Tower. $250

IV Double Union Station, reproduced dome. $750

IV No. 99-2-3 Bridge, with original box. $675

IV Two-Light Target Signal. $150

Ives/American Flyer Rolling Stock

I/AF No. 20-192, 20-195, 20-198 Freight Cars, with original box, 1929. $625

Ives/Lionel

Train Sets and Locomotives: 1930–1932

IV/LI No. 10 Locomotive, peacock finish with 337-338 cars bearing "Ives Railway Lines," decals. $475

IV/LI No. 408E Locomotive, apple green. $750

IV/LI No. 1764E Locomotive, with 1766-1767-1768 cars with maroon roofs and terra-cotta sides. *$4,100*

IV/LI No. 1770E Locomotive and Tender. *$800*

IV/LI No. 1770E Locomotive, with 1760 tender, 1771 lumber car, 1772 gondola, and 1777 caboose, 1932. *$1,600*

IV/LI No. 1082 "Interstate Limited," with black/orange 3236 and 184-185-186 passenger cars, in original boxes, including set box, 1929. *$1,750*

Rolling Stock

IV/LI No. 190 Tank Car, 1932. *$400*

IV/LI No. 192 Box Car. *$425*

IV/LI No. 195 Caboose. *$200*

IV/LI No. 198 Gondola. *$200*

IV/LI No. 199 Crane. *$350*

IV/LI No. 1779 Crane. *$1,000*

IV/LI No. 246-247-248-249 Passenger Cars, black, restored by Joshua Cohen (President of Lionel in 1932). *$1,200*

Lionel

Train Sets and Locomotives

LI No. 392 Locomotive and Tender, 424-425-426 "Girard" passenger set. *$3,600*

LI No. 390E "Blue Comet," 420-421-422 passenger set, original box and set box. *$6,200*

LI No. 400E Locomotive and Tender, original box for locomotive.
$1,700

LI No. 400E Black Locomotive and Tender, 212-219-217-220 work train, original box.   *$5,500*

LI No. 384E Locomotive and Tender, 309-312 passenger set, terra cotta/maroon, original box.   *$1,400*

LI No. 402 Twin Locomotive, mojave.   *$525*

LI No. 400E Locomotive and Tender, gray.   *$2,500*

LI No. 385E and 384 Tender, gray.   *$850*

LI No. 8E Electric Locomotive, olive, original box.   *$190*

LI No. 8, mojave, with 337-337-338 passenger set.   *$375*

LI No. 8E, red, 337-338 passenger set.   *$200*

LI No. 9, green, 328-329-330 passenger set.   *$3,400*

LI No. 9E Electric Locomotive and Tender, gunmetal, original box.
$1,400

LI No. 9E 0-4-0 Electric Locomotive, orange.   *$1,600*

LI No. 9U 0-4-0 Electric Locomotive, orange.   *$1,100*

LI No. 10E, 332-339-341 passenger set, peacock finish.   *$440*

LI No. 318E, mojave, 309-310-312 passenger set.   *$500*

LI No. 385E Locomotive and Tender, gunmetal, 309-310-312 two-tone blue passenger set.   *$1,450*

LI No. 400E Locomotive and Tender, crackle black (restored).
$1,400

LI No. 392 Locomotive and Tender, gunmetal, original box.
$1,400

LI No. 381E 4-4-4 Electric Locomotive. $2,500

LI 400E Locomotive and Tender, black with display board, case, and original box. $2,800

LI No. 385E Locomotive and Tender, 1766-1767-1768 passenger set, original box, 1934. $210

LI No. 390E Locomotive and Tender, 515-516-516-517 coal train set. $2,200

LI No. 400E Locomotive and Tender, gunmetal. $2,300

LI No. 384 Locomotive and Tender. $775

LI No. 392 Locomotive With Early Short Tender, black. $1,200

LI No. 384 Hand-Reverse Locomotive and Tender. $650

LI No. 390 Hand-Reverse Locomotive and Tender (restored).
$600

LI No. 392 Locomotive and Tender, 424-425-426 "Girard" passenger set. $3,600

Passenger Car Sets

LI No. 1766-1767-1768 Passenger Set, original box (two), red/maroon, 1934. $1,500

LI No. 390E, 420-421-422 "Blue Comet" Passenger Train Set, original box and set box. $6,200

LI No. 41 Set Box, 112-113-114-116-117 freight cars, minus locomotive. $750

LI No. 408E, 412-413-414-416 "State" Set, two-toned brown.
$8,500

LI No. 4684 Three-Car "Bunker Hill" Passenger Set, orange.
$600

LI No. 10E, 332-339-341 Passenger Set, peacock. $440

LI No. 8E, 337-338 Passenger Set, red. $200

LI No. 400E, 420-421-422 "Blue Comet" Passenger Train Set (restored). $3,500

LI No. 412-413-416 "State" Cars, green (restored). $2,700

LI No. 1766-1766-1768 Passenger Car Set, two original boxes.
$1,500

LI No. 402, 418-419-490-432 Passenger Set, mojave. $1,900

LI No. 408E, 418-419-490-431 Passenger Set, apple green.
$3,500

LI No. 318E, 309-310-312 Passenger Set, cars in original box, green.
$600

LI No. 318, 309-310-312 "Baby State" Passenger Set, two-toned brown. $1,300

Rolling Stock

LI No. 213 Stock Car, maroon/mojave, original box. $500

LI No. 214R Refrigerator Car, ivory/peacock, original box.
$900

LI No. 215 Tank Car, green. $150

LI No. 216 Hopper, dark green, original box. $500

LI No. 217 Caboose, maroon/orange. $425

LI No. 218 Dump Car, mojave, original box. $250

LI No. 219 Crane Car, peacock, original box. $200

LI No. 318E, No. 516 hoppers (three), black/red, No. 517 caboose coal train. $1,800

LI No. 219 Crane Car, yellow/red. $250

LI No. 219 Crane Car, cream/red. $275

LI No. 211 Lumber Car, nickel journals. $90

LI No. 212 A.G. Gondola, nickel plates, original box. $250

LI No. 213 Cattle Car, cream/maroon, nickel plate, original box.
                                                        $1,000

LI No. 214 Box Car, nickel plate, yellow/brown. $1,250

LI No. 214R Refrigerator, nickel plate, white/light blue, original box. $750

LI No. 215 "Sunoco" Tank Car, nickel plate, aluminum. $800

LI No. 216 Hopper, brass plate, green, original box. $375

LI No. 217 Caboose, nickel plate, red, original box. $500

LI No. 218 Dump Car, nickel journals, mojave. $215

LI No. 219 Crane, nickel plate, red/ivory. $300

LI No. 220 Floodlight Car, nickel plate, green. $425

LI No. 511 Lumber Car. $45

LI No. 513 Stock Car. $110

LI No. 515 Tank Car, terra cotta.   *$130*

LI No. 515 Tank Car, terra cotta.   *$155*

LI No. 515 Tank Car, terra cotta, original box.   *$160*

LI No. 384T Tender, olive, plus passenger car.   *$160*

LI No. 217 Caboose, orange.   *$300*

LI No. 212 Gondola, with three No. 205 containers, maroon.
                                                       $350

LI No. 212 Gondola, with barrels, apple green.   *$160*

LI No. 212 Gondola, gray.   *$120*

LI No. 213 Stock Car.   *$400*

LI No. 214 Box Car, cream/orange.   *$300*

LI No. 215 "Sunoco" Tank Car, ivory.   *$875*

LI No. 220 Floodlight Car, terra cotta.   *$275*

LI No. 217 Caboose, peacock.   *$220*

LI No. 211 Lumber, original box.   *$75*

LI No. 212 Gondola, gray.   *$150*

LI No. 511 Lumber Car.   *$80*

LI No. 512 Gondola Car, green.   *$60*

LI No. 513 (Early) Stock Car.   *$80*

LI No. 513 (Late) Stock Car.   *$150*

LI No. 514 Refrigerator Car.   *$125*

LI No. 514R Refrigerator Car. $125

LI No. 515 Tank Car, white. $180

LI No. 517 Caboose, red/green. $85

LI No. 520 Floodlight Car. $220

LI No. 514 Box Car, yellow/brown, nickel trim. $150

LI No. 515 "Sunoco" Tank Car, silver, nickel trim. $180

LI No. 520 Searchlight Car, nickel trim. $220

Accessories/Lineside Equipment

LI No. 78 Train Control. $70

LI No. 80 Semaphore. $65

LI No. 82 Semaphore Train Control. $100

LI No. 83 Traffic Signal. $95

LI No. 92 (Late) Floodlight Tower, original box. $500

LI No. 92 Floodlight Tower. $140

LI No. 124 Station, original box. $250

LI No. 129 Platform, original box. $1,400

LI No. 99N Train Control Signal, original box. $90

LI No. 99 Train Control Signal. $65

LI No. 97 Coal Elevator. $100

LI No. 124 "Lionel City" Station. $175

LI No. 134 "Lionel City" Station.   *$350*

LI No. 97 Coal Loader, original box.   *$150*

LI No. 222 Switches With Controls, pair 223 switches with controls.   *$140*

LI No. 223 Switches, original box.   *$170*

LI No. 223 Right-Hand Switches (three), complete.   *$100*

LI No. 280 Bridge, original box.   *$60*

LI No. 58 Lamp Posts (eight), original box.   *$325*

LI Double Lamp Posts (four).   *$165*

LI Single Lamp Posts (four).   *$210*

LI Single-Span Bridge, green.   *$45*

LI Standard Gauge Tunnel.   *$85*

LI No. 134 Station With Automatic Train Control, original box.
                                                            $450

LI No. 186 Accessory Set of Five Bungalows, lithographed, original box.   *$525*

LI No. 184 Bungalows, original box.   *$350*

LI No. 440 Signal Bridge With 440 C Control Panel.   *$350*

LI No. 440 Signal Bridge With 440 C Control Panel, original box.
                                                            $400

LI No. 441 Railroad Track Scale, original box.   *$850*

LI Standard Gauge Tunnel.   *$85*

LI No. 840 Power Station.   *$2,300*

LI No. 911 Scenery Plot.   *$210*

Reproductions by Miscellaneous Manufacturer

Williams No. 94 High-Tension Towers (six), original box.   *$275*

Miscellaneous U.S. Train Manufacturers

Classic Model Train Sets and Locomotives

CM No. 201 Locomotive "CMSTP & P," three passenger cars.
                                                               $125

CM Bicentennial 2-6-0 Locomotive and Tender.   *$125*

CM Erie R.R. Camelback, locomotive and tender kits, original
box.   *$200*

McCoy

Train Sets and Locomotives

MC Cascade R.R. 4-4-0 Locomotive and Tender, six-car passenger
set.   *$350*

MC Cascade R.R. Twin-Motor Electric Locomotive.   *$250*

*MC No. 4643 T.C.A. (Train Collectors of America) 4-4-4 Loco-
motive.*   *$160*

Rolling Stock

MC No. 251 Canadian Pacific Gondola, original box.   *$25*

MC No. 252 *"Schutz Brau" Box Cars.* $30

MC No. 257 *Northern Pacific Box Car.* $35

MC No. 260 *Great Northern Caboose*, original box. $30

MC No. 261 *"Virginian" Stock Car*, original box. $30

MC No. 262 *New Haven Box Car*, original box. $30

MC No. 263 *"Union" 76 Tank Car*, original box. $30

MC No. 264 *"Hooker" Tank Car*, original box. $25

MC No. 265 *Erie R.R. Hopper*, original box. $35

MC No. 266 *"Anheuser-Busch" Box Car*, original box. $25

MC No. 267 *"Linde" Box Car*, original box. $25

MC No. 268 *"Yamika" Box Car*, original box. $25

MC No. 269 *Boston & Maine R.R. Box Car*, original box. $35

MC No. 271 *Great Northern Box Car*, original box. $35

MC No. 274 *Minneapolis & St. Louis Box Car*, original box.

$30

MC No. 275 *"Twin Pine Lumber" Car*, original box. $25

MC No. 276 *"Pig Palace" Stock Car*, original box. $20

MC No. 1001 *T.C.A. Western Division Box Car*, original box.

$20

MC No. 1003 *T.C.A. Eastern Division Box Car*, original box.

$20

MC 1006 *T.C.A. Pacific Northwest Division Box Car*, original box.

$20

MC 1009 T.C.A. Great Lakes Division Box Car, original box.

$20

MC 1020 T.C.A. Lake Erie Chapter Box Car, original box. $20

MC 1021 T.C.A. W.B.E.A. Chapter Box Car, original box. $20

MC 1972 T.C.A. Convention Car, original box. $25

MC 1974 T.C.A. Convention Car, original box. $20

MC 1976 T.C.A. Convention Car, original box. $35

MC 1977 T.C.A. Convention Car, original box. $20

Sotheby's Collectors' Carousel

The following train lots from the estate of Paul Bidonde were sold at Sotheby's Collectors' Carousel in New York City, December 16, 1986. *Note:* Train manufacturers are listed alphabetically. Each maker's models are arranged sequentially by catalog number. If catalog numbers remain unlisted, models are then listed chronologically. References to "DNS" mean item did not sell.

American Flyer

AF Standard-Gauge Electric Train Set, a No. 4039 mojave locomotive, a mail car, a "Valley Forge" passenger car, a "Washington" passenger car; also a standard-gauge No. 4000 green locomotive (wheels and engine detached); locomotive: 14 in.
Catalog Est. $800–$1,200 (DNS)

AF Standard-Gauge Train Set, comprising a No. 4637 "Shasta" locomotive (wheels disengaged but there, lacking rails), No. 4693 black tender, No. 4010 yellow and blue tank car, No. 4017 green gondola, No. 4020 two-tone blue cattle car, No. 4021 red caboose, No. 4018 beige and blue box car, and No. 4023 orange lumber car with wood; locomotive: 14½ in. 1. *$550*

Boucher Standard-gauge "Blue Comet" locomotive and tender, ca. 1930, No. 2500 with 4-6-2, $1,980 at Sotheby's 1986 Bidonde Auction.

AF Standard-Gauge *"President's Special" Train Set,* ca. 1928; No. 4689 locomotive, No. 4392 "Army-Navy" observation car, No. 4390 "Academy" club car, No. 4391 "Academy" club car, and No. 4390 "West Point" club car, all finished in two-tone blue; also a standard-gauge Pullman car, finished in two-tone blue; locomotive: 18 in. 1.   *$2,090*

Boucher

BO *Standard-Gauge "Blue Comet" Electric Locomotive and Tender,* ca. 1930; No. 2500 locomotive with a 4-6-2 wheel arrangement and a tender (the two pieces have been repainted black); locomotive: 21 in. 1.   *$1,980*

BO *Standard-Gauge "Blue Comet" Electric Locomotive and Tender,* the locomotive with a 4-6-2 wheel arrangement and a replaced tender (the whole locomotive repainted black); locomotive: 22 in. 1.   *$1,045*

Boucher Standard-gauge "Blue Comet" locomotive and tender, 4-6-2, 1930s, $1,045 at Sotheby's 1986 Bidonde Auction.

Dorfan

DO Standard-Gauge Passenger Cars, Four, a dark green observation car, No. 770 "American Railway Express" car, No. 772 "Washington" car, and No. 771 "San Francisco" car; the last two cars with passengers and lights and the last three cars finished in yellow and orange; also a gauge-O train set: a cast-iron orange locomotive and tender, No. 492 green "American Railway Express," No. 493 "Seattle" passenger car and blue observation car, and a red locomotive, the last two cars with passengers and lights (locomotive split apart). *$495*

DO Standard-Gauge Freight Cars, Five, No. 486751 brown caboose car, No. 29325 light blue tank car, No. 11701 red hopper car, No. 121499 green "Santa Fe" car, No. 253761 orange gondola. *DNS*

Ives

IV Cast-Iron Clockwork Locomotive, ca. 1884; the locomotive embossed "Pat. Aug. 19. '84," two lithographed tin, gauge-1 passenger cars, No. 72 "Chicago" car, and No. 71 buffet/baggage car; also Bing cast-iron clockwork locomotive finished in black with orange trim (the first locomotive lacking bell); locomotives: 9½ in. and 11 in. l. *$935*

IV Gauge-1 "President Washington" Electric Locomotive, the cast-iron locomotive with 4-4-0 wheel arrangement and an engineer at cab window, finished in green; locomotive: 13 in. l. *$605*

IV Lithographed Tin "Union" Stations, Two, ca. 1914; glass and cast-iron dome supported by wooden columns above four tin benches; locomotive: 22 in. l. *$495*

IV Gauge-1 Electric Cast-Iron Locomotive, No. 1129, finished in black; locomotive: 13 in. l. *DNS*

IV Standard-Gauge Electric Locomotive and Tender, No. 1134, finished in black; also reproduction Ives standard-gauge electric locomotive, No. 3245R, wheel arrangement 4-4-4, finished in black.
$660

IV Electric Locomotive, No. 3239, finished in dark green with red trim; locomotive: 12 in. 1.
$660

IV Gauge-1 Gray No. 3240 Locomotive, with a 0-4-4-0 wheel arrangement; locomotive: 12½ in. 1.
$770

IV Standard-Gauge Electric Locomotive and Freight Cars, a No. 3243 orange locomotive, two No. 190 "Texas Oil" tank cars, No. 193 brown cattle car, No. 191 brown coke car, No. 197 green lumber car, No. 196 dark green flat car, No. 194 hopper, three No. 192 brown box cars and gray flat car.
$715

Lionel

LI Standard-Gauge No. 1 "Electric Rapid Transit" Trolley Motor Car, ca. 1906–1910; the trolley finished in blue and cream (wheels and motor detached, lacks light); 9¾ in. 1.
$1,210

LI Steam-Type Locomotive and Tender, early 1900s; No. 6 locomotive, 4-4-0 wheel arrangement; together three standard-gauge passenger cars, comprising three No. 29 "New York Central Lines" observation cars (one passenger car minus wheels).
$1,100

LI Standard-Gauge Brass Locomotive, ca. 1913; No. 54 locomotive, 0-4-4-0 wheel arrangement, finished in red on the wheels, ventilators, and pilots; locomotive: 14 in. 1.
$1,750

LI Lot of Standard-Gauge Passenger Cars, ca. 1920; No. 10 "Interurban" green car, No. 18 green parlor car, No. 18 orange Pullman car, No. 19 orange baggage/passenger car, No. 190 orange observation car.
$1,100

LI Standard-Gauge, Five-Piece, Passenger Train Sets, Two, No. 256 locomotive, No. 712 Pullman car, two No. 710 observation cars (all above finished in orange), No. 318E locomotive, No. 310 mail car, No. 309 Pullman car, and No. 312 observation car, the last four cars finished in green.   *$1,045*

LI Standard-Gauge, Painted Metal, No. 300 "Hell Gate" Bridge, finished in orange, cream, and green, miscellaneous lot of accessories, four No. 77 automatic crossing gates, No. 89 flag pole, two No. 67 cast-iron double lamp posts, and four train traffic lights.
$1,100

LI Standard-Gauge "State Set," ca. 1929; No. 381E locomotive (lacking electrical motor and several railings), No. 413 "Colorado" passenger car, No. 412 "California" passenger car, and a No. 416 "New York" passenger car.   *$4,400*

LI Standard-Gauge Electric Locomotive, No. 390E locomotive with a 2-4-2 wheel arrangement, three No. 516 hopper cars and a No. 517 pea green and a red caboose; locomotive: 13 in. 1.   *$550*

LI Standard-Gauge "Blue Comet" Five-Piece Passenger Train Set, No. 390E locomotive, No. 390T tender, No. 422 "Temple" observation car, No. 420 "Faye" passenger car, No. 421 "Westphal" passenger car (locomotive lacking one railing).   *$2,090*

LI Standard-Gauge Electric Train Set, No. 402 locomotive, No. 402E locomotive (without wheels), a No. 419 baggage car, two No. 490 observation cars, and two No. 418 parlor cars, all finished in mojave.   *$660*

LI Standard-Gauge Electric Train Set, No. 402 locomotive, No. 490 observation car, No. 418 parlor car, No. 419 baggage/parlor car, all finished in mojave, the three passenger cars in their original boxes; locomotive: 14 in. 1.   *$1,100*

LI Standard-Gauge Electric Locomotive, No. 408E locomotive with 0-4-4-0 wheel arrangement, No. 431 dining car, both finished in mojave; locomotive: 15½ in. 1.   *$1,000–$1,500 (DNS)*

Lionel No. 402 Standard-gauge electric outline locomotive, No. 490 observation car, No. 418 parlor car, No. 419 baggage/parlor car, three cars in original box; locomotive: 14 in. 1.; mojave, $1,000–$1,500.

LI Standard-Gauge Electric Locomotive, No. 408E mojave locomotive with a 0-4-4-0 wheel arrangement, No. 490 mojave observation car, No. 418 mojave passenger car; locomotive: 15½ in. 1.
$550

LI Hudson-Type, Super-Detail Scale Model, No. 700E Locomotive, the locomotive from class J-IE series 5344 with 4-6-4 wheel arrangement, a No. 700T "New York Central" tender mounted on display tracks; locomotive: 24 in. 1. $2,750

Rolling Stock

LI Gondola, No. 2652, O gauge, terra cotta. $35

LI Gondola, No. 2652, O gauge, small series, orange and black, nickel trim, white painted lettering, original box. $65

LI Caboose, No. 2657, red with brown roof, black frame, original box. $35

LI Shell Tank Car, No. 2654, O gauge, orange with nickel trim on black, original box. $85

LI Shell Tank Car, No. 2654, O gauge, orange on black, nickel trim.   *$40*

LI Shell Tank Car, No. 2654, O gauge, orange on black, nickel trim, original box.   *$65*

LI Caboose, No. 2657, O gauge, red, yellow windows, silver ends, black base, original box.   *$60*

LI Caboose, No. 2672, O gauge, Tuscan red, original box.   *$45*

LI Gondola, No. 2812, O gauge, white, rubber-stamped, barrels, terra cotta, black frame, original box.   *$90*

LI Gondola, No. 2812, light green on black, nickel trim, O gauge, barrels, original box.   *$90*

LI Automobile Furniture Car, No. 2814, O gauge, yellow with maroon roof and trim, black frame, nickel trim, original box.
$125

LI Shell Tank Car, No. 2815, orange on black, nickel trim, original box.   *$250*

LI Sunoco Tank Car, No. 2815, O gauge, silver with decals, nickel trim, original box.   *$200*

LI Shell Tank Car, No. 2815, O gauge, yellow, black frame, nickel trim, Shell decal, original box.   *$225*

LI Coal Hopper, No. 2816, O gauge, black with white rubber-stamped letters, litho tin.   *$300*

LI Coal Car, No. 2816, O gauge, black with rubber-stamp, original box.   *$180*

LI Caboose, No. 2817, O gauge, red, white windows, brown roof, black base, rubber-stamped, original box marked No. 817 blue caboose.   *$210*

LI Pennsylvania Box Car, No. 2954, O gauge, semiscale, Tuscan red, plastic, prewar. $500

LI Lot of Standard-Gauge Freight Cars, three No. 218 brown dump cars, No. 216 green hopper car, No. 212 maroon gondola holding three green safes, two No. 213 orange and green cattle cars (one with roof repainted and other with roof lacking), two No. 211 black flat cars with wood loads, a green cattle car, two No. 215 green tank cars, No. 214R green and white refrigerator car, No. 217 orange and red caboose, and No. 219 peacock green crane. $1,000–$1,500 (DNS)

LI Lot of Three Freight Cars, semiscale, O gauge, original boxes, No. 2954 plastic Tuscan red box car, No. 2956 die-cast black hopper with No. 206 load of coal, No. 2957 Tuscan red die-cast caboose. $1,750

LI Sunoco Tank Car, No. 2955, O gauge, gray on black with decals, original box. $175

LI Sunoco Tank Car, No. 2955, semiscale, black with decals. $600

LI Sunoco Tank Car, No. 2955, semiscale, O gauge, black with decals. $800

LI Semiscale B. & O. Coal Hopper, No. 2956, O gauge, black, white lettering, with No. 160 bin, original box. $300

LI Lot of Two Semiscale Cabooses, No. 2957, O gauge, Tuscan brown. $375

LI Remote-Control Lumber Car, No. 365L, O gauge, black with nickel trim, original box. $55

LI Remote-Control Dump Car, No. 3659, O gauge, red on black. $55

LI Remote-Control Lumber Car, No. 3811, O gauge, black, nickel trim, scarce raised coupler, original box. $70

LI Remote-Control Lumber Car, No. 3811, O gauge, with No. 160 bin, black with nickel trim, original box.   *$80*

LI Box Car, No. 3814, brown on black, O gauge, remote control, box of three N.P.C.I. tools in original box No. 812T.   *$200*

LI Merchandise Remote-Control Box Car, No. 3814, O gauge, decals, nickel trim, brown on black.   *$110*

LI Operating Merchandise Car, No. 3854, semiscale, O gauge, Tuscan red, white lettering, original box.   *$225*

LI Remote-Control Dump Car, No. 3859, O gauge, red on black with nickel trim, original box.   *$85*

LI Remote-Control Dump Car, No. 3859, O gauge, red on black with nickel trim, no box.   *$65*

LI Remote-Control Dump Car, No. 3859, O gauge, red on black, original box.   *$90*

LI Tender, No. 0047, OO gauge, No. 0043 black Southern Pacific hopper car, missing one hopper door.   *$125*

LI Silver Sunoco Tank Car, No. 0045, OO gauge, die-cast, original box, No. 0077 red caboose in original wrappers from factory, original box.   *$200*

LI Track Cleaning Car, No. 3927, orange with nickel horn, aluminum rails, two lilac and gray track cleaning bottles with a circle sponge, has No. 004T box.   *$70*

Märklin

MK Gauge-1 Clockwork Locomotive, ca. 1902; 0-4-0 locomotive finished in dark green with orange trim, side embossed with "GM & C," also a gauge-1 tender, blue passenger car, and green and orange freight car; locomotive: 7½ in. 1. (Similar locomotive is illustrated in *The Trains on Avenue de Rumine,* Count Antonio Giansanti Coluzzi, London, page 50, bottom color plate; see Bibliography.)   *$935*

MK Gauge-1 Clockwork Painted Tin Locomotive, ca. 1902; the 0-4-0 locomotive finished in dark green with orange trim, side embossed with "GM & C," also gauge-1 "PRR 90309" red caboose, two flat cars, tender without wheels, and red passenger car; locomotive: 7½ in. 1.   *$1,100*

MK Painted Tin Warehouse, 1902; No. 1045, with four sliding doors, a hinged side door, two cranes; finished in orange, yellow, and brown to simulate bricks; 15½ in. 1.   *$935*

MK Gauge-1 Clockwork Painted Tin Locomotive, ca. 1907; locomotive finished in black with orange and green trim (lacking one set of wheels, a smoking funnel, a bell, and a side rail; some areas resoldered); also a gauge-1 maroon passenger car, two green flat cars, orange passenger car with eagle decal at side (last car with areas repainted); locomotive: 14 in. 1.   *$935*

MK Tin Steam-Operated Fountain, ca. 1909–1912; No. 4223, the central fountain with three birds; also a painted tin tunnel, ca. 1909–1912, No. 2525, the tunnel in the shape of a mountainside.   *$660*

MK Painted Tin Roundhouse, ca. 1910; two hinged doors and sides painted to simulate stone; 24 in. 1.   *$800–$1,200 (DNS)*

MK Gauge-O Passenger Cars, ca. 1929; a sleeping car complete with beds, sinks; second car, a dining car complete with cafeteria, seats and tables; both finished in dark green with gold and maroon trim; also model of the "Companie Internationale des Wagons-Lits," probably Elettren, 1950–1960, inside complete with bunk beds, sinks, toilets, mirrors; gauge-1 "NYCRR 2926" green box car.   *$2,750*

MK Gauge-O Passenger Cars, Four, ca. 1930; two blue dining cars, a blue sleeping car, and a green baggage car, all in original boxes; also four gauge-O passenger cars, ca. 1935, comprising "Nevada" Pullman, a "Firefly" Pullman, a "Florence" Pullman, and observation car (all repainted).   *$9,075*

MK Gauge-O, No. 5273, Electric Locomotive and Tender, ca. 1934; 4-6-4 locomotive finished in black with a "New York Central" tender, mounted on display tracks; locomotive: 13½ in. 1.

$6,600

MK Gauge-O P.L.M. Model Locomotive, ca. 1938; with 4-8-2 wheel arrangement, in original box with transformer, controls; also three "Mitropa" gauge-O passenger cars, ca. 1926: a dining and sleeping car with passengers and a third passenger car.   *$3,080*

Voltamp

VO Gauge-2, No. 2100 Locomotive and "B & O" Tender, early 1900s; with 4-4-0 wheel arrangement, finished in black, embossed on wheels: "Voltamp"; locomotive: 14 in. 1. (See similar example in *The Toy Collector,* Louis Hertz, New York, 1976, illustrated, p. 40; see Bibliography.)   *$2,090*

VO Standard Gauge, "Royal Blue Limited" No. 2210 Locomotive, ca. 1911; "Suburban" locomotive with a 0-4-4-0 wheel arrangement; also standard-gauge No. 210 "Interurban" trolley car (repainted trolley); locomotive: 13 in. 1.   *$2,970*

Miscellaneous

Buddy "L" Outdoor Train Set, No. 963 locomotive, a tender, No. 35407 black flat car, a black gondola, a red box car, a red tank car, a cattle and caboose car, and a wrecking crane (some rust, an erosion hole in tank car); locomotive: 26 in. 1.   *$2,750*

Gauge No. 1 Electric Locomotive and Tender, probably Carlisle and Finch, white metal locomotive with a 4-4-2 wheel arrangement and a brass passenger car; locomotive: 18 in. 1.   *$4,125*

Knapp Standard-gauge, cast-iron electric locomotive and tender, ca. 1905, 0-4-0, black with red trim. Estimated at $600–$800; brought $1,760. (Courtesy of Sotheby's, New York)

Knapp Standard-Gauge, Cast-Iron Electric Locomotive and Tender, ca. 1905; No. 222 locomotive with 0-4-0 wheel arrangement, finished in black trimmed in red; locomotive: 13½ in. 1.   *$1,760*

Lot of Gauge-1 Freight Cars, German, two "Budweiser" refrigerator cars, "Old Dutch Cleanser" refrigerator car, "Swift" refrigerator car, "Hocking Valley" gondola, "PRR 96774" box car, "NYC & HR" caboose car, all with lithographed details.   *$935*

Two American Cast-Iron Locomotives, the first Wilkins, ca. 1890, and the second Kenton, late 19th century; both finished in black with red trim; 14 in. and 10 in. 1.   *$935*

German Painted Tin Tunnel, ca. 1910; tunnel simulates a mountain with bridges and houses tucked within mountainside; 23 in. h.

$440

Lloyd Ralston Auction

The following train lots were offered at the May 6, 1989, Lloyd Ralston Auction in Fairfield, Connecticut. This was a collection of Lionel and Ives toy trains owned by Everett "Red" Chapman of Barrington, Rhode Island. *Note:* Train lots appear in numerical sequence by manufacturer's catalog number.

Ives

Locomotives and Tenders

IV Locomotive and Tender, No. 17, O gauge, plates on locomotive, painted CI, windup, working, no key, black with red and gold stripes on roof, red steam chest; new No. 11 L.V.E. tender, litho tin, black, red, and green.   *$300*

IV Locomotive and Tender, No. 17, O gauge, in white letters on black plates, painted CI, windup, working, no key, red and gold stripes on roof; tender is new No. 11 L.V.E., red, black, and green.   *$350*

IV Locomotive and Tender, No. 20, O gauge, plated on locomotive, painted CI, windup, not working, no key, black with red and gold stripes on roof, C6, new No. 11 L.V.E. tender, red and black.   *$400*

IV Locomotive and Tender, No. 1, O gauge, painted CI, windup, working, no key, on red plate with white letters, smooth boiler; tender F.E. No. 1, four wheels, red and black, faded. $700

IV Locomotive and Limited Vestibule Express Eight-Wheel Tender, No. 1125, black with blue interior, early electric locomotive has white on black plates, boiler has unusual detail and whistle.
$1,000

IV Locomotive and Tender, O gauge, locomotive No. 2 on plates, painted CI, windup, working, no key, tender is L.V.E. II, litho tin, red and black. $378

Rolling Stock

IV Lot of Two Cars, litho tin, O gauge, No. 50 baggage, Pennsylvania Lines, yellow with red, brown, and black, dark gray roof, C6; No. 51 Newark Coach, Pennsylvania Lines, yellow with red, brown, and black, dark gray roof. $400

IV Gondola With Wood-Grained Sides, No. 54, red with black, O gauge, litho tin, C6; Pennsylvania Lines No. 56 caboose, O gauge, litho tin, wood-grained sides, red with black, gray roof and white cupola. $375

IV Limited Vestibule Express, No. 60, and "Express" service baggage, O gauge, red with white and orange clerestory roof, C6; Pennsylvania Lines No. 67 caboose, O gauge, white with orange and black trim, roof is gray and white. $600

IV Limited Vestibule Express, "Empress" parlor car, No. 62, O gauge, red with gold and black, black clerestory roof, original box. $1,400

IV Refrigerator/Dairy Line Express, No. 124, O gauge, large series, litho tin, white with red and blue, litho striped roof, early couplers, T-trucks. $500

IV Fast Freight Line, No. 125, "General Merchandise" car, O gauge, litho tin, yellow with red and black striped roof, slightly faded, inside truck frame.   *$1,300*

IV Livestock Transportation Car, No. 127, O gauge, litho tin, gray with blue, roof faded, red and black striped, inside truck frame, doors missing.   *$1,100*

IV Livestock Transportation, No. 127, O gauge, large series, wood-grained siding, litho tin, white with red, gray, and blue, litho striped roof, Märklin-style truck.   *$375*

IV Limited Vestibule Express, No. 130 buffet, O gauge, litho tin, wood-grained red with yellow, black, and green trim, gray and green clerestory roof.   *$600*

IV Lot of Two Iroquois-Type Parlor Cars, O gauge, litho tin, four wheels, No. 1 "Mohawk" Fast Express, red with black roof, incomplete ends, C3; No. 51 "Hiawatha," Limited Vestibule Express, yellow, black, and red, roof missing.   *$400*

IV Limited Vestibule Express, "Philadelphia," O gauge, litho tin, white with gold and blue trim, black and silver clerestory roof.
                                        $1,900

IV Limited Vestibule Express, baggage car, "Chicago," O gauge, white with gold and blue trim, black and silver clerestory roof, one side door missing.   *$1,700*

IV Limited Vestibule Express, baggage car, "Chicago," O gauge, yellow with black and red trim, black and silver clerestory roof.
                                        $2,200

IV Limited Vestibule Express, "Empress," parlor car, O gauge, yellow with brown, red, and black, black clerestory roof, original box.   *$1,600*

IV Livestock Car, No. 20–193, Standard gauge, orange with red roof, painted tin, original box.   *$600*

Accessories

IV Crossing Gate, litho tin, mechanical, base 20½ in. × 7¼ in., O gauge, yellow, red is faded, blue and white roof.   *$2,000*

Lionel

Locomotives and Train Sets

LI Train Set, No. 204 locomotive, black, die-cast 1689T tender, litho tin black, no whistle, two No. 610 Pullmans, No. 612 observation, red with silver roofs, missing one journal box, four original boxes and set box, prewar, department store special.   *$550*

LI Freight Set, O gauge, No. 224E black die-cast locomotive; No. 2224W tender; No. 3659 black and red remote-control dump car with No. 160 bin; No. 167 whistle controller; remote-control track set; No. 2660 yellow, red, green crane car with electric couplers; No. 3652 yellow remote-control gondola with barrels and No. 160 bin; No. 3651 remote-control lumber car with No. 160 bin; No. 2657 red caboose with white windows; original boxes except one, set box, grease tube.   *$475*

LI Passenger Set, O gauge, No. 225E, black die-cast locomotive, No. 2245 tender, three cars: No. 2600 Pullman, No. 2601 observation, No. 2602 baggage, red with cream windows and doors, nickel trim, original boxes.   *$1,000*

LI Prewar Freight Set, O gauge, No. 226E, black die-cast locomotive, nickel trim, No. 226W black tender, No. 2810 yellow, red, and green crane car with black frame, one knob missing and one cracked, No. 2812 green gondola with barrels, No. 2820 green searchlight car, missing both lenses, No. 2817 red caboose with silver trim, original boxes except one, set box, nickel trim.   *$1,550*

LI Locomotive and Tender, O gauge, semiscale, 0-6-0 Pennsylvania switcher, boiler front, No. 228 locomotive, cab No. 8976, Pennsylvania tender No. 2228, ringing bell, die-cast black, one original box.   *$2,100*

LI Pennsylvania Streamline Locomotive, No. 238E, die-cast, No. 265W tender, O gauge, gray, original box.   *$500*

LI Train Set, O gauge, No. 249, gray, die-cast and steel locomotive, bell missing, No. 265 tender, litho tin, electric lights, No. 602 double-door baggage, No. 600 Pullman, No. 601 observation is gray with red roof.   *$700*

LI Freight Set, O gauge, No. 254E locomotive, olive green on black with brass and nickel trim, No. 812 mojave on black gondola, brass plates, No. 811 lumber, maroon, rubber-stamped in gold, brass and nickel trim, No. 817 caboose, peacock, dark green roof, black frame, orange windows, brass trim, original boxes and set box, directions missing pages and cover, No. 81 rheostat and box of connecting ties.   *$750*

LI Passenger Set, O gauge, No. 256 locomotive, orange, green trim on black, brass trim, locomotive wheels and headlights deteriorated, two No. 710 Pullmans, No. 712 observation, cars are orange with olive trim, brass and nickel trim.   *$3,000*

LI Locomotive, O gauge, No. 256, orange on black, rubber-stamped, headlights crazed, original box.   *$1,500*

LI Freight Set, O gauge, No. 259E locomotive with No. 2689T tender, gunmetal gray and nickel trim, No. 2651 light green lumber, No. 2660 operating work crane, yellow, dark green crane, red roof, black body, No. 2654 Sunoco tank car, silver on black, nickel trim, No. 2657 caboose, red with yellow windows, silver ends, black base, all original boxes, set box with operating instructions and catalog, missing covers.   *$700*

LI Freight Set, O gauge, No. 259E locomotive, No. 1689T tender, pressed steel, gunmetal gray, nickel trim, No. 654 Sunoco tank, silver on black, nickel trim, No. 651 lumber car, light green, nickel trim, No. 657 caboose, red with yellow windows, nickel trim, original boxes and set box. $450

LI Locomotive and Tender, O gauge, No. 260 gray with nickel-trim locomotive, missing two flags, die-cast and steel, No. 263 tender, missing one handrail. $575

LI Locomotive and Vanderbilt Tender, No. 260E, black with yellow stripe on frame, copper and brass trim, matching tender, die-cast and painted tin, boiler front incomplete, unusual box. $750

LI Freight Set, O gauge, No. 261E, black die-cast and steel locomotive, litho tin tender, No. 654 Sunoco tank car, silver, No. 659 green tipple dump car, No. 651 green flat car with lumber, No. 652 yellow gondola, No. 657 red caboose, all original boxes except one, set box. $500

LI Train Set, O gauge, litho tin, No. 262 locomotive, black with copper trim, one flag missing, No. 262T tender, No. 812 gondola, green with original box and barrels, No. 814 automobile furniture, missing brake wheel, yellow and orange, No. 817 caboose, two-tone green, original box, set box. $550

LI Passenger Set, No. 262, black with copper trim, die-cast and pressed steel locomotive, two flags missing, No. 262T tender, two No. 613 Pullmans, one missing a handrail and has rusting on side, No. 614 observation, terra cotta and maroon with copper trim, original boxes and set box, instruction booklet. $850

LI "Blue Comet" Locomotive and Vanderbilt Tender, No. 263E, O gauge, die-cast and pressed steel, original box, repair to tender. $675

LI "Blue Comet," O gauge, two-tone blue, No. 263E locomotive, whistle tender has water spot the size of a quarter and a 3-in. discoloration leading to rust, No. 615 baggage, No. 613 Pullman coach, No. 614 observation, original boxes and set box. $2,600

LI Locomotive and Tender, O gauge, No. 263E locomotive, No. 226W tender, gunmetal gray with nickel trim, litho tin and die-cast, original boxes.   *$1,100*

LI Passenger Set, O gauge, locomotive No. 263W, gunmetal, No. 2263R whistle tender, "Vanderbilt," six-wheel, gunmetal gray, locomotive and tender are die-cast and pressed steel, nickel trim, No. 615 baggage, No. 613 Pullman, No. 614 observation, red bodies, silver and red roofs, doors, windows, observation end, and number plates, nickel trim, original boxes, all rubber-stamped R, original boxes and set box.   *$2,000*

LI Passenger Set, O gauge, "Commodore Vanderbilt" engine No. 265-E, die-cast and tin, No. 265W tender, litho tin, No. 602 baggage, No. 600 Pullman, No. 601 observation, blue with silver, original boxes and set box.   *$900*

LI Union Pacific, City of Denver, Streamline Train Set, No. 636W die-cast locomotive, yellow and brown, two No. 637 coaches, No. 638 observation, original boxes and set box, some wheel rust.
                                                           $1,050

LI Locomotive and Tender, No. 763E, black die-cast locomotive, No. 226WX tender, O gauge, original boxes.   *$1,050*

LI Mechanical Freight Train Set, No. 1545, O gauge, black No. 1511 locomotive on red base, copper trim, red No. 1516 tender, No. 1515 Sunoco oil car, silver with blue lettering on red frame, No. 1514 box car, "Baby Ruth," yellow litho, brown trim, peacock roof, red frame, original box.   *$375*

LI Freight Set, No. 1688, streamlined locomotive, flat black, No. 1689 tender, No. 2680 Shell tank car, orange with black frame, No. 1682 red on black caboose, original boxes and set box. *$350*

LI Junior Streamline Train Set, litho tin, No. 1700 locomotive, No. 1701 coach, No. 1702 observation, silver on red, original boxes.   *$500*

LI Freight Set, OO gauge, No. 003 locomotive, No. 003T tender, black die-cast, No. 0045 Shell tank car, black, No. 0044 Tuscan red box car, No. 0047 red caboose, two No. 022 plug and control wire sets, all original boxes and set box, 16 pieces of track. *$800*

LI Locomotive and Tender, OO gauge, No. 5342 black die-cast locomotive, No. 001T-5 tender, original box No. 0091W. *$375*

LI Canadian National GP7 Diesel, postwar, No. 8031, O gauge, original box, plastic and steel. *$230*

Rolling Stock

LI Lumber Loader/Shed, No. 164, original box. *$300*

LI Remote-Control Crane Car, No. 165, with directions, original box. *$400*

LI Remote-Control Crane, No. 165, operating "Gantry" crane, yellow and red crane on silver structure with green base, original instructions, rubber-stamped. *$225*

LI Observation Car, No. 604, O gauge, rubber-stamped, orange wood-grained doors and windows, gold observation end rails, original box. *$100*

LI Lot of Three Passenger Cars, O gauge, two No. 607 Pullmans, No. 608 observation, two-tone green with yellow windows, original boxes and set box. *$350*

LI Lot of Three Passenger Cars, two No. 610 Pullmans, No. 612 observation, olive with red trim, original box, O gauge. *$350*

LI Lot of Two "Blue Comet" Passenger Cars, No. 613 Pullman, No. 615 baggage, original box, O gauge. *$450*

LI Baggage Car, No. 615, terra cotta, maroon and yellow trim, original box, O gauge, rubber-stamped. *$200*

LI Hopper, No. 652, O gauge, terra cotta, nickel trim, original box.   *$70*

LI Coal Hopper, No. 653, O gauge, light green, black trim, small series, nickel trim, original box.   *$80*

LI Lot of Box Car and Caboose, No. 655 box car, O gauge, yellow with maroon roof and trim, black frame, brass trim, missing a door handle, No. 657 caboose, O gauge, red with yellow trim, brass trim, black frame.   *$100*

LI Box Car, No. 655, O gauge, small series, yellow and maroon, nickel trim, original box.   *$70*

LI Cattle Car, No. 656, O gauge, small series, gray and red, nickel trim, original box.   *$100*

LI Coal Tender, No. 26ITR, red, brass and nickel trim, original box.   *$250*

LI Coal Tender, No. 265T, O gauge, red with nickel trim, original box.   *$245*

LI Coal Tender, No. 265T, O gauge, gray with nickel trim, original box.   *$135*

LI Hopper, No. 803, O gauge, peacock, brass and copper trim, missing two journal boxes.   *$20*

LI Shell Tank Car, No. 804, O gauge, orange, decals, nickel trim, four wheels.   *$175*

LI Caboose, No. 807, O gauge, dark red with peacock roof and windows, brass and copper trim.   *$50*

LI Tip Car, manual, No. 809, O gauge, orange, rubber-stamped, brass, nickel and copper trim, black base.   *$90*

LI Operating Derrick Car, No. 810, O gauge, terra cotta, maroon roof, peacock crane, black base, brass, copper and nickel trim, original box. $275

LI Derrick Car, No. 810, O gauge, large crane, yellow with red roof, green crane, black base, nickel trim, original box. $200

LI Lumber Car, No. 811, O gauge, silver, with load, nickel trim, original box. $100

LI Gondola, No. 812, O gauge, green on black, brass trim, original box. $70

LI Gondola, No. 812, O gauge, light green, nickel trim on black, two barrels, original box. $140

LI Stock Car, No. 813, O gauge, yellow, maroon trim, black base, nickel trim, one brake wheel disconnected, one sliding door top missing, original box labeled No. 814 box car. $175

LI Livestock Car, No. 813, O gauge, orange, green roof and trim, black frame, brass and copper trim, original box. $120

LI Automobile Furniture Car, No. 814, O gauge, yellow, orange roof and trim, black, brass and copper trim, original box. $110

LI Automobile Furniture Car, No. 814, O gauge, yellow with brown roof and trim, black, nickel trim, original box. $175

LI Ventilated Refrigerator Car, No. 814R, O gauge, white with blue roof, silver frame, original box. $400

LI Ventilated Refrigerator Car, No. 814R, O gauge, white, peacock roof, black frame, brass and copper trim, original box. $400

LI Tank Car, No. 815, O gauge, green with brass and nickel trim, original box. $225

LI Sunoco Tank Car, No. 815, O gauge, silver with decals, brass trim, original box. $170

LI Sunoco Tank Car, No. 815, O gauge, silver with decals, nickel trim, original box.   *$175*

LI Sunoco Tank Car, No. 815, O gauge, silver with black frame, original box.   *$130*

LI Coal Hopper, No. 816, O gauge, red, nickel trim, original box.
$120

LI Hopper Car, No. 816, O gauge, red, brass and copper trim, original box.   *$150*

LI Caboose, No. 817, O gauge, red on black, nickel trim, original box.   *$50*

LI Searchlight Car, No. 820, O gauge, terra cotta on black, brass and copper trim, rubber-stamped lettering.   *$140*

LI Searchlight Car, No. 820, O gauge, green on black, original box.   *$150*

LI Lumber Car, No. 831, O gauge, light green, nickel trim.   *$30*

LI Gondola, No. 902, O gauge, green on black, brass and nickel trim.   *$15*

LI Coal Tender, No. 2224W, O gauge, die-cast, black, rubber-stamped, original box.   *$140*

LI Tender, No. 2225TV, O gauge, gunmetal gray, nickel trim, original box.   *$100*

LI Coal Tender, No. 2226W, O gauge, black, rubber-stamped, whistle, original box.   *$220*

LI Three "Blue Comet" Cars, No. 2615 baggage, two No. 2613 Pullmans, two-tone blue with white trim, wheels show wear, two original boxes, operating couplers.   *$450*

LI Lot of Three Passenger Cars, O gauge, No. 2615 baggage, No. 2613 Pullman, No. 2614 observation, two-tone green with yellow windows and doors, rubber-stamped, original boxes.   *$1,400*

LI Searchlight Car, No. 2620, O gauge, die-cast, gray and black searchlight, red platform, nickel trim, missing lens.   *$110*

Accessories

LI Early Railroad Crossing, signal, die-cast and tin.   *$135*

LI Switches, No. 021, original box.   *$40*

LI Lot of Two Boxes of Remote-Control Switches, No. 022, O gauge, one box missing a switch.   *$70*

LI Lot of Illuminated Bumper and Automatic Crossing Gate, No. 025 illuminated bumper, die-cast on rail, original box; No. 47 automatic crossing gate, with illuminated lanterns, green base, cream crossing, original box.   *$180*

LI Remote-Control Log Dumper, No. 38LL, and No. 160 bin, black, original box, O gauge.   *$100*

LI Whistling Station, No. 48W, lithographed building with lithographed tile roof, original box.   *$100*

LI Lamp Post, No. 52, painted cast iron and die-cast, olive, original box.   *$70*

LI Lamp Post, No. 54, prewar, cast iron and pot metal, green, original box.   *$150*

LI Lamp Post, No. 57, die-cast and tin, orange, original box, No. 91 signal, die-cast, brown.   *$190*

LI Lot of Two Lamp Posts, No. 58 lamp post, yellow, original box; No. 56 lamp post, green, original box.   *$120*

LI Whistle Controller, No. 65, multi-volt transformer, No. 1038, original box.   *$30*

LI Whistle Controller, No. 66, three No. 167 whistle controllers, No. 76 lamp post, two No. 012 lamp and signal case lights, original box.   *$40*

LI Lot of Two Electric Warning Signals, No. 69N, red base, nickel-plated bell and crossing sign, original box, No. 069 white base, nickel-plated bell with red and brass crossing sign, original box.
                                                               $190

LI Accessory Set, No. 71, No. 60 telegraph posts, original box.
                                                               $475

LI Black Signal, No. 076, O gauge, litho tin, white, original box, No. 58 lamp post, yellow, die-cast, original box.   *$100*

LI Railroad Crossing Sign, No. 077, light green arm on maroon stand on dark green base, original box.   *$55*

LI Semaphore Signal, No. 82, red base, silver pole, black ladder.
                                                               $185

LI Train Control Automatic Signal, No. 82, green signal semaphore, green, silver, black ladder, nickel trim, original box. *$160*

LI Telegraph Post Set, No. 86, original box.   *$550*

LI Flag and Cord, No. 89, original box.   *$85*

LI Floodlight Tower, No. 92, red and silver, missing one lens, original box.   *$140*

LI Water Tank, No. 93, silver on red base, original box.   *$95*

LI Remote-Control Coal Elevator, No. 97, yellow with red roof and silver trim, black base, original box.   *$200*

LI Coal Loader, No. 98, handoperated, O gauge, yellow with red roof, black base, silver girders.   *$175*

LI City Station, No. 115, white with red windows, base and roof, original box.   *$375*

LI Tunnel, No. 119, painted brass, paint is flaky, original box.
   $140

LI Tunnel, No. 123, O gauge, painted papier-mâché, original box, has small hole and crack in back.   *$150*

LI City Illuminated Station, No. 124, brown building, cream trim, green base, red roof, silver lamp posts, original box.   *$450*

LI Lionelville Station, No. 136, mojave, green base, red roof and trim, white doors and windows, original box.   *$425*

LI Town Station, No. 137, white building, mojave base, green and yellow trim, original box.   *$225*

LI Crossing Gate, No. 152, die-cast and tin, original box.   *$55*

LI Lot of Automatic Black Signal and Highway Lamp Post, No. 153 automatic black signal, die-cast and litho tin, green, silver and orange, original box; No. 64 highway lamp post, die-cast, green, original box.   *$100*

LI Station Platform, No. 156, green with red roof, original box.
   $135

LI Freight Station Set, No. 163, includes baggage truck, dump truck, and two hand trucks, original box taped.   *$350*

LI Single-Span Bridge, No. 270, red, original box.   *$55*

LI Bridge, No. 271, O gauge, red, original box.   *$85*

LI Bascule Bridge, No. 313, silver with green trim, yellow house, orange windows, red roof, original box.   *$575*

LI Power Station, No. 436, terra cotta with gray base, yellow roof, orange windows, green trim, original box.   *$300*

LI Switch-Signal Tower, No. 437, litho tin, terra cotta, orange, yellow, green roof, has paper instructions on building bottom, original box.   *$600*

LI Switch Signal Tower, No. 437, terra cotta, maroon, peacock, red, white and green, paper direction label on bottom.   *$395*

LI Illuminated Diner, No. 442, cream with red roof and trim, original box.   *$350*

LI Panel Board, No. 439, red, black panel, nickel trim, original box.   *$230*

LI Accessory Set, No. 808, O gauge, No. 831 green lumber, No. 803 peacock coal, No. 804 silver oil, No. 805 green-with-orange box car, No. 806 orange-with-red-roof cattle car, No. 807 red-with-green roof, original set box.   *$400*

LI Accessory Set, No. 818, O gauge, No. 812 green gondola, No. 816 maroon coal, No. 814 yellow-with-brown-roof automobile/furniture, No. 817 red caboose, original box.   *$500*

Miscellaneous

Dorfan S182999 N.Y.C. Box Car, O gauge, litho tin, yellow, C6; Dorfan Lumber Car, O gauge, black and red, litho tin.   *$60*

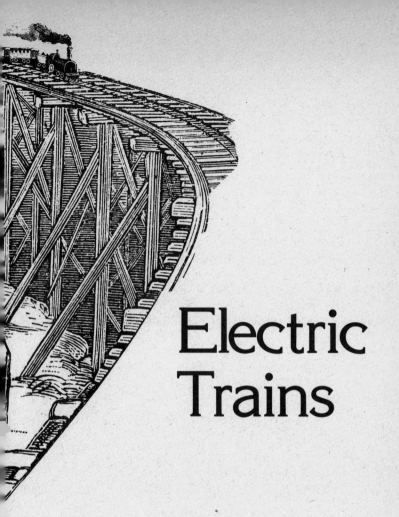

Electric
Trains

American Flyer Trains

American Flyer, Chicago, Illinois
1907–1966
(Originally known as "Chicago
Flyer"; acquired by A.C. Gilbert in
1938)
Founders: W.O. Coleman, Sr., John
Hafner
Specialty: Produced inexpensive cast-iron windup trains, competing head-on with Bing and Ives in the U.S. market, until 1920. Truly came of age in 1938 when A.C. Gilbert acquired the firm on a royalty arrangement.

Milestones:

- 1907: American Flyer makes locomotives patterned closely after the Ives cast-iron steam outline 0-4-0s, but selling for considerably less. It is generally believed that the Edmonds-Metzel Manufacturing Co. actually produced and distributed the first train sets.
- 1910: The first reference is made to the American Flyer Manufacturing Co. in the annual catalog.
- 1918–1919: American Flyer produces its first electric trains.

- 1925: American Flyer entered the Standard-gauge market; purchased passenger coaches from Lionel and dressed them in their own livery.
- 1925: American Flyer introduced a British outline series of trains to the English market, the "British Flyer," a venture that soon floundered.
- 1928–1930: Ives, which was under receivership, was placed under the control of American Flyer and Lionel.
- 1929–1939: This decade marked a drastic departure for American Flyer. Beginning with steam outline locomotives with cast-iron boilers with little approximation of scale, the era ends with models with die-cast boilers, much closer attention to scale, and far greater detail.
- 1938–1940: American Flyer, then under A.C. Gilbert, completely redesigned its line, bringing out an HO-gauge railway with rails 16.5 mm apart and a 1:87 scale. The 4-6-4 "Hudson" and a rake of die-cast coaches were headliners.
- 1946: After World War II, American Flyer abandoned HO gauge for another gauge, a two-rail system known as "S." The distance between the rails was reduced to 24 mm, smaller than the O 1:43 scale. Proportions and detail were vastly improved.
- 1946–1956: American Flyer enjoyed a decade of record sales following World War II. But less expensive HO-gauge train sets were glutting the market; relatively expensive O-gauge trains experienced a sharp decline and the entire industry experienced a severe slump.
- 1961: A.C. Gilbert was acquired by the Wrather Corp. and moved from Chicago to New Haven.
- Gilbert was forced out of business in 1966 and sold its American Flyer trains to Lionel.

Summary: From the late 1920s through the mid-1950s, American Flyer's astute marketing strategy and vastly improved quality and performance standards made them a worthy competitor to Lionel in dominating the hobby on these shores. Such headliners as the "Atlantic," Pennsylvania Railroad "K-5," "Hudson," "Northern," plus an 0-8-0 switcher and superbly scaled passenger and freight cars are especially sought after by collectors.

Locomotives and Train Sets

Hummer: 1916–1939

Note: The "Hummer" name was used to designate economy line.

AF No. Type 1 "Hummer," 1916–1918.   *$100–$125*

AF No. Type 2 "Hummer," 1919–1926, "50" tender. *$100–$125*

AF No. Type 3 "Hummer," with applied boiler piping.
                                                                    $100–$125

AF "The Hummer," 1916–1921, "500" yellow numerals and lettering on dark green.   *$75–$100*

2nd Version, green winged "A.F.L." logo on green background, dark geen roof.   *$75–$100*

3rd Version, dark green/orange, chartreuse lettering.
                                                                    $75–$100

4th Version, black lettering and details on yellow.   *$80–$110*

5th Version, red/yellow, yellow lettering and winged "A.F.L." logo.   *$75–$100*

AF "Empire Express," white lettering on red background, green roof and frame.   *$50–$75*

2nd Version, yellow details.   *$50–$75*

American Flyer "Empire Express" (uncat.) O-gauge (uncat.) locomotive and No. 328 tender, "Chicago" Hummer-type passenger car, 1925, $125–$150.

3rd Version, white on orange.   *$50–$75*

4th Version, red and black on yellow.   *$50–$75*

5th Version, red on yellow or orange, red roof and frame.
                                                  $50–$75

6th Version, has "517" numerals, white on red.   *$50–$75*

7th Version, yellow litho, black dots and stripes on brown, black roof, "517" on side.   *$50–$75*

8th Version, "Pennsylvania Lines" yellow on red, green roof with red piping, "500" numerals.   *$75–$100*

9th Version, "Continental Limited" white on dark blue, white lettering on dark blue legend.   *$75–$100*

AF No. 15 Blue Car Train Set, 1938, four streamlined cars with four-wheel trucks, No. 4622-6 locomotive, light blue sides, dark blue roof, darker blue decal stripes, yellow lettering, black piping.

No. 16216B Coach, celluloid windows with yellow stripe.
                                                  $175–$200

No. 1622B Observation Car, same decoration as coaches but boat-tailed rear end, black trucks.   *$175–$200*

AF No. 1621R Coach, Red Car Train Set, 1939, red sides, roofs, and vestibules, darker red decal stripes, yellow lettering, black piping.   *$125–$150*

AF No. 1622R Observation Car, decorated as above with boat-tail end, six-wheel type-14 trucks.   *$125–$150*

AF No. 16216C Chromed Car Set, 1938, chrome-plated sides, dark gray roofs, semivestibules, silver decal stripes, black lettering, celluloid windows with blue stripe.   *$125–$150*

AF No. 16216C Observation Car, decorated as above. *$125–$150*

AF "Union Pacific" Streamliner, 1936, power car, two coaches and observation car, black tracks, whistle, 51 in. 1. *$500–$550*

AF "Union Pacific" Streamliner, 1937, minus whistle.

$400–$450

AF No. 11 Train Set "Union Pacific" Streamliner, 1938, four-wheeled trucks on coaches. $500–$550

AF No. 11, 1939 (identical to 1938). $500–$550

AF No. 1322-RT "Illinois Central" Streamliner, 1935, a.k.a. "The Green Diamond"; power car, three coaches and observation car, green with broad tan legend bearing "American Flyer Lines" decals (two), 46 in. l. overall.

No. 9962 Power Car. $275–$300

No. 9954 Coach. $125–$150

No. 9955 Observation Car. $700–$750

AF No. 1741W "Hiawatha" Locomotive (No. 1683), 1936–1937, gray/orange, tender and coaches, type-8 trucks, matching colors and gray roof, yellow-on-maroon decals, observation car with beveled end.

No. 1741-RW Passenger Set, 1936. $1,500–$2,000

No. 1742 (Deluxe) Passenger Set, 1937. $1,500–$2,000

AF No. 1641 Coach, 1936–1937, orange body with gray roof, maroon frame and stripe, lighted car, type-8 trucks, 12 in. l.

$150–$200

AF No. 1642 Observation Car, 1936–1937, same colors as No. 1641 coach, 13½ in. l. $150–$200

AF No. 1770-RW and No. 1773 Train Sets, green car sets (for diecast "Hudson"), four car sets, two-toned green, dark green decal stripes with yellow lettering, black piping. $200–$225

No. 1621 G. Coach, decorated as above, black. $175–$200

No. 1622 Observation Car, boat-tail end, black. $175–$200.

AF No. 1321RT "Burlington Zephyr" Set, 1935, power car with electric motor, coach and observation car, economy version, lithographed aluminum.   *$150-$200*

AF No. 830 "Burlington Zephyr" Set, 1935, power car with clockwork motor, coach and observation car.   *$175-$225*

AF No. 832/833 "Burlington Zephyr" Set, 1935, power car with clockwork, coaches (two) and observation car, 90-degree crossover track.   *$200-$250*

AF No. 7378T "Burlington Zephyr" Set, 1935, power car, reverse electric motor, coaches (three), observation car.   *$200-$250*

> *Note:* All the above four cars bore identical lithography.

AF "Comet" Set, ca. 1935, bears strange likeness to "Burlington Zephyr" sets, blue and silver lithography, gray/black details, "American Flyer" appears in band above windows on coaches.
                                                          $450-$500

AF "Comet" Power Car, blue, silver, gray and black lithograph, remote-control reverse motor, 11½ in. 1.   *$150-$175*

AF "Comet" Coach, type-13 truck at rear end.   *$150-$175*

AF "Comet" Trailing Car, type-13 truck at rear end. *$175-$200*

Electric Outline Locomotives: 1920–1924

AF No. 1090 Box-Cab Locomotive, ca. 1929, "Empress Express," solid wheels, black frame, orange sides, green roof, gold numerals, two pantographs, 6½ in. 1.   *$50-$75*

2nd Version, includes red pilot light.   *$50-$75*

3rd Version, spoked wheels, two pickups.   *$50-$75*

AF No. 1093 Box-Cab Locomotive, 1930, headlight, black frame, green body.   *$50–$75*

2nd Version, spoked wheels, red body, one pantograph.
                                                               $50–$75

3rd Version, green body, solid wheels.   *$50–$75*

AF No. 1094 Box-Cab Locomotive, 1928, headlight, black frame, brass pilots, red lithographed body, bell, one pantograph.
                                                               $50–$75

AF No. 1095 Box-Cab Locomotive, 1922–1924, "American Flyer Lines" and "1095 A.F.M.C." rubber-stamped in yellow, brown body.   *$50–$75*

2nd Version, green body.   *$50–$75*

AF No. 1096 Box-Cab Locomotive, 1925–1927, "New York Central" cab in 1925, a "New Haven"-type lithographed cab in 1926–1927, rubber-stamped numerals, 6½ in. 1.   *$50–$75*

2nd Version, black body.   *$50–$75*

3rd Version, 1926, maroon.   *$75–$100*

4th Version, 1927, red, double pantograph.   *$75–$100*

5th Version, 1927, single pantograph (otherwise same as 4th version).   *$75–$100*

AF No. 1097 Box-Cab Locomotive, 1928, old-style roof-mounted cast headlight, stamped bell, lithographed dark orange body, green roof, "American Flyer" in cartouche on side, two pantographs, solid wheels.   *$75–$100*

2nd Version, 1929, new-style spoked wheels, dual pickup.
                                                              $75–$100

3rd Version, red sides, green roof, green numerals and lettering on white oval.   *$75–$100*

4th Version, gilt lettering on black cartouches.   *$75–$100*

AF No. 1101 Box-Cab Locomotive, 1922, Montgomery Ward as set No. 48010, black, yellow rubber-stamping of letters and numerals, "1095."   *$50–$75*

2nd Version, two-piece cast-iron frame, smaller motor.

$50–$75

AF No. 1196 Box-Cab Locomotive, "Empress Express" and "1096," two pantographs.   *$75–$100*

AF No. 1201 Steeple-Cab Locomotive, 1921–1924, bell at rear, 1924 has bell at front, black, orange rubber-stamp lettering.   *$50–$75*

2nd Version, dark green body.   *$75–$100*

AF No. 1211 Steeple-Cab Locomotive, "American Flyer Lines" and "Motor 1211."   *$75–$100*

AF No. 1217 Steeple-Cab Locomotive, 1920–1921, red windows, bell at rear, black, orange rubber-stamping.   *$75–$100*

2nd Version, brown, yellow rubber-stamping.   *$75–$100*

3rd Version, dark green, gold stamping.   *$75–$100*

AF No. 1218 Steeple-Cab Locomotive, orange with red stamping.
$100–$125

2nd Version, red window frames.   *$100–$125*

3rd Version, red with yellow stamping and frames. *$100–$125*

4th Version, green with yellow stamping and frames.
$100–$125

5th Version, black with yellow frames and stamping.
$100–$125

6th Version, black with black window frames.   *$100–$125*

AF No. 3011 Box-Cab Locomotive, 1926–1927, red/brown lithographed, yellow window frames, brown roof.   *$100–$150*

2nd Version, black roof.   *$100–$150*

3rd Version, enameled sides.   *$100–$150*

AF No. 3012 Box-Cab Locomotive, 1925–1927, black enameled body, 1926.   *$100–$125*

2nd Version, 1927, orange lithographed body.   *$100–$125*

3rd Version, 1927, no reverse.   *$100–$125*

4th Version, 1927, reddish-brown lithographed with black roof.   *$100–$125*

5th Version, same as 4th with cast headlight in front of bell.   *$100–$125*

AF No. 3013 Box-Cab Locomotive, 1927, blue lithographed cab with yellow window frames, reverse unit.   *$100–$125*

2nd Version, no reverse.   *$100–$125*

AF No. 3019 Box-Cab Locomotive, 1923–1924, "New York Central"-type body, black with maroon window frames, yellow rubber-stamping.   *$175–$200*

2nd Version, same as above but with latch couplers fore and aft.   *$175–$200*

3rd Version, dark green with red window trim, yellow stamping, vertical twisted rear hook coupler.   *$175–$200*

AF No. 3020 Box-Cab Locomotive, 1922–1925, American Flyer's most upscale O-gauge electric outline locomotive, modeled after "New York Central" T-type, black with yellow stamping.   *$425–$500*

2nd Version, black with dark red window frames, yellow stamping.   *$300–$400*

3rd Version, dark green, red window trim, yellow stamping.   *$300–$400*

4th Version, yellow window trim.   *$300–$400*

5th Version, brown, orange window trim.   *$350–$425*

AF No. 3109 Center-Cab Locomotive, 1928–1929, "New Haven"-style, orange lithography, blue-green window frames, bell and pantograph, brass journals.   *$110–$135*

AF No. 3116 Center-Cab Locomotive, 1928–1929, modeled after "St. Paul" style, green, red-painted pilots, goldenrod frame, brass handrails.   *$200–$223*

AF No. 3117 Center-Cab Locomotive, 1928–1929, same as above with flag holders, red body on black frame, wire handrails, 10¼ in. 1.; also a version with stamped brass handrails.   *$100–$200*

AF No. 7011 Steeple-Cab Locomotive, 1929, Montgomery Ward, green body, yellow stamping, gilt window frames and grilles, no reverse.   *$250–$300*

　2nd Version, dark green, normal reverse.   *$275–$300*

Wide-Gauge Train Sets: 1925–1935

American Flyer's Wide-gauge (2¼ in.) sets proved to be strong competition for Lionel's 2⅛ in. Standard gauge. American Flyer's top-of-the-line grouping represented below comprises some of the most coveted sets in the hobby.

AF No. 1316 Set, 1931, 3110-3013-3012-3014.   *$225–$275*

AF No. 1350 Set, 1932, 3316-3171-3171-3172.   *$275–$325*

AF No. 1366RT Set, O gauge, 1934, 3193-1214-1213-1217.
                    $250–$300

AF No. 1433 Set, 1925, "The All-American," maroon, 4019-4040-4041-4042.   *$850–$1,000*

AF No. 1448 Set, 1935, "The Warrior," 4681-4695-4671-4331-4331-4331-4332.   *$2,000–$3,000*

American Flyer 2-4-0 train set, 1933, O gauge, eight-wheel coaches with brass trim, $250–$300.

AF No. 1453 Set, 1926, "The President's Special," 4039-4080-4081-4081.   *$6,000–$8,000*

AF No. 1466 Set, 1927 (second), "The President's Special," 4687-4080-4081-4082.   *$6,000–$8,000*

AF No. 1473 Set, 1928, "The Statesman," orange with orange car roofs, 4654-4151-4151-4152.   *$2,000–$3,000*

AF No. 1473 Set, 1930, "The Statesman," orange with green car roofs, 4654-4151-4151-4152.   *$2,000–$3,000*

American Flyer "Presidential" set, locomotive No. 4689, $7,000–$9,000. (Courtesy of Sotheby's, New York)

AF No. 1474 Set, 1933, "The Brigadier," red 4644R/C locomotive, 4331-4332.   *$1,000–$1,500*

AF No. 1489 Set, 1929, "The President's Special," two-tone blue, 4689-4390-4391-4393-4392.   *$7,000–$9,000*

AF No. 1491 Set, 1931, "The Iron Monarch," 4694-4693-4340-4341-4342.   *$2,500–$4,000*

AF No. 1493 Set, 1932, "The New Minute-Man," 4694-4695-4693-4390-4391-4392.   *$2,500–$4,000*

Standard-Gauge Locomotives: 1925–1936

AF No. 4000 Locomotive, black.   *$400–$425*

AF No. 4000 Locomotive, maroon.   *$425–$450*

AF No. 4039 Locomotive, 0-4-0, brown, black with brass trim.
$750–$850

AF No. 4635 "Shasta" Locomotive, red with brass trim.
$525–$625

AF No. 4637 Locomotive, 0-4-0, bell, green, beige with brass trim.
$500–$550

AF No. 4637 "Shasta" Locomotive, green.   *$625–$700*

AF No. 4644 "Shasta" Locomotive, red/gray.   *$575–$650*

AF No. 4653 Locomotive, 0-4-0, red, black with brass trim.
$325–$375

AF No. 4654 Locomotive, black.   *$375–$450*

AF No. 4660 Locomotive, black.   *$400–$475*

AF No. 4667 Locomotive, red, black with brass trim. $375–$425

AF No. 4670 Locomotive, 2-4-2, and Tender, black, green stripe with brass trim. $450–$500

AF 4670 Locomotive, 4-4-2, and Tender, black, green stripe with brass, nickel trim. $725–$800

AF No. 4671 Locomotive, cast iron, black. $625–$700

AF No. 4672 Locomotive, 4670, and Tender, 4671. $725–$800

AF No. 4678 Locomotive, 0-4-0, red, gray with brass trim.
$400–$450

AF No. 4680 "Golden State" Locomotive. $750–$800

AF No. 4682 Locomotive, 4680, and Coal Tender, 4671, 1933.
$750–$800

AF No. 4683 Locomotive. $550–$600

AF No. 4684 Locomotive. $550–$600

AF No. 4686 "The Ace" Locomotive, 4-4-4, two-tone blue, black, red with brass trim. $550–$600

AF No. 4687 "President's Special" Locomotive, blue lithograph.
$2,000–$3,000

AF No. 4687 Locomotive, 4-4-4, blue, black with brass trim.
$2,500–$3,000

AF No. 2689 "The Commander" Locomotive, 4-4-4, peacock blue, black with brass and nickel trim. $3,000–$3,500

AF No. 4692 American Flyer-Ives Locomotive. $2,500–$3,000

AF No. 4693 Locomotive, 4-4-2, blue, with brass and copper trim.
$750–$850

AF No. 4694 American Flyer-Ives Locomotive.   *$650–$700*

AF No. 4694 Locomotive.   *$850–$900*

AF No. 4695 Locomotive.   *$850–$900*

Clockwork Locomotives: 1930–1937

AF No. 615 Clockwork Locomotive, 1932–1934, 0-4-0, "American Flyer" decal, with No. 121 tender.   *$50–$75*

AF No. 616 Clockwork Locomotive, 1932, 0-4-0, with No. 941T "Dictator," No. 940T "Chief," tender rubber-stamped "Champion," black.   *$50–$75*

AF No. 618 Clockwork Locomotive, 1933, 0-4-0 manual reverse switch.   *$50–$75*

AF No. 619 Clockwork Locomotive, 1932, 2-4-2, round headlight shield, "Champion" tender, black.   *$50–$75*

AF No. 620 Clockwork Locomotive, embossed domes. *$75–$100*

AF No. 621 Clockwork Locomotive, includes tender. *$75–$100*

AF No. 1084 Clockwork Locomotive, 1931, with No. 119 tender, red with gold trim, solid disc wheels.   *$50–$75*

AF No. 1085 Clockwork Locomotive, 1931, die-cast O gauge with No. 121 tender (lithographed).   *$75–$100*

AF No. 3303 Clockwork Locomotive, 1934, 2-4-0, continuous whistle mechanism, rubber-stamped "A.F."   *$100–$125*

AF No. 4403/403 Clockwork Locomotive, "American Flyer Lines" decal on side toward boiler front, black.   *$75–$100*

   2nd Version, gunmetal gray boiler.   *$75–$100*

AF No. (Uncataloged) Clockwork Electric Locomotive, 1932 with "Champion" tender. *$100–$125*

AF No. (Uncataloged) Clockwork Locomotive, 1934, 0-4-0, part of Set No. 717 in 1934 and No. 831 coal loader in 1935 with late 5½-in. freight cars, red locomotive. *$75–$100*

Locomotives and Tenders: 1930–1939

AF No. 427 Locomotive and Tender, 1939, 2-6-4, "425" rubber-stamped on cab in silver, Type 5 "Vanderbilt" tender, Type 15 boiler cab. *$100–$125*

AF No. 4614-4 Locomotive and Tender, 1938, 2-4-2, Type 3 tender, Type 15 boiler cab. *$100–$125*

AF No. 4614-6 Locomotive and Tender, 1938, 2-6-4, Type 5 "Vanderbilt" tender, Type 15 boiler cab. *$125–$150*

AF No. 1683 Locomotive and Tender "Hiawatha," 1936, "Milwaukee Road" decal, black, turned-brass leading wheels, 4-4-2, tender with whistle. *$800–$1,200*

  2nd Version, 1937, leading wheels are cast. *$800–$1,200*

AF No. 9915 Locomotive and Tender, swiveled four-wheel motor unit with Type 11 truck, "Burlington Zephyr," 1934–1937 spinoff in cast aluminum. *$1,000–$1,500*

AF No. 437 Locomotive and Tender, 1939, 420-type locomotive, 403-type locomotives and tenders as set, original part of American Flyer Set No. 310, double-header freight. *$125–$150*

AF No. 1710-RT Locomotive and Tender, 1936, Type 11 boiler, Type 9 eight-wheel tender, 0-4-2, remote-control reverse, operating headlight, black. *$100–$150*

AF No. 1686 Locomotive and Tender, 1937, Type 11 boiler, Type 9 eight-wheel tender, 2-4-4, gunmetal gray. $150–$175

AF No. 4629 Locomotive and Tender, 1939, Type 11 boiler, Type 9 eight-wheel tender, 2-4-4, operating headlight. $150–$175

AF No. 419 Locomotive and Tender, 1939, Type 11 boiler, Type 9 eight-wheel tender, 2-4-4, operating headlight. $150–$175

AF No. 1681 Locomotive and Tender, 1936–1938, Type 8 tender, whistle, beige-trimmed windows, running board with white stripes.
$250–$300

2nd Version, dark gray-trimmed windows. $250–$300

3rd Version, red-trimmed windows, "1680" decal.
$250–$300

AF No. 4321 Locomotive and Tender, 1938–1939, "American Flyer Lines" rubber-stamped in silver, "429" cab rubber-stamped in silver. $325–$375

2nd Version, five-digit white decal rather than "1429."
$325–$375

3rd Version, black matte finish, "American Flyer" and "429" rubber-stamped. $400–$450

AF No. 424 Locomotive and Tender, 1939, 2-4-2, Type 3 tender, Type 15 boiler cab. $100–$125

AF No. 616 Locomotive, 1932, 0-4-0, black tender with "Champion" rubber-stamped in white. $75–$100

AF No. 619 Locomotive, 1932, 2-4-2, "Champion" tender.
$75–$100

AF No. 1084 Locomotive, 1931, No. "119" lithographed tender, red and gold, solid disc wheels. $75–$100

AF No. 618 Locomotive, 961-T (620 is No. for pairing), 0-4-0, manual reverse switch. $75–$100

AF No. 623 Locomotive, 1934, with Set No. 831 coal loader, red locomotive, same boiler stamping as locomotives No. 614 and No. 618.   *$75–$100*

AF No. 620 Locomotive, embossed domes.   *$75–$100*

AF No. 1225 Electric (Steam-Type) Locomotive, 1918, 1919–1924, No. 119 or No. 120 tender, locomotive with gold trim and red, Type 1 boiler cab.   *$100–$125*

AF No. 3188 Locomotive and Tender, No. 319B locomotive and No. 3189 tender (four wheels), Type 4 boiler cab, headlight 1930–1931.   *$75–$100*

AF No. 3192 Locomotive and Tender, 1930–1931, brass plate has No. on cab, Type 3 boiler cab, headlight.   *$75–$100*

AF No. 3191 Locomotive, 1931, 2-4-0, remote reversing, brass tanks.   *$75–$100*

AF No. 3194 Locomotive and Tender, 1931, 0-4-0, numbered brass plate appears on cab, manual reversing.   *$75–$100*

AF No. 3302 Locomotive and Tender, 1931, wheel die-cast "Vanderbilt"-type tender, rubber-stamped "3300" on cab, visor over headlight.   *$200–$300*

AF No. 3324/3326 Locomotive and Tender, 1932–1935, ringing brass bell, 2-4-2, remote-control reverse, black.   *$75–$100*

AF No. 641–1687 Locomotive and Tender, 1936, 2-4-2, Type 3B coal tender, black.   *$100–$150*

   2nd Version, with Type 8 rectangular tender, black.

                                                              $125–$175

AF No. 3308 Locomotive and Tender, 1932–1934, 2-4-2, Type 7 boiler, "Vanderbilt" Type 6 four-wheel oil tender, locomotive numbered "3307," ringing bell.   *$100–$125*

   2nd Version, locomotive unnumbered.   *$100–$125*

AF No. 3309 Locomotive and Tender, 1934, minus bell and remote-control reverse. $100–$125

AF No. 4677 Locomotive and Tender, 1938, 2-4-2, Type 6 boiler, Type B eight-wheel coal tender, black "420" rubber-stamped on cab in silver. $100–$125

AF No. 422 Locomotive and Tender, 1939, Type 3B eight-wheel coal tender. $100–$125

2nd Version, nickel trim, extra lead weight in cab. $125–$150

AF No. 3316 Locomotive and Tender, 1932–1935, 2-4-2, Type 8 boiler, Type 7B eight-wheel tender, brass trim on headlight, gilt slotted front coupler. $125–$150

2nd Version, minus front coupler. $125–$150

AF No. 3310 Locomotive and Tender, 1934, 2-4-2, Type 8 boiler, Type 7B eight-wheel "Vanderbilt" oil tender, ringing bell, remote-control reverse. $125–$150

AF No. 1688 Locomotive and Tender, 1937, 2-4-2, Type 8 boiler, Type 7B eight-wheel tender, brass whistle. $125–$150

AF No. 617 Locomotive and Tender, 1933–1934, Type 9 boiler, Type 5 four-wheel coal tender, copper bell. $50–$60

AF No. 3304 Locomotive and Tender, 1934, 2-4-2, Type 10 boiler, Type 4 four-wheel coal tender, copper dome and pipe. $50–$60

AF No. 3313 Locomotive and Tender, 1935, Type 10 boiler, Type 4 four-wheel coal tender. $50–$60

AF No. 4603 Locomotive and Tender, 1938, 2-4-4, Type 10 boiler, Type 9 eight-wheel tender. $30–$50

AF No. 403 Locomotive and Tender, 1939, 2-4-4, Type 10 boiler, Type 7 eight-wheel coal tender. $30–$50

Locomotives and Rolling Stock ($^3/_{16}$-in.): 1940–1941

AF No. 531 "New York Central" J-3, 1940–1941, Hudson 4-6-4, black with white lettering, cab rubber-stamped "531."

$200–$250

AF No. K531 "New York Central," ca. 1940–1941, kit version of No. 531, locomotive decal "5640," "New York Central" tender decal. $150–$200

AF No. 534 "Union Pacific," 1940, 4-8-4, black with white lettering, includes No. 567 12-wheel tender, 21½-in.-1. cab is stamped "533." $300–$400

  2nd Version, "571" stamped on cab. $300–$400

AF No. K534 "Union Pacific," same as above in kit form.

$250–$300

AF No. 545 "Pennsylvania," 1940, 4-4-2, black with silver "545" rubber-stamping on cab. $250–$300

Note: The following three train sets are uncataloged and are known as the "Minne-Ha-Ha" sets.

AF No. 960T "New York Central" Sheet Metal Set, electric locomotive/tender and streamliner coach/observation car, 27 in. overall. $350–$400

AF No. 964T "Minne-Ha-Ha" Set, same as above with additional coach, burnt orange and silver. $350–$400

AF No. 816 Steam Streamline Set, locomotive (clockwork), tender with two coaches, observation car, orange/red. $350–$400

S-Gauge Postwar Locomotives and Tenders: 1946–1966

AF No. 293 Steam Locomotive, NYNH & Hartford, Pacific 4-6-2, 1953–1958. $75–$100

AF No. 295 Steam Locomotive, Pacific 4-6-2, 1951. *$100–$125*

AF No. 296 Steam Locomotive, New Haven, Pacific, 4-6-2, 1955.
$200–$250

AF No. 299 Steam Locomotive, Reading, Atlantic 4-4-2, 1954.
$150–$175

AF No. 300 Steam Locomotive, Reading, Atlantic 4-4-2, 1946–1947. *$50–$75*

AF No. 300 Steam Locomotive, Reading, Atlantic 4-4-2, 1949–1951. *$50–$75*

AF No. 301 Steam Locomotive, Reading, Atlantic 4-4-2, 1946–1953. *$30–$50*

AF No. 302 Steam Locomotive, Reading, Atlantic 4-4-2, 1948–1953. *$30–$50*

AF No. 302 Steam Locomotive, Reading, Atlantic 4-4-2, 1950–1951. *$30–$50*

AF No. 303 Steam Locomotive, Reading, Atlantic 4-4-2, 1954–1955. *$30–$50*

AF No. 307 Steam Locomotive, Reading, Atlantic 4-4-2, 1954–1955. *$30–$50*

AF No. 308 Steam Locomotive, Reading, Atlantic 4-4-2, 1956.
$30–$50

AF No. 310 Steam Locomotive, Pennsylvania. *$30–$50*

AF No. 310 Steam Locomotive, Pennsylvania 4-6-2, 1947.
$75–$100

AF No. 312 Steam Locomotive, Pennsylvania, K-5, 4-6-2, 1946–1948, 1952. *$65–$75*

AF No. 312 Steam Locomotive, Pennsylvania, K-5, 4-6-2, 1949–1951. *$75–$100*

AF No. 313 Steam Locomotive, Pennsylvania, K-5, 4-6-2, 1955–1957. *$100–$125*

AF No. 314AW Steam Locomotive, Pennsylvania, K-5, 4-6-2, 1949–1950. *$150–$200*

AF No. 315 Steam Locomotive, Pennsylvania, K-5, 4-6-2, 1952. *$75–$100*

AF No. 316 Steam Locomotive, Pennsylvania, K-5, 4-6-2, 1953–1954. *$125–$150*

AF No. 320 Steam Locomotive, New York Central, Hudson 4-6-4, 1946–1947. *$125–$150*

AF No. 321 Steam Locomotive, New York Central, Hudson 4-6-4, 1946–1947, tender: "New York Central System." *$150–$175*

AF No. 321 Steam Locomotive, New York Central, Hudson 4-6-4, 1946–1947, tender: "New York Central." *$200–$250*

AF No. 322 Steam Locomotive, New York Central, Hudson 4-6-4, 1947–1948, tender: "New York Central System." *$125–$150*

AF No. 322 Steam Locomotive, New York Central, Hudson 4-6-4, 1946, tender: "New York Central." *$200–$250*

AF No. 322 AC Steam Locomotive, New York Central, Hudson 4-6-4, 1948–1952. *$100–$125*

AF No. 324 AC Steam Locomotive, New York Central, Hudson 4-6-4, 1950. *$100–$125*

AF No. 325 AC Steam Locomotive, New York Central, Hudson 4-6-4, 1951. *$90–$110*

AF No. K325 Steam Locomotive, New York Central, Hudson 4-6-4, 1952.   *$90–$110*

AF No. 326 Steam Locomotive, New York Central, Hudson 4-6-4, 1953–1957.   *$90–$110*

AF No. 332 Steam Locomotive, Union Pacific, Northern 4-8-4, 1946–1949, tender: "Union Pacific."   *$1,000–$1,500*

AF No. 332 Steam Locomotive, Union Pacific, Northern 4-8-4, 1946–1949, "Union Pacific" on tender shield logo.   *$175–$200*

AF No. 332 AC Steam Locomotive, Union Pacific, Northern 4-8-4, 1950–1951.   *$175–$200*

AF No. 334 DC Steam Locomotive, Union Pacific, Northern 4-8-4, 1950.   *$200–$225*

AF No. K335 Steam Locomotive, Union Pacific, Northern, 1952.
$175–$200

AF No. 336 Steam Locomotive, Union Pacific, Northern 4-8-4, 1953–1957.   *$175–$200*

AF No. 342 Steam Locomotive, nickel-plated, Switcher 0-8-0, 1946, tender: "Nickel Plate Road."   *$800–$1,000*

AF No. 342 Steam Locomotive, nickel-plated, Switcher 0-8-0, 1947–1948, 1952, tender: "A.F.L. & Nickel Plate Road."
$100–$150

AF No. 342 AC Steam Locomotive, nickel-plated, Switcher 0-8-0, 1949–1951.   *$100–$150*

AF No. 342 DC Steam Locomotive, nickel-plated, Switcher 0-8-0, 1948–1950.   *$100–$125*

AF No. 343 Steam Locomotive, nickel-plated, Switcher 0-8-0, 1953–1958.   *$125–$150*

AF No. 346 Steam Locomotive, nickel-plated, Switcher 0-8-0, 1955.   *$200–$250*

AF No. 350 Steam Locomotive, B & O, Pacific 4-6-2, 1948–1950.
$100–$125

AF No. 353 Steam Locomotive, Circus, royal blue, Pacific 4-6-2, 1950–1951.   *$125–$150*

AF No. 354 Steam Locomotive, "Silver Bullet," Pacific 4-6-2, 1954.   *$100–$125*

AF No. 355 Switcher, C & NW, 1957.   *$75–$100*

AF No. 356 Steam Locomotive, "Silver Bullet," Pacific 4-6-2, 1953, chrome.   *$150–$200*

AF No. 356 Steam Locomotive, "Silver Bullet," Pacific 4-6-2, 1953.   *$75–$100*

AF No. 360–361 Alco A & B, Santa Fe Set, silver and chrome, 1950–1952; priced as set.   *$200–$250*

AF No. 360-364 Alco A & B, Santa Fe, silver finish, 1951–1952.
$200–$250

AF No. 372 GP-7, Union Pacific, Road Switcher, 1955–1957, "Built by Gilbert" on side.   *$125–$150*

AF No. 372 GP-7, Union Pacific, Road Switcher, 1955–1957, minus "Gilbert" identification.   *$150–$175*

AF No. 374-375 GP-7, Texas & Pacific, Road Switcher Set, 1955; priced as set.   *$175–$200*

AF No. 375 GP-7, GM A.F., Road Switcher, 1953.   *$350–$450*

AF No. 377-78 GP-7, Texas & Pacific, Road Switcher Set, 1956–1957.   *$150–$200*

AF No. 405 Alco A, "Silver Streak," 1952.   *$100–$150*

AF No. 466 Alco A, "Silver Comet," 1953–1955.   *$75–$100*

AF No. 470-471-473 Alco A-B-A, Santa Fe Set, 1953–1957.
$225–$275

AF No. 472 Alco A, Santa Fe, 1956.   *$150–$200*

AF No. 474-475 Alco A-A, "Silver Rocket," 1953–1955.
$175–$200

AF No. 477-478 Alco A-B, "Silver Flash," 1953–1954.
$200–$225

AF No. 479 Alco A, "Silver Flash," 1955.   *$100–$125*

AF No. 480 Alco B, "Silver Flash," 1955.   *$350–$400*

AF No. 481 Alco A, "Silver Flash," 1956.   *$125–$150*

AF No. 484-485-486 Alco A-B-A, Santa Fe Set, 1956–1957.
$250–$300

AF No. 2104 Steam Locomotive, Pennsylvania, Switcher 0-6-0,
1957.   *$150–$175*

AF No. 21005 Steam Locomotive, Pennsylvania, Switcher 0-6-0,
1958.   *$200–$250*

AF No. 12084 Steam Locomotive, Canadian & Northwest, Pacific
4-6-2, 1957.   *$100–$125*

AF No. 21085 Steam Locomotive, Canadian & Northwest, Pacific
4-6-2, 1958.   *$75–$100*

AF No. 21095 Steam Locomotive, New Haven, Pacific 4-6-2, 1958
(one of the toughest AF postwar engines to track down).
$600–$700

AF No. 21099 Steam Locomotive, New Haven, Pacific 4-6-2, 1958.
$200–$250

AF No. 21100 Steam Locomotive, Reading, Atlantic 4-4-4, 1957.
$50–$75

AF No. 21105 Steam Locomotive, Reading, Atlantic 4-4-2, 1957–1960.
$50–$75

AF No. 21106 Steam Locomotive, Reading, Atlantic 4-4-2, 1959.
$50–$75

AF No. 21107 Steam Locomotive, Pennsylvania, Atlantic 4-4-2, 1964–1966.
$40–$60

AF No. 21107, same as above but Burlington, Atlantic, 1965.
$50–$75

AF No. 21129 Steam Locomotive, New York Central, Hudson 4-6-4, 1962–1963.
$250–$350

AF No. 21139 Steam Locomotive, Union Pacific, Northern 4-8-4, 1958.
$250–$300

AF No. 21140 Steam Locomotive, Union Pacific, Northern 4-8-4, 1959–1960.
$300–$350

AF No. 21145 Steam Locomotive, nickel-plated, Switcher 0-8-0, 1958.
$250–$300

AF No. 21155 Steam Locomotive, Docksider, Switcher 0-6-0, 1959.
$200–$250

AF No. 21156 Steam Locomotive, Docksider, Switcher 0-6-0, 1959.
$200–$250

AF No. 21158 Steam Locomotive, Reading, Atlantic 4-4-2, 1960.
$50–$75

AF No. 21161 Steam Locomotive, Reading, Atlantic 4-4-2, 1960.
$30–$50

AF No. 21161 Steam Locomotive, Reading, Atlantic 4-4-2, "Prestone Car Care Express," 1960. *$100–$125*

AF No. 21166 Steam Locomotive, Burlington "Casey Jones" 4-4-0, 1963–1964 (there were other "Casey Jones" variations from 1961–1965 in the same value range). *$50–$75*

AF No. 21205/21205-1, F9, Boston & Maine, 1961; priced as set.
$100–$125

AF No. 21206/21206-1, F9, Santa Fe, 1962; priced as set.
$100–$125

AF No. 21207/21207-1, F9, Great Northern, 1963–1964; priced as set. *$100–$125*

AF No. 21215/21215-1, F9, Union Pacific, 1961–1962; priced as set. *$100–$125*

AF No. 21551 Alco A, Northern Pacific, 1958. *$175–$200*

AF No. 21573 General Electric, New Haven with two pantographs, 1958–1959. *$200–$250*

AF No. 21720 Alco B, Santa Fe, 1958. *$350–$400*

AF No. 21813, Minneapolis & St. Louis, Switcher, 1958.
$250–$275

AF No. 21831 GP-7, Texas & Pacific, 1958. *$300–$350*

AF No. 21910/21910-2 Alco A-B-A, Santa Fe, 1957–1958; priced as set. *$450–$500*

AF No. 21920/21920-1 Alco A-A, Missouri Pacific, 1963, single motor in 21920; priced as set. *$200–$250*

AF No. 21922/21922-1 Alco A-A, Missouri Pacific, 1959–1960; priced as set.   *$350–$400*

Rolling Stock

Standard-Gauge Rolling Stock: Prewar

AF No. 4006 Hopper Car.   *$350–$400*

AF No. 4010 Tank Car, yellow.   *$275–$300*

AF No. 4011 Caboose.   *$200–$250*

AF No. 4012 Lumber Car, blue, black, brass trim.   *$125–$150*

AF No. 4017 Gondola, green.   *$125–$150*

AF No. 4018 Box Car, beige/blue.   *$300–$350*

AF No. 4019 Engine, 0-4-0, maroon, black, brass trim.
$375–$425

AF No. 4020 Cattle Car, green/blue.   *$325–$350*

AF No. 4020 Cattle Car, two-tone blue.   *$325–$350*

AF No. 4021 Caboose, two-tone red, brass trim.   *$225–$250*

AF No. 4022 Lumber Car, with load.   *$225–$250*

AF No. 4023 Lumber Car, with load.   *$225–$250*

AF No. 4039 Locomotive, 0-4-0, brown, black, brass trim.
$135–$225

AF No. 4040 Mail Car, lithographed, red.   *$225–$250*

AF No. 4040 "United States Mail Railway Post Office," green, orange, black lithograph.   *$200–$225*

AF No. 4040 Baggage Car, maroon. $225–$250

AF No. 4041 Pullman, maroon. $225–$250

AF No. 4042 Observation Car, maroon. $225–$250

AF No. 4080 Baggage Car. $325–$350

AF No. 4081 "Washington" Car. $325–$350

AF No. 4082 "Valley Forge" Car. $325–$350

AF No. 4122 Mail Car, two-tone blue. $225–$250

AF No. 4250 "Lone Scout" Club Car, turquoise, red lithograph, brass trim. $250–$275

AF No. 4251 "Lone Scout" Observation Car, turquoise, red, brass trim. $250–$275

AF No. 4252 "Lone Scout" Observation Car, turquoise, red, brass trim. $250–$275

AF No. 4331 Pullman Car, red. $250–$275

AF No. 4331 Observation Car, red with brass doors. $250–$275

AF No. 4331 Pullman Car, two-tone red, brass inserts and brass windows. $250–$275

AF No. 4332 Passenger Car, red. $225–$250

AF No. 4332 Observation Car, red with brass doors. $250–$275

AF No. 4340 "Pocahontas" Club Car, beige/green, green trucks, brass plates and windows. $250–$275

AF No. 4340 "Hamiltonian" Club Car, two-tone red, brass trim. $250–$275

American Flyer "Pocahontas," 1928, No. 4637 Wide-gauge bi-polar loco-motive, Lionel-style coaches with internal lighting, coaches: 14 in. 1.; overall length: 6 ft., 7 in., $1,500–$2,000. (Courtesy of Sotheby's, New York)

AF No. 4341 Pullman Car, beige/green, green trucks, brass plates and windows. $250–$275

AF No. 4341 "Hamiltonian" Pullman Car, two-tone red, brass trim. $250–$275

AF No. 4341 "Pocahontas" Pullman Car, two-tone red, brass trim.
$275–$300

AF No. 4342 "Pocahontas" Observation Car, beige/green, green trucks, brass plates and windows. $250–$275

AF No. 4342 "Hamiltonian" Observation Car, two-tone red, brass trim. $250–$275

AF No. 4343 "Pocahontas" Observation Car, beige/green, brass trim. $250–$275

AF No. 4350 Club Car, blue/green with red roof. $250–$275

AF No. 4351 Club Car, blue/green with red roof. $250–$275

AF No. 4352 Club Car, blue/green with red roof. $250–$275

AF No. 4380 "Hancock" Baggage Car, beige/green, brass trim.
$350–$400

AF No. 4381 "Flying Colonel-Adams," blue, brass trim.
$350–$400

AF No. 4381 "Hancock" Pullman Car, green/beige, brass trim.
$350–$400

AF No. 4382 "Flying Colonel-Hancock" Observation Car, blue, brass trim.
$350–$400

AF No. 4382 "Hancock" Observation Car, beige/green, brass trim.
$350–$400

AF No. 4390 "West Point" Club Car, two-tone blue. $550–$600

AF No. 4391 "Annapolis" Pullman Car, two-tone blue.
$550–$600

AF No. 4392 "Army-Navy" Observation Car, two-tone blue.
$550–$600

AF No. 4393 "Army-Navy" Observation Car, two-tone blue.
$550–$600

AF No. 4393 "President's Special" Academy Diner, two-tone blue.
$750–$800

AF No. 4642 Box Car, red/black. $325–$350

AF No. 4644 "Eagle" Pullman Car, lithographed. $225–$250

AF No. 4644 "Eagle" Observation Car, lithographed.
$225–$250

Uncataloged

AF No. "Bunker Hill" Passenger Car, orange, maroon, black lithographed, brass trim. $200–$250

S-Gauge Rolling Stock: Postwar

Note: A.F.L. signifies American Flyer Lines.

AF No. 50 (247 & 250), FY & PRR, 1960–1961.   *$60–$75*

AF No. 55 Box Car, "G. Fox & Co.," brown, 1947.   *$1000+*

AF No. 55 (240 & 55) Box Car, "Gold Belt Line," 1960–1961.
$50–$75

AF No. 65 (245 & 65) Flat Car, FY & PRR, cannon load, 1960–1961.   *$125–$150*

AF No. 88 (210) Steam Locomotive, FY88 & P, "Franklin" 4-4-0, 1959.   *$100–$125*

AF No. 234 (21 & 234) GP-7, Chesapeake & Ohio, 1961–1962.
$175–$200

AF No. 500 Combine, A.F.L., chrome finish, 1952.   *$150–$175*

AF No. 500 Combine, A.F.L., silver finish, 1952.   *$150–$175*

AF No. 501 Coach, A.F.L., chrome finish, 1952.   *$100–$125*

AF No. 501 Coach, A.F.L., silver finish, 1952.   *$100–$125*

AF No. 502 Vista-Dome Car, A.F.L., chrome finish, 1952.
$100–$125

AF No. 502 Vista-Dome Car, A.F.L., silver finish, 1952.
$100–$125

AF No. 503 Observation Car, A.F.L., silver finish, 1952.
$100–$125

AF No. 503 Observation Car, A.F.L., chrome finish, 1952.
$100–$125

AF No. 583 Electro Magnetic Crane (single button control), 1946–1949. $75–$100

AF No. 583A Electro Magnetic Crane (double-button control), 1950–1953. $75–$100

AF No. 605 Flat Car, A.F.L., log loader, 1953. $25–$50

AF No. 606 Crane Car, A.F.L., 1953. $30–$60

AF No. 607 Work Caboose, A.F.L., 1953 $15–$30

AF No. 609 Flat Car, A.F.L., girder load, 1953. $20–$30

AF No. 613 Box Car, Great Northern, brown, 1953. $25–$50

AF No. 620 Gondola, Southern, black, 1953. $15–$30

AF No. 622 Box Car, GAEX, 1953. $25–$50

AF No. 623 Reefer, Illinois Central, orange, 1953. $25–$50

AF No. 625G Tank Car, "Gulf," silver, 1952–1953. $20–$25

AF No. 627 Flat Car, A.F.L., girder load, 1950. $25–$35

AF No. 627 Flat Car, Canadian & Northwest, girder loader, 1947–1950. $25–$30

AF No. 629 Stock Car, Missouri Pacific, red, 1943–1953.
$25–$30

AF No. 630 Caboose, A.F.L., red, 1946–1953. $15–$25

AF No. 630 Caboose, Reading, red, 1946–1953. $10–$15

AF No. 631 Gondola, Texas & Pacific, 1946–1953. $10–$15

AF No. 632 Hopper, Lehigh-New England, gray, 1946–1953.
$20–$30

AF No. 633 Reefer, B & O, two color variations: red or brown, 1948–1953. *$25–$35*

AF No. 633 Box Car, B & O, three color variations on sides: white, red or brown, 1948–1953. *$25–$35*

AF No. 634 Floodlight, C & NW, 1946–1949, 1953. *$30–$40*

AF No. 635 Crane Car, C & NW, 1946–1949. *$30–$40*

AF No. 636 Flat Car, Erie, depressed center, with spool load, 1948–1953. *$25–$35*

AF No. 637 Box Car, Missouri, Kansas, Texas, red, 1949–1953.
$10–$15

AF No. 638 Caboose, A.F.L., red, 1949–1953. *$10–$15*

AF No. 639 Box Car, A.F.L., brown or yellow, 1949–1952.
$20–$25

AF No. 639 Reefer, A.F.L., yellow, 1951–1952. *$20–$25*

AF No. 640 Hopper, Wabash, black, 1953. *$25–$35*

AF No. 641 Gondola, Frisco, brown, 1953. *$30–$40*

AF No. 641 Gondola, A.F.L., red or green, 1949–1951. *$10–$20*

AF No. 642 Box Car, Seaboard, Coast Line, light brown, 1953.
$25–$30

AF No. 642 Box Car, A.F.L., brown or red, 1950–1952.
$25–$30

AF No. 642 Reefer, A.F.L., brown or red, 1952. *$25–$30*

AF No. 643 Flat Car, A.F.L., Circus, with circus supplies, 1950–1953. *$75–$100*

AF No. 644 Crane Car, industrial brown hoist, A.F.L., 1950–1953. $35–$50

AF No. 645 Work Caboose, A.F.L., 1950–1951. $20–$30

AF No. 645A Work Caboose, A.F.L., 1951–1953. $20–$25

AF No. 647 Refrigerator Car, Northern Pacific, orange side, 1952–1953. $25–$30

AF No. 648 Track Cleaning Car, A.F.L., depressed center, 1952–1954. $25–$30

AF No. 649 Coach, Circus, yellow, 1950–1952. $60–$70

AF No. 650 Coach, New Haven, green or red, 1946–1953.
$30–$40

AF No. 651 Baggage Car, New Haven, green or red, 1946–1952.
$30–$40

AF No. 651 Baggage Car, A.F.L., green or red, 1953. $30–$40

AF No. 652 Pullman Car, green or red, 1946–1953. $60–$70

AF No. 653 Combine, green or red, 1946–1953. $60–$70

AF No. 654 Observation Car, green or red, 1946–1952. $60–$70

AF No. 655 Coach, A.F.L., green or red, 1953. $30–$40

AF No. 655 Coach, "Silver Bullet," silver or chrome, 1953.
$30–$40

AF No. 660 Combine, A.F.L., aluminum or chrome, 1950–1952.
$40–$50

AF No. 661 Coach, A.F.L., aluminum or chrome, 1950–1952.
$40–$50

AF No. 662 Vista-Dome Car, A.F.L., aluminum or chrome, 1950–1952.   *$40–$50*

AF No. 663 Observation Car, A.F.L., aluminum or chrome, 1950–1952.   *$40–$50*

AF No. 714 Log Unloading Car, with log load, 1951–1954.
                                                                       $25–$30

AF No. 715 Auto Unloading Car, 1946–1954.   *$30–$40*

AF No. 716 Operating Hopper, 1946–1951.   *$20–$25*

AF No. 717 Log Unloading Car, with log load, 1946–1952.
                                                                       $25–$30

AF No. 718 Mail Pickup Car, A.F.L./New Haven, red or green, 1946–1954.   *$30–$35*

AF No. 719 Coal Dump Car, CB & Q, maroon, 1950–1954.
                                                                       $35–$40

AF No. 732 Operating Baggage Car, green or red, 1950–1954.
                                                                       $50–$60

AF No. 734 Operating Box Car, brown/red, 1950–1954. *$25–$30*

AF No. 735 Animated Coach, New Haven, red, 1952–1954.
                                                                       $50–$60

AF No. 751/751A Log Loader, 1946–1950.   *$100–$125*

AF No. 752 Seaboard Coaler, 1946–1950.   *$125–$150*

AF No. 752A Seaboard Coaler, 1951–1952.   *$110–$135*

AF No. 801 Hopper Car, B & O, black, 1956–1957.   *$20–$25*

AF No. 802 Refrigerator Car, Illinois Central, orange, 1956–1957.
                                                                       $25–30

AF No. 803 Box Car, Santa Fe, 1956.   *$25–$30*

AF No. 804 Gondola, Norfolk & Western, black, 1956–1957.
                                                         $10–$15

AF No. 805 Gondola, Pennsylvania, 1956–1957.   *$10–$15*

AF No. 806 Caboose, red, 1956.   *$10–$15*

AF No. 807 Box Car, Rio Grande, white, 1957.   *$30–$40*

AF No. 900 Combine, Northern Pacific, green, 1956. *$125–$150*

AF No. 901 Coach, Northern Pacific, green, 1956.   *$125–$150*

AF No. 902 Vista-Dome Car, Northern Pacific, green, 1956.
                                                       $125–$150

AF No. 903 Observation Car, Northern Pacific, green, 1956.
                                                       $125–$150

AF No. 904 Caboose, red, 1956.   *$10–$15*

AF No. 905 Flat Car, with log load, 1954.   *$20–$25*

AF No. 906 Crane Car, 1954.   *$25–$30*

AF No. 907 Work Caboose, A.F.L., 1954, K/C.   *$20–$25*

AF No. 909 Flat Car, girder load, 1954.   *$20–$25*

AF No. 910 Tank Car, "Gilbert Chemical," green, 1954.
                                                        $75–$100

AF No. 911 Gondola, C & O, black, with pipe load, 1955–1957.
                                                         $15–$20

AF No. 912 Tank Car, "Koppers," black, 1955–1956.   *$50–$75*

AF No. 913 Box Car, Great Northern, 1953–1958.   *$30–$40*

AF No. 914 Log Unloading Car, with log load, 1953–1957.
$25–$30

AF No. 915 Auto Unloading Car, car load, 1953–1957. $25–$30

AF No. 916 Gondola, D & H, with canister load, 1955–1957.
$15–$20

AF No. 918 Mail Pickup Car, A.F.L./New Haven, red, 1953–1956.
$25–$30

AF No. 919 Coal Dump Car, CB & Q, black, 1953–1957.
$50–$60

AF No. 920 Gondola, Southern, black, 1953–1957. $15–$20

AF No. 921 Hopper, C B & Q, coal load, 1953–1957. $20–$25

AF No. 922 Box Car, GAEX, green, 1953–1956. $30–$35

AF No. 923 Refrigerator Car, Illinois Central, orange, 1954–1955.
$25–$30

AF No. 924 Hopper, Jersey Central, coal load, gray, 1953–1957.
$20–$25

AF No. 925 Tank Car, "Gulf," silver, 1955–1956. $20–$25

AF No. 926 Tank Car, "Gulf," silver, 1955–1956. $30–$35

AF No. 928 Flat Car, New Haven, with lumber load, 1956–1957.
$20–$25

AF No. 928 Flat Car, New Haven, log load, 1954. $20–$25

AF No. 929 Stock Car, Missouri Pacific, red, 1952–1956.
$25–$30

AF No. 930 Caboose, A.F.L., red, 1952. $20–$25

AF No. 931 Gondola, Texas & Pacific, green, 1952–1955.
$15–$20

AF No. 933 Box Car, Baltimore & Ohio, white sides, 1953–1954.
$25–$30

AF No. 934 Caboose, red, 1955. $35–$50

AF No. 935 Caboose, brown, 1957. $20–$25

AF No. 936 Flat Car, Erie, spool load, 1953–1954. $25–$30

AF No. 936 Flat Car, Pennsylvania, spool load, 1953–1954.
$50–$60

AF No. 937 Box Car, MKT, yellow, 1953–1955. $25–$30

AF No. 938 Caboose, red, 1954–1955. $10–$15

AF No. 940 Hopper, Wabash, black, 1953–1957. $15–$20

AF No. 941 Gondola, Frisco, 1953–1957. $12–$15

AF No. 942 Box Car, Seaboard, 1954. $20–$25

AF No. 944 Crane Car, 1952–1957. $30–$35

AF No. 945 Work Caboose, 1953–1957. $20–$25

AF No. 946 Floodlight, Erie, depressed center, 1953–1954.
$25–$30

AF No. 947 Refrigerator Car, Northern Pacific, orange, 1953–1958.
$30–$40

AF No. 951 Baggage, "Railway Express Agency," green or red, 1953–1956. $25–$30

AF No. 952 Pullman Car, "Pikes Peak," green or red, 1953–1956.
$60–$75

AF No. 953 Combine, "Niagara Falls," green or red, 1953–1956.
$60–$75

AF No. 954 Observation Car, "Grand Canyon," green or red, 1953–1956.
$60–$75

AF No. 955 Coach, A.F.L., green or red, 1954.   *$30–$40*

AF No. 956 Flat Car, "Monon," piggyback van load, 1956–1957.
$35–$45

AF No. 957 Operating Box Car, Erie, with aluminum barrels, 1957, K/C.
$60–$75

AF No. 958 Tank Car, "Mobilgas," red, 1957.   *$20–$30*

AF No. 960 Combine, A.F.L., "Columbus," chrome or silver, 1953–1957.
$35–$45

AF No. 960 Combine, as above, "New Haven," with orange stripe.
$40–$50

AF No. 960 Combine, as above, "Santa Fe," red stripe.
$45–$50

AF No. 960 Combine, as above, "Silver Comet," blue stripe.
$30–$40

AF No. 960 Combine, as above, "Silver Flash," brown stripe.
$55–$65

AF No. 960 Combine, as above, "Silver Rocket," green stripe.
$40–$50

AF No. 961 Coach, "Jefferson," chrome or silver, no color stripe, 1953–1957.
$35–$40

AF No. 961 Coach, as above, orange stripe.   *$40–$50*

AF No. 961 Coach, as above, red stripe.   *$40–$50*

AF No. 961 Coach, as above, brown stripe.   *$50–$60*

AF No. 961 Coach, as above, green stripe.   *$30–$35*

AF No. 962 Vista-Dome "Hamilton," chrome or silver, no color stripe, 1953–1957.   *$35–$40*

O-Gauge Rolling Stock

AF No. 120 Tender.   *$25–$50*

AF No. 121 Tender, black, white, "No. 121."   *$75–$85*

AF No. 404 Pullman Car.   *$85–$100*

AF No. 405 Observation Car.   *$85–$100*

AF No. 421 Tender.   *$68–$80*

AF No. 476 Gondola.   *$20–$40*

AF No. 478 Box Car.   *$25–$50*

AF No. 480 Tank Car, "Shell," yellow.   *$25–$50*

AF No. 482 Lumber Car, red.   *$20–$40*

AF No. 484 Caboose.   *$20–$40*

AF No. 486 Hopper, black.   *$20–$40*

AF No. 488 Floodlight.   *$20–$40*

AF No. 490 Whistle Car, red.   *$60–$80*

AF No. 494 Baggage Car.   *$20–$40*

AF No. 495 Coach Car, red.   *$60–$80*

AF No. 500 Pullman Car, lithographed. $50–$75

AF No. 500 Tank Car, HO-gauge. $25–$50

AF No. 501 Hopper, HO-gauge. $25–$50

AF No. 506 Caboose, HO-gauge. $25–$50

AF No. 513 Observation Car. $150–$175

AF No. 515 Coach Car, tinplate lithograph, yellow, red, black, orange. $60–$80

AF No. 555 Tender, black. $20–$30

AF No. 564 Tender, black. $25–$50

AF No. 736 Missouri Pacific Closed Cattle Car, with cattle corral and two cattle, has button. $60–$80

AF No. 1025 Railway Express Mail Car. $50–$75

AF No. 1026 Passenger Car. $100–$125

AF No. 1102 Coach. $125–$150

AF No. 1103 Passenger Car. $60–$80

AF No. 1105 American Express Baggage Car, dark green with orange trim. $70–$80

AF No. 1105 Canadian National Railways "Dominion Flyer," red with yellow logo and black/yellow lettering, black roof. $225–$250

AF No. 1106 "Dominion Flyer" Coach, brown, black lithograph. $60–$80

AF No. 1106 "Dominion Flyer" Parlor Car, yellow, black, green lithograph, 1914–1916. $60–$80

AF No. 1106 Canadian National Parlor Car, "Winged Engine" logo, green lithograph/black roof, four wheels. $60–$80

AF No. 1106 Rawlings Lumber Car, black, 1930. $30–$50

AF No. 1107 Coach Car, lithograph. $60–$80

AF No. 1108 Baggage Car, lithograph. $60–$80

AF No. 1112 Box Car, red lithograph, 1925. $60–$80

AF No. 1112 Box Car, yellow lithograph, 1930. $60–$80

AF No. 1113 Gondola, green lithograph, 1925. $30–$50

AF No. 1114 Caboose, red, green, white lithograph, brass trim.
$40–$60

AF No. 1118 Tank Car, lithograph, gray, white, black. $50–$75

AF No. 1122 "Bluestreak" Passenger Car, 6½ in. 1. $50–$75

AF No. 1123 Tuscan Passenger Car. $50–$75

AF No. 1127 Caboose. $30–$50

AF No. 1200 Baggage Car, lithograph, four-wheel. $75–$100

AF No. 1200 Baggage Car, lithograph eight-wheel. $75–$100

AF No. 1201 Passenger Car, red lithograph/black roof. $75–$100

AF No. 1202 "Lightning Bolt" Baggage Car, 1921. $75–$100

AF No. 1203 "Lightning Bolt" Passenger Car, blue lithograph/ black roof, five-panel door, eight wheels. $75–$100

AF No. 1203 "Lightning Bolt" Coach Car, lithograph, four-wheels, 1921. $75–$100

Dorfan No. 55 locomotive (late 1920s), with 14048 gondola and 607 caboose, $300–$400.

Ives No. 1 locomotive (cast iron), with F. E. 1 tender, and "Newark" Pennsylvania Lines coach, $350–$450.

Ives No. 0 locomotive, No. 1 tender, baggage car, and "Hiawatha" Limited Vestibule Express, 1901–1912, $550–$650.

American Flyer "Empire Express" (uncataloged) O gauge locomotive and 328 tender, "Chicago" Hummer-type passenger car, 1925, $125–$150.

Lionel Winner No. 1010 locomotive, with pair of 1011 "Winner Lines" Pullmans, 1931–1932, $250–$350. "Winnertown Station," $75–$100.

Ives New York Central 3238 locomotive, 1930s, with Santa Fe and Swift refrigerator cars, caboose, NY, NH & H box car, 1025 tanker and gondola, $650–$750.

Keystone Ride 'Em No. 6400 locomotive, $500–$600.

Buddy "L" 12-wheel locomotive riding toy, early 1930s, $900–$1,000. (Includes photo of matching tender.)

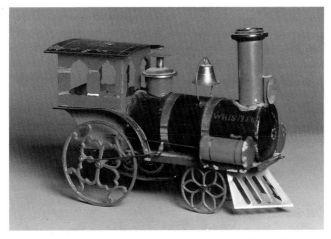

"Whistler" painted tin clockwork locomotive, Ives, 1880s, $2,000-plus. *(Photo courtesy of Carl Burnett)*

Lionel Express No. 752W Union Pacific diesel streamliner set, 1934–1941, $175–$250. American Flyer trestle bridge.

American Flyer No. 4686 "Flying Colonel" 4-4-4, 1925–1930 locomotive, Standard gauge with two Pullmans and observation car, $2,500–$3,000.

Lionel No. 8 0-4-0 locomotive, with 337 passenger coaches pulling into Lionel City Station, 1925–1932, $200–$250.

Early 1900s Ives and 1920s Ives Standard gauge on double-track layout, with Lionel City Station; other vintage train sets mingle with variety of toys on shelves. *(Photo courtesy of Carl Burnett)*

"Moon Mullins and Kayo" hand car, Marx, early 1930s, lithographed wind-up, $250–$300.

PGA golf pro Ed Dougherty, of Philadelphia, displays rare, silver 628 Northern Pacific; center front: pink MKT boxcar (6464-350); lower right: gray-nose Union Pacific FA mirrored by 209 New Havens. Third shelf from top, right: MSTL No. 229 Alco FA in olive drab. Second shelf from top, center: yellow dump car. Lionel display is No. D-103, 1953.

Stepped display holds Dougherty's F units, Geeps, 44 Tonners and Hudsons. Note cases below filled with accessories.

Fulgerex O & HO gauge 241 locomotives and tenders (from the French scale model firm owned by Count Giansanti Coluzzi). Priced in Alexander Gallery's Christmas 1988 Catalog at $22,000 the pair. *(Photo courtesy of Alexander Gallery, New York)*

Lionel No. 2025 "Pacific" 2-6-2, 1947, steam outline, with whistling tender. *(Photo courtesy of A. L. Schmidt,* Classic Toy Trains*)*

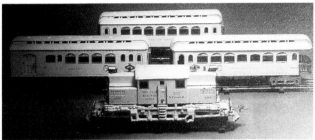

Ives White set, 1922–1927, No. 3243 electric outline locomotive, buffet, parlor, and observation cars. Offered by Alexander Gallery at $9,500. *(Photo courtesy of Alexander Gallery, New York)*

Ted Maurer March 1989 Train Auction represented a number of exceptional sets in the hobby. The American Flyer "Flying Colonel," $6,000; "Pocahontas," $1,900; Ives "Prosperity Special," $12,000; "President Washington," $2,200, and "Black Diamond Express Senior," $5,000; Lionel "Blue Comet," $6,200, and No. 408E "State" set, $3,500.

Four classic Lionel locomotives from Lloyd Ralston's Everett "Red" Chapman Collection Sale, May 1989. No. 256 O gauge, orange, $1,500; No. 262, black (complete set), $850; No. 263E "Blue Comet" (complete set), $2,600; black and red locomotive (unidentified); Lionel signal bridge No. 440N, $850.

Märklin armored train, 1904; an open car for Boer War soldiers and a cannon car (not shown) make up complete set. Today, it's priced in the $50,000 bracket.

AF No. 1204 "Lightning Bolt" Baggage Car, yellow with red lettering.   *$75–$100*

AF No. 1205 Baggage Car, dark green.   *$75–$100*

AF No. 1205 Mail Car.   *$100–$120*

AF No. 1206 Coach Car, red.   *$75–$100*

AF No. 1206 Passenger Car, orange, maroon.   *$75–$100*

AF No. 1206 Pullman Car.   *$75–$100*

AF No. 1207 Observation Car, 1926.   *$75–$100*

AF No. 1223 Coach Car.   *$35–$55*

AF No. 1306 Passenger Car.   *$50–$75*

AF No. 3001 "Illini" Pullman Car, dark green, orange trim.
                                                                        $75–$100

AF No. 3001 "Columbia" Pullman Car, dark brown body and roof, black frame.   *$75–$100*

AF No. 3001 Observation Car, lettered "Pullman," rear deck with railing, 1925–1927.   *$85–$100*

AF No. 3004/3014 Caboose, red body and cupola, orange roof, 1930–1935.   *$25–$35*

AF No. 3008 Box Car, yellow, black lithographed.   *$60–$80*

AF No. 3009 Dump Car, decaled, peacock blue.   *$40–$60*

AF No. 3010 Tank Car, gray, black, nickel trim.   *$60–$80*

AF No. 3012 Box Car, rubber-stamped, decaled set, orange, green door and roof.   *$60–$80*

AF No. 3013 Gondola, decaled set. $40–$60

AF No. 3014 Caboose, decaled set. $40–$60

AF No. 3016 Sand Car, green. $25–$50

AF No. 3017 Caboose, eight wheels, red body. $40–$60

AF No. 3018 Tank Car, eight wheels, gray, orange roof. $40–$60

AF No. 3018 Tank Car, yellow, black, copper trim, brass dome.
$40–$60

AF No. 3019 Dump Car, eight wheels, blue/green. $50–$75

AF No. 3025 Wrecker Crane Car, red with black room, 1936–1938.
$50–$60

AF No. 3046 Lumber Car, eight wheels, silver/red, 1930–1932.
$50–$60

AF No. 3113 Box-Cab Locomotive. $300–$500

AF No. 3141 Coach Car, red, black, gold, brass trim, 1930–1932.
$50–$60

AF No. 3141 Pullman Car, red, black, brass trim. $50–$60

AF No. 3142 Observation Car, red/maroon roof, gold, brass trim.
$100–$125

AF No. 3150 Baggage Car, two-tone green, 1930–1933.
$100–$125

AF No. 3151 Passenger Car, two-tone green, 1930–1935.
$75–$100

AF No. 3152 Observation Car, two-tone green, brass trim.
$75–$100

AF No. 3161 Pullman Car, two-tone green. $75–$100

AF No. 3162 Observation Car, turquoise, blue, gray, brass trim.
                                                             $75–$100

AF No. 3171 Pullman Car, tan, green, brass trim, "The Potomac." $75–$100

AF No. 3172 Observation Car, tan, green, brass trim, red body, maroon roof. $75–$100

AF No. 3180 Club Car, "Potomac," tan, green, brass trim.
                                                             $85–$120

AF No. 3180 Club Car, tan with green roof, "Potomac," 1928–1930. $85–$120

AF No. 3181 Pullman Car, "Potomac," tan, green, brass trim.
                                                             $85–$120

AF No. 3182 Observation Car, "Potomac," tan, green, brass trim.
                                                             $85–$120

AF No. 3189 Tender, tin, 1933. $50–$75

AF No. 3206 Flat Car, with lumber, orange. $50–$75

AF No. 3207 Sand Car. $30–$40

AF No. 3208 Box Car, orange/peacock, 1928–1938. $35–$40

AF No. 3210 Tank Car, silver/green, 1928–1938. $50–$75

AF No. 3211 Caboose, red, 1928–1938. $35–$50

AF No. 3212 Milk Car, white, 1938. $75–$100

AF No. 3216 Log Car, 1930–1938. $25–$50

AF No. 3219 Dump Car, blue, 1938.   *$25–$50*

AF No. 3280 Club Car, ''Golden State,'' turquoise/teal blue.
$100–$125

AF No. 3281 Pullman Car, two-tone red, green.   *$125–$150*

AF No. 3281 Pullman Car, turquoise/teal blue.   *$200–$225*

AF No. 3282 Observation Car, turquoise/teal blue, ''Golden State.''   *$125–$150*

AF No. 3282 Observation Car, turquoise/teal blue, ''Jeffersonian,'' 1928–1932.   *$100–$125*

AF No. 3380 Club Car, red/dark red roof, brass window inserts and decals, 11 in. l.   *$125–$150*

AF No. 3381 Coach Car, ''Ambassador,'' red/dark red roof, brass window insert and decal, lighted.   *$125–$150*

AF No. 3382 Observation Car, ''Ambassador,'' red/dark red roof, brass window insert and decal, eight wheels, lighted. *$150–$175*

S-Gauge Accessories/Lineside Equipment: Postwar

AF No. 8B 100-Watt Transformer, 1946–1952.   *$30–$35*

AF No. 9B 150-Watt Transformer, 1946.   *$30–$35*

AF No. 12B 250-Watt Transformer, 1946–1952.   *$35–$40*

AF No. 15B 110-Watt Transformer, 1953–1956.   *$25–$30*

AF No. 16B 190-Watt Transformer, 1953.   *$30–$35*

AF No. 16B 175-Watt Transformer, 1954–1956   *$30–$35*

AF No. 17B 190-Watt Transformer.   *$30–$35*

AF No. 18B 190-Watt Transformer, dual controls, 1953. *$35–$40*

AF No. 19B 300-Watt Transformer, dual controls, 1952–1955.
                                                      $50–$60

AF No. 21/21A Imitation Grass Plot, 1½-lb. bag, 1949–1956.
                                                      $4–$6

AF No. 22 Scenery Gravel, 22-oz. bag.   *$4–$6*

AF No. 23 Artificial Coal Lumps, ½-lb. bag.   *$4–$6*

AF No. 24 Multicolor Wire, roll of 25 ft.   *$6–$7*

AF No. 25 Smoke Fluid Cartridges, box of 12, 1947–1956. *$5–$6*

AF No. 26 Service Kit, 1952–1956.   *$7–$8*

AF No. 30/30A Highway Sign Set, eight, three yellow, five red, in
box.   *$14–$16*

AF No. 30B 300-Watt Transformer, dual control, 1953–1955.
                                                      $50–$70

AF No. 31/31A Railroad Signs, eight, all white, in box. *$15–$20*

AF No. 32 City Street Set, eight pieces in box, 1949–1950.
                                                      $15–$20

AF No. 32A Park Set, 12 pieces in box, 1951.   *$20–$25*

AF No. 33 Passenger and Train Figure Set, eight, in box, 1953.
                                                      $25–$30

AF No. 34 Railway Figure Set, 25 pieces, 1953.   *$40–$50*

AF No. 35 Brakeman Figures With Lantern, three, in box.
                                                      $25–$30

AF No. 40 Smoke Set, 1953–1955. $5–$7

AF No. 50 Illuminated District School, 1953–1954. $50–$60

AF No. 160 Station Platform, not illuminated, 1953. $65–$70

AF No. 161 Illuminated Bungalow, 1953. $65–$70

AF No. 162 "Mysto-Magic Company" Factory. $80–$85

AF No. 163 "Flyerville Station," 1953. $65–$70

AF No. 164 Illuminated Barn, 1953. $75–$80

AF No. 165 Illuminated Grain Elevator, 1953. $75–$80

AF No. 166 Illuminated Church, 1953. $75–$85

AF No. 167 Illuminated Town Hall, 1953. $75–$85

AF No. 168 Illuminated Hotel, 1953. $75–$85

AF No. 247 Tunnel, 11 in. l., 1946–1948. $15–$20

AF No. 248 Tunnel, 14 in. l., 1946–1948. $20–$25

AF No. 249 Tunnel, 11½ in. l., 1947–1956. $15–$20

AF No. 270 News and Hotdog Stand, 1952–1953. $65–$75

AF No. 271 "Whistle Stop Set," newsstand, hotdog stand, passenger waiting stand, 1952–1953. $80–$90

AF No. 272 Illuminated "Glendale Station." $65–$75

AF No. 273 Illuminated Suburban Station, 1952–1953. $65–$75

AF No. 274 Illuminated "Harbor Junction Freight Station," 1952–1953. $65–$75

AF No. 275 Illuminated "Eureka" Diner, 1952–1953.

$75–$100

AF No. 561 Billboard, Santa Fe Alco diesel pictured, 1955–1956.

$20–$25

AF No. 561 Billboard Horn, Santa Fe Alco pictured, 1955–1956.

$20–$25

AF No. 566 Whistling Billboard, Santa Fe Alco pictured.

$15–$20

AF No. 568 Whistling Billboard, 1956. $15–$20

AF No. 571 Truss Girder Bridge, 1955–1956. $5–$7

AF No. 577 Whistling Billboard, "Ringling Bros. Barnum & Bailey," 1946–1950. $25–$30

AF No. 578 Station Figure Set, in box. $40–$50

AF No. 579 Single Street Lamp, 1946–$1949. $10–$12

AF No. 580 Double Street Lamp, 1946–1949. $12–$15

AF No. 581 Girder Bridge, "Lackawanna" or "American Flyer," 1946–1956. $10–$15

AF No. 582 Automatic Blinker Signal, 1946–1948. $45–$50

AF No. 584 Bell Danger Signal, 1946–1947. $35–$40

AF No. 585 Tool Shed, 1946–1952. $20–$25

AF No. 586F Wayside Station, 1946–1956. $45–$50

AF No. 587 Block Signal, 1946–1947. $20–$25

AF No. 588 Semaphore Signal, 1946–1948. $45–$50

AF No. 589 Illuminated Passenger/Freight Station, 1946–1956.
$20–$25

AF No. 590 Illuminated Control Tower, by Bachman for A.C. Gilbert, 1955–1956. $45–$50

AF No. 591 Single-Arm Crossing Gate, 1946–1948. $30–$35

AF No. 592A Double-Arm Crossing Gate. $30–$35

AF No. 593 Illuminated Signal Tower, 1946–1954. $45–$50

AF No. 594 Animated Track Gang Set, 1946–1947. $800–$900

AF No. 596 Water Tank, 1946–1956. $40–$45

AF No. 598 and 599 Talking Station Records (replacements), 1946–1956; price for each. $15–$20

AF No. 668 Manual Switch, left, nonilluminating. $10–$15

AF No. 669 Manual Switch, right, nonilluminating. $10–$15

AF No. 690 Track Terminal, 1945–1946. $1–$3

AF No. 694 Automatic Link Coupler Truck Unit, 1946–1953.
$3–$5

AF No. 700, 701, and 702 Sections of Straight Track; price for each. $.50–$1

AF No. 703 Curve Track, ½ section. $.50–$1

AF No. 704 Manual Uncoupler. $1–$2

AF No. 705 and 706 Remote Uncouplers, 1946–1947 and 1948–1956 respectively; price for each. $2–$3

AF No. 707 Track Terminal. $1–$2

AF No. 708 Diesel Whistle Control.   *$5–$6*

AF No. 709 Lockout Eliminator, 1950–1956.   *$5–$6*

AF No. 711 Mail Pickup, for No. 718 and 719 mail cars.   *$5–$6*

AF No. 713 Mail Hook, including track terminal, 1953–1955.
                                                        $8–$10

AF No. 720/720A (Left and Right) Remote-Control Switches.
                                                        $25–$30

AF No. 722/722A (Left and Right) Manual-Control Switches.
                                                        $10–$12

AF No. 726 Road Bed, rubber, black or gray, straight.   *$2–$3*

AF No. 727 Road Bed, rubber, black or gray, curved.   *$1–$2*

AF No. 728 Rerailer, 1956.   *$7–$10*

AF No. 730 Bumper, green or red, 1946.   *$5–$7*

AF No. 731 Pike Planning Kit, 1952–1956.   *$12–$15*

AF No. 748 Overhead Footbridge.   *$20–$25*

AF No. 749 Street Lamp Set, three, plastic, 1950–1952. *$12–$15*

AF No. 750 Trestle Bridge, black, silver, and metallic blue.
                                                        $30–$35

AF No. 753 Trestle Bridge, with beacon, 1952.   *$35–$40*

AF No. 754 Double-Trestle Bridge, 1950–1952.   *$40–$45*

AF No. 755 Illuminated Talking Station, green roof, record and player; also came with brown roof, which is much scarcer.
                                                        $60–$70

AF No. 758 "Sam the Semaphore Man," 1949–1950.   *$25–$30*

AF No. 758A, same as above, 1950–1956.   *$60–$70*

AF No. 759 Bell Danger Signal, 1953–1956.   *$25–$30*

AF No. 760 Automatic Highway Flasher Signal, 1949–1956.
$10–$12

AF No. 761 Semaphore, two track trips, 1949–1956.   *$25–$30*

AF No. 762 Two-in-One Whistle Billboard, with two-button control, 1949–1950.   *$25–$30*

AF No. 763 Mountain Set, three items, 1949–1950.   *$30–$35*

AF No. 764 Illuminated Express Office.   *$65–$75*

AF No. 766 Animated Station, with four plastic passenger figures, 1952.   *$45–$50*

AF No. 767 Roadside Diner, illuminated "Branford Diner," 1950–1954.   *$45–$50*

AF No. 768 "Gulf" Oil Supply Depot, 1950–1953.   *$40–$50*

AF No. 768 "Shell" Oil Supply Depot.   *$35–$45*

AF No. 769/769A Revolving Aircraft Beacon, 1951–1956.
$25–$30

AF No. 770 Baggage Loading Platform, 1950–1952.   *$50–$60*

AF No. 771 Operating Stockyard Set, eight black and white rubber cattle with bases, also No. 736 cattle car.   *$50–$60*

AF No. 771K, same as above except set accompanies No. 976 cattle car.   *$45–$50*

AF No. 772 Plain Tank Water Tower, 1950–1956.   *$30–$40*

AF No. 772, similar to above but with checkerboard design on tank.   *$35–$45*

AF No. 773 Oil Derrick, with glass bubble road and light, gray tower, red base, 1950–1952.   *$20–$25*

AF No. 773, same as above, gray tower, gray base.   *$25–$30*

Dorfan Trains

The Dorfan Company, Newark, New Jersey **DORFAN**
1924–1933 *TRAINS*
Founder: Joseph Kraus, who started the
    firm in his own name in Nuremberg,
        Germany. Kraus used ''Fandor'' as a trade name. Kraus moved
        to the United States in 1923. ''Dorfan'' is simply ''Fandor'' in
        garbled form.
Specialty: Produced its first electric model train in 1925, the
    ''Electric Constructive Locomotive.'' Also marketed the first
    practical construction set in the hobby. By 1926 Dorfan loco-
    motives could outperform the field, but their innovative die-
    castings soon showed signs of metal fatigue. (This is one of the
    telltale clues in identifying early model Dorfans.) In the late
    1920s, the firm added a small line of appealing O-gauge trains.
    The stock market crash of 1929 and failure to keep up with the
    giants—American Flyer and Lionel—in mass-producing toy
    trains hastened its demise. For all intents and purposes, pro-
    duction ceased in 1933. Because of sizable inventory backlog,
    sales continued sporadically until 1938.

Summary: Of all the major U.S. manufacturers, Dorfan was
arguably the most innovative. Many rail fans place it among the
big four train makers (in lieu of Marx), joining Lionel, Ives, and

American Flyer. The following are some of Dorfan's many "firsts."

- First die-cast locomotive bodies.
- First readily assembled locomotion construction sets.
- First switch or panel board.
- First to construct both locomotive and engine from same parts.
- First to feature inserted window frames in passenger cars.
- First with drive wheels and axles removable as one unit.
- First die-cast passenger car wheels.
- First ball-bearing locomotive.
- First die-cast steam outline locomotive.
- First remote-controlled train-stop signals.
- First directional remote-control for locomotives.
- First remote-control uncoupler.

Standard-Gauge Locomotives and Train Sets

DO "Chicago" Gray Locomotive, 1930s, two gray cars marked "Chicago" in set box.   *$550–$650*

DO Locomotive, with No. 770 baggage, No. 772 "Washington," No. 773 observation car with Dorfan set original box.
                                                      $700–$750

DO Green Locomotive, with two maroon No. 789 "Mountain Brook" Pullmans and No. 790 "Pleasant View" observation car.
                                                      $700–$800

Dorfan No. 890 "Champion Limited," orange.

DO Electric-Style Locomotive, with Lionel No. 10 series trucks attached. $200–$300

DO Orange Locomotive, 1928, with pair of "Pleasant View" Pullmans, brass trim, orange cars with green roofs, 0-4-0 wheel configuration. $750–$850

DO Super Dorfan Set, locomotive, lumber car, two passenger cars, caboose. $1,500–$2,000

DO No. 3930 Locomotive, with five freight cars, in Dorfan set box, known as "Loco Builder" engine, in green or black, 14½ in. 1.
$900–$1,100

DO No. 3930, same as above, in red engine, 13 in. 1.
$900–$1,100

DO No. 3931 Electric Locomotive, 4-4-4, green. $1,100–$1,500

DO No. 3931, same as above, in black. $1,100–$1,500

O-Gauge Locomotives

DO No. 51 0-4-0 Locomotive, green, yellow. $125–$150

DO No. 52 0-4-0 Locomotive, green. $125–$150

DO No. 53 0-4-0 Locomotive, peacock, yellow, with brass trim.
$325–$350

DO No. 53 0-4-0 Locomotive, green, maroon.   · $325–$350

DO No. 53 0-4-0 Locomotive, red. $325–$350

DO No. 54 0-4-0 Locomotive, silver, gray, with brass trim.
$325–$350

DO No. 54 0-4-0 Locomotive, silver, blue. $325–$350

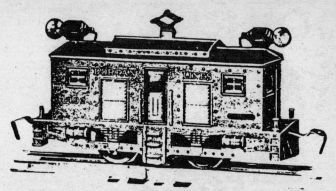

LOCO-BUILDER ENGINE No. 54 (Silver Blue)
Reversible. This is the dandiest engine of its type ever put on the market. With its rich brass trimmings, silver colored finish, headlights at each end, and pennant holders at front and rear platforms, it has an outstanding eye appeal. Swift, powerful, flashing action. Length of engine, 9¾ inches. Shipping weight, 2¾ pounds.
Retail price, each   **$8.95**
No. 54-RC—Distance Remote Control. Retail price, each $13.45

Catalog illustration of Dorfan No. 54 Builder engine. $325–$350.

DO No. 55 0-4-0 Locomotive, black or red.   *$325–$350*

DO No. 490 0-4-0 Locomotive, 1926, with "Pleasant View" Pullman, die-cast zinc alloy.   *$800–$900*

DO No. 510 0-4-0 Locomotive, green, yellow, brass trim, rivet detail.   *$330–$360*

DO No. 530 0-4-0 Locomotive, green, maroon.   *$325–$350*

Rolling Stock

Narrow-Gauge Rolling Stock

DO No. 600 Gondola.   *$20–$30*

DO No. 601 Box Car.   *$20–$30*

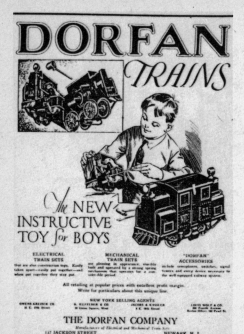

Dorfan advertisement features No. 51 New York Central locomotive, 0-4-0, green, 1925. Valued at $125–$150.

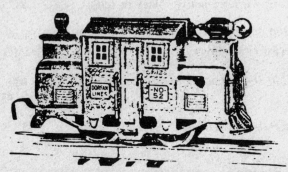

LOCO-BUILDER ENGINE No. 52 (Red)
Reversible. Electric headlight and brass hand rails. A most powerful engine for its size. Length, 7¼ inches. Shipping weight, 2½ pounds. Retail price, each   **$5.95**
LOCO-BUILDER ENGINE No. 51 (Green)
Not Reversible. Otherwise same as No. 52. Length, 7¼ inches. Shipping weight, 2 pounds 6 ounces. Retail price, each   **$4.95**

Catalog illustration of Dorfan Nos. 52 and 51 engines, $125–$150 each.

DO No. 604 Tanker.   *$25–$35*

DO No. 605 Hopper.   *$25–$35*

DO No. 607 Caboose.   *$20–$30*

DO No. 609 Lumber Car.   *$20–$30*

DO No. 610 Derrick Car.   *$75–$100*

Standard-Gauge Rolling Stock

DO No. 770 Baggage Car, red, black, green, nickel trim.
$325–$350

DO No. 771 Coach, black, orange, passengers in windows.
$335–$360

DO No. 771 "San Francisco" Passenger Car, green, red, black, nickel trim.   *$425–$450*

DO No. 772 "Washington" Coach, red, yellow, with brass and nickel trim.   *$325–$350*

DO No. 772 Coach, brown and green (crackle).   *$325–$350*

DO No. 773 Observation Car, black, red, green (crackle), with brass and nickel trim.   *$425–$450*

DO No. 789 Coach, green, orange.   *$300–$325*

DO No. 789 Pullman, with green window frames.   *$100–$125*

DO No. 789 "Mountain Brook" Coach, light brown, green.
$175–$200

DO No. 789 "Mountain Brook" Coach, red, black.   *$225–$250*

DO No. 789 "Pleasant View" Coach, yellow, maroon.

$150–$175

DO No. 800 Gondola. $75–$100

DO No. 801 Box Car. $100–$125

DO No. 804 Tanker. $100–$125

DO No. 805 Hopper. $125–$150

DO No. 806 "Pennsylvania" Caboose. $75–$100

DO No. 809 Lumber Car. $75–$100

O-Gauge Rolling Stock

DO No. 70 Automatic Electric Crane Car, red, yellow.

$900–$1,100

DO No. 160 Tender, black. $75–$100

DO No. 492 Baggage Car, green, maroon, with brass trim.

$85–$110

DO No. 493 "Seattle" Coach, maroon, green, with brass trim.

$75–$100

DO No. 493 "Seattle" Coach, peacock. $100–$125

DO No. 496 Passenger Car, silver or red. $75–$100

DO No. 497 Observation Car, red or silver. $75–$125

DO No. 498 Passenger Car, brown or red. $75–$100

DO No. 499 Observation Car, brown or red. $75–$100

DO No. 5402 "Washington" Coach, black, red, yellow.

$125–$150

DO No. 11201 Hopper, gray. $50–$75

DO No. 14048 Gondola, yellow lithograph, nickel trim.

$75–$100

DO No. 21499 "Sante Fe" Box Car, black litho, green, red, brown, with brass trim. $375–$400

DO No. 126432 Box Car, green, black. $75–$100

DO No. 234561 Gondola, black, orange. $375–$425

DO No. 29325 Tanker, aqua, red, black, white. $375–$425

DO No. 486751 Caboose, red, brown, green, black, yellow.

$375–$425

DO No. 517953 Box Car, brown, orange. $75–$100

DO No. S182999 Box Car, black, yellow lithograph. $75–$100

Dorfan freight cars (five): No. 486751 caboose, brown; No. 29325 tanker, light blue; No. 11701 hopper, red; No. 121499 "Santa Fe" car, green; No. 253761 gondola, orange, $1,200–$1,500.

Uncataloged

DO "Chicago" Coach, green with brass window inserts.
$100–$125

DO "Pennsylvania" Hopper, 1930s. $250–$300

DO Hopper, Box Car, Gondola, with Lionel No. 10 Series trucks.
$250–$300

DO "Chicago" Pullman. $150–$200

Accessories/Lineside Equipment

DO No. 410 Bridge, O gauge. $35–$50

Uncataloged

DO Champion 100-Watt Transformer. $10–$20

DO Champion 50-Watt Transformer. $5–$10

DO Trestle Bridge. $35–$45

DO Tunnel, with cows, horse, wagon, car, house, mountains, trees, O gauge, lithographed. $15–$20

Ives Trains

Ives, Blakeslee & Co., Bridgeport, Connecticut
1872–1932

Founders: Edward R. Ives and Cornelius Blakeslee. Ives had started E.R. Ives & Co. in Ply-
mouth, Connecticut, in 1868 and originally
produced baskets and hot-air toys. Most of the
Ives' early trains bore the
initials "I.M.C." for
Ives Manufacturing Com-
pany.

Specialty: Clockwork toys
and trains in tin and cast iron (later die-cast metal). Ives continued to make clockwork toys long after its entry into the electrical train field.

Milestones:

- Made O gauge its standard in 1904, producing almost identical copies of models by Märklin and Issmayer in the European 1 gauge.
- From 1901–1910, Ives was the German train makers' most
  intense competition; Ives' superiority centered on its large
  cast-iron locomotives.

- In 1910, Ives added electric-drive locomotives to its line, patterned after the New York Central's "S-class" electrics.
- Ives innovated a special kind of catalog in 1909 by departing from distributor- and retailer-oriented text and directing their sales pitch to 12-year-old boys.
- In 1912, Ives added to its gauge-1 range the most atypical and widely copied of all its U.S. passenger coaches, the "Observation," with its unique and decorative open-end platform. Ironically, Ives didn't add this coach type to its O-gauge line until 1923.
- In 1921, Ives abandoned 1 gauge and adopted Wide gauge—their version of Lionel's Standard gauge (which was the latter's copyrighted phase). Ives improved upon Lionel styling, but at a higher manufacturing cost.
- In the mid-1920s, Ives borrowed large sums to finance a switch from cast iron to light strong die-castings.
- In 1928, Ives' finances were not strong enough to sustain them; they declared bankruptcy.
- From 1928 to 1930, Ives continued under the joint control of Lionel and American Flyer. From 1930–1932, the Ives name was carried by Lionel only.

Summary: Ives has the most revered name in the toy world, particularly when it comes to clockwork models. In model trains as well, their name is consistent with quality. Their cast-iron No. 3239 and No. 3240 series rank among the all-time 1-gauge classics and their "swan song," "The Prosperity Special" from 1929, is one of the most scarce and desirable of all train sets.

Most Ives train sets were not large production runs. Many of these examples rarely surface at auction or shows, making it more difficult to assess a value rating.

Locomotives and Tenders

IV No. OO Locomotive, 1930, cast iron, black, Ives' smallest locomotive.   *$150–$175*

Ives early 1900s, cast-metal clockwork locomotive and "Limited Vestibule Express" tender with gilt imprint under cab window, "F.A.O.S." (F.A.O. Schwarz, the NYC toy emporium), $175-$225.

IV No. O Locomotive With No. 1 Tender, 1901, tin, painted black, red.   *$125-$150*

2nd Version: No. O, 1902-1904, with F.E. No. 1 tender, litho.
                                                              $125-$150

3rd Version: No. O, 1930, cast iron with F.E. No. 1 tender, black, gold litho.   *$100-$125*

4th Version: No. O, 1917, cast iron with No. 11 tender, black, gold.   *$85-$100*

IV No. 1 Locomotive With No. 11 Tender, 1903-1929, cast iron, black and gold.   *$85-$100*

IV No. F.E. 1 Tender, 1901-1912, tin, black.   *$100-$125*

IV No. 3 Locomotive With "Chicago Flyer" Tender, 1902-1909, tin, black, gray.   *$150-$200*

IV No. 3 Locomotive With No. 1 Tender, 1911, cast iron, black, gold.   *$100-$125*

IV No. 4 Locomotive With No. 1 Tender, 1910-1912, cast iron, black, gold.   *$100-$125*

Ives No. 1 locomotive, black cast iron with red trim; "F.E. 1" tender, red, black, and yellow "Newark" PRR Lines coach, $350–$450.

IV No. 5 Locomotive With No. 11 Tender, 1915, cast iron drivers, black, gold. $125–$150

IV No. 6 Locomotive With No. 11 Tender, 1912–1926, cast iron, black, gold. $125–$150

IV No. 9 Locomotive With New York Central No. 25 Tender, cast iron, black. $100–$125

IV No. 10 Locomotive, 1930, cast-iron black clockwork.
$200–$225

IV No. 10E Locomotive, electric outline, 1931–1932, tin, peacock finish, Standard gauge (Lionel's designation after taking over Ives).
$300–$350

IV No. 11 Locomotive With L.V.E. No. 11 Tender, 1901–1916, cast iron, black, gold. $100–$125

IV No. 11 L.V.E. Tender, tin, black. $100–$125

IV No. 12 Tender, black, 1910. $75–$100

IV No. 17 Locomotive With No. 11 Tender, cast iron, black with gilt-embossed boiler bands. $100–$125

IV No. 17 Locomotive With No. 11 Tender, 1901–1905, cast iron with tin boiler bands. $150–$175

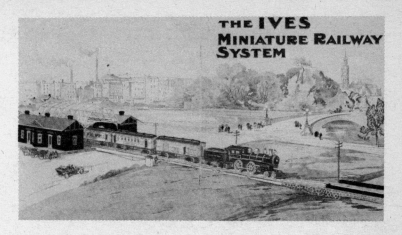

Ives 1909, wrap-around catalog cover illustrating cast-iron clockwork locomotive with "Twentieth Century Limited" passenger cars.

IV No. 17 Locomotive With No. 11 Tender, 1908, cast iron, black, gold, red brake and boiler bands.   *$100–$125*

IV No. 19 Locomotive With No. 17 Tender, cast-iron black, red brake.   *$175–$200*

IV No. 20 Locomotive With No. 25 Tender, 1914, with reverse, black.   *$125–$150*

IV No. 21 Locomotive, 1921 steel clockwork, black.   *$300–$325*

IV No. 25 Locomotive With L.V.E. No. 11 Tender, locomotive is cast iron, boiler bands, two brakes, black.   *$500–$550*

IV No. 25 Locomotive With No. 25 Tender, 1906–1911, cast iron.
                                                $150–$175

IV No. 25 Locomotive With No. 25 Tender, 1912–1914, black.
                                                $125–$150

IV No. 25 Locomotive With No. 25 Tender, 4-4-0, 1911, cast iron.
                                                $150–$175

IV No. 26 Locomotive, 1930, clockwork, cast iron, black.

$250–$275

IV No. 30 Locomotive, 1926, electric outline, cast frame, dummy headlight, clockwork, green, gold.   *$250–$275*

IV No. 31 Locomotive, 1925, electric outline, clockwork, bell, dummy headlight, cast frame.   *$200–$250*

IV No. 40 Locomotive With No. 40 Tender, 4-4-0, 1904–1909, 1 gauge, cast iron.   *$800–$900*

IV No. 40 Locomotive With No. 40 Tender, 4-4-0, 1910–1916, cast iron, 1 gauge.   *$800–$900*

IV No. 40 Tender, 1929, tin/cast iron, Standard gauge.

$175–$200

2nd Version: same as above, but 1 gauge.   *$172–$200*

IV No. 41 Locomotive With No. 40 Tender, 0-4-0, Standard gauge, black.   *$800–$900*

IV No. 66 Locomotive, 1930, cast metal, clockwork, brake, black.

$125–$150

IV No. 176 Locomotive, 0-4-0, cast iron, clockwork, brake, black.

$200–$250

IV No. 257 Locomotive With No. 257 Tender, 1931, steel cast frame, black.   *$225–$250*

IV No. 258 Locomotive With No. 258 Tender, 1931–1932, steel cast frame, black.   *$225–$250*

IV No. 417 Locomotive With Tender, 4-4-0, cast iron, black, red.

$275–$325

IV No. 1100 Locomotive With No. 11 Tender, 0-4-0, 1914–1923, cast iron, black, red, gilt.   *$125–$150*

IV No. 1100 Locomotive With No. 1 Tender, 2-2-0, 1910–1913, O gauge, cast iron, red, black, gilt. $125–$150

IV No. 1116 Locomotive With No. 11 Tender, 0-4-0, 1916–1918, cast iron, red, black, gilt. $125–$200

IV No. 117 Locomotive With No. 11 Tender, 0-4-0, 1910–1918, cast iron, black, gilt, red. $125–$175

IV No. 1118 Locomotive With No. 17 Tender, 0-4-0, 1910–1925, cast iron, tin bands on boiler, black. $75–$125

IV No. 1120 Locomotive With No. 25 or No. 1117 Tender, 1916–1917, black. $150–$175

IV No. 1122 Locomotive With No. 25 Tender, 4-4-2, 1928–1930, black with copper trim. $275–$325

IV No. 1125 Locomotive With No. 25 Tender, 4-4-0, 1910–1916, tin boiler bands, black, gilt. $275–$325

IV No. 1125 Locomotive With No. 17 Tender, 0-4-0, 1930, O gauge, black, blue. $150–$200

IV No. 1129 Locomotive With No. 40 Tender, 2-4-2, 1915–1920, cast iron, black. $900–$1,000

IV No. 1132 Locomotive, 0-4-0, 1925, Standard gauge, manual reverse, red, black. $550–$650

IV No. 1134 "President Washington" Locomotive With No. 40 Tender, 4-4-0, 1927, black, olive. $750–$850

IV No. 1134 "Ives Flyer" Locomotive, 4-4-2, 1929, black.
                    $750–$850

IV No. 1501 Locomotive With No. 1502 (Lionel No. 257) Tender, 1932, steel, four wheels, red. $100–$125

IV No. 1502 Tender, 1931–1932, four wheels, steel, red. *$50–$75*

IV No. 1506 Locomotive With No. 1507 Tender, 1931–1932, steel, bell, brake. *$50–$75*

IV No. 1507 Tender, 1932, four wheels, steel, black. *$25–$50*

IV No. 1651 Locomotive, 1932, electric, steel, blue, red, yellow, maroon. *$150–$200*

IV No. 1661 Locomotive With No. 1661 Tender, 2-4-0, 1932, O gauge, steel, red, black. *$75–$125*

IV No. 1661 Tender, 1932, four wheels, O gauge, black. *$25–$50*

IV No. 1663 Locomotive, 2-4-2, 1931, O gauge, cast frame, black. *$125–$150*

IV No. 1760 Locomotive (Lionel No. 384) With No. 1760 Tender, Standard gauge, black. *$325–$375*

IV No. 1760 Tender, 1931, eight wheels, steel, black, copper trim. *$100–$125*

IV No. 1764 Locomotive, 1932, electric outline, Standard gauge, black. *$325–$375*

IV No. 1770 Locomotive (Lionel No. 390), 2-4-2, 1932, Standard gauge. *$325–$375*

IV No. 1810 Locomotive, 1931–1932, box cab, electric, O gauge, blue, orange. *$75–$100*

IV No. 3200 Locomotive, 1910, electric outline, cast iron, olive. *$350–$400*

IV No. 3200 Locomotive, 1914, electric outline, O gauge, cast iron, black, gilt. *$100–$125*

IV No. 3200 Locomotive, 1911, O gauge, cast iron, embossed lettering, black.   *$150–$175*

IV No. 3216 Locomotive, 1917, with pilot headlight (headlight is integrally cast), cast iron, O gauge, gray.   *$175–$200*

IV No. 3217 Locomotive, 1912–1916, cast iron, maroon, red, gilt.
$150–$175

IV No. 3218 Locomotive, 1910–1917, headlight, letters embossed, maroon.   *$175–$200*

IV No. 3220 Locomotive, 1916, cast iron, headlight, black, red.
$150–$175

IV No. 3235 Locomotive, 1924–1927, steel, Standard gauge, brown, gilt, brass plates.   *$150–$200*

IV No. 3235R Locomotive, 1925–1927, Standard gauge, steel, brown, gilt, brass plates.   *$150–$175*

IV No. 3236 Locomotive, 1925–1930 (later Lionel No. 8 in 1929), Standard gauge, brown.   *$150–$175*

IV No. 3236R Locomotive, 1925–1930, same as above with automatic reverse.   *$175–$200*

IV No. 3237 Locomotive, 1926–1930, Standard gauge, black, brass plates.   *$500–$550*

Ives tin clockwork train set from 1895 catalog, $1,000–$1,500.

IV No. 3237R Locomotive, same as above with automatic reverse.
$525-$575

IV No. 3238 Locomotive, 1912–1917, cast iron, headlight, embossed lettering.
$300-$325

IV No. 3239 Locomotive, 1913–1920, cast metal, electric outline, 1 gauge, black.
$700-$800

IV No. 3240 Locomotive, 1913–1920, 1 gauge, cast iron, electric outline, black, brass trim.
$1,000-$1,500

IV No. 3241 Locomotive, 1921–1925, electric outline, Standard gauge, maroon.
$200-$250

IV No. 3241R Locomotive, 1924–1925, Standard gauge, automatic reverse, olive.
$250-$300

IV No. 3242 Locomotive, 1921–1930, Standard gauge, manual reverse, black, orange, green.
$250-$275

IV No. 3242R Locomotive, same as above with automatic reverse.
$275-$325

IV No. 3243 Locomotive, 4-4-0, 1921–1927, electric outline, Standard gauge, green, orange, red.
$350-$400

IV No. 3243R Locomotive, 1924–1927, Standard gauge, orange, black with brass plates.
$350-$400

IV No. 3245 Locomotive, 1928, short cab, manual reverse, Standard gauge, black.
$800-$900

IV No. 3245R Locomotive, same as above with automatic reverse.
$800-$900

IV No. 3245 Locomotive, 1929–1930, long cab, manual reverse, Standard gauge.
$1,500-$2,000

IV No. 3245R Locomotive, same as above with automatic reverse.
$1,500–$2,000

IV No. 3250 Locomotive, 1919–1924, O gauge, brown with red bell. *$75–$100*

IV No. 3250 Locomotive, 1924–1927, O gauge, red headlight and bell, brown. *$75–$100*

IV No. 3251 Locomotive, 1919–1927, electric outline, green with red handrails. *$75–$100*

IV No. 3251 Locomotive, 1919–1927, electric outline, green with red handrails. *$75–$100*

IV No. 3252 Locomotive, 1919–1924, maroon, green, manual reverse. *$85–$110*

IV No. 3252 Locomotive, 1924–1925, manual reverse, green, maroon, brass plates. *$85–$110*

IV No. 3253 Locomotive, 1919–1927, O gauge, olive with maroon headlight. *$100–$150*

IV No. 3254 Locomotive, 1925–1928, headlight, red, blue, brass plates. *$85–$110*

IV No. 3255 Locomotive, 1926–1930, steel frame, headlight, red, blue with brass plates. *$175–$200*

IV No. 3255R Locomotive, 1926–1930, cast frame, headlight, orange with brass plates. *$150–$175*

IV No. 3257 Locomotive, 1926–1930, twin headlights, manual reverse, red, gray, brass plates. *$300–$325*

IV No. 3257R "Olympian" Locomotive, 1927–1930, manual reverse, twin headlights, gray with brass plates. *$325–$350*

IV No. 3258 Locomotive, 1928–1930, box cab, green, gilt, litho or brass plates. *$100–$125*

IV No. 3259 Locomotive, 1927–1929, manual reverse, headlight, white, maroon. *$125–$150*

IV No. 3260 Locomotive, 1929–1930, headlight, O gauge, blue/green litho. *$125–$150*

IV No. 3261 Locomotive, 1929–1930, headlight, peacock, olive litho. *$125–$150*

Train Sets

IV No. 30 Set, "Mohican" No. 00 Locomotive, No. 11 tender, Nos. 51, 51 chair cars. *$300–$350*

IV No. 31 Set, "Seneca" No. 00 Locomotive, No. 11 tender, Nos. 50, 51, 51 (one) baggage and (two) chair cars. *$350–$400*

IV No. 32 Set, "Pequoit" No. 10 Locomotive, 1930, No. 11 tender, Nos. 551, 551 chair cars. *$200–$250*

IV No. 33 Set, "Apache" No. 176 Locomotive, 1930, No. 11 tender, Nos. 551, 558 chair and observation cars. *$250–$300*

IV No. 34 Set, "Sioux" No. 66 Locomotive, 1930, No. 12 tender, Nos. 53, 54, 56 freight, gravel cars, caboose. *$250–$300*

IV No. 35 Set, "Iroquois" No. 176 Locomotive, 1930, No. 12 tender, Nos. 550, 551, 558 baggage, chair, observation cars. *$400–$425*

IV No. 36 Set, No. 176 Locomotive, 1930, No. 12 tender, Nos. 563, 564, 567 gondola, box car, caboose. *$300–$350*

IV No. 37 Set, "Mohawk" No. 176 Locomotive, 1930, No. 12 tender, Nos. 551, 558 chair and observation cars. *$225–$250*

IV No. 38 Set, "Blackfoot" No. 176 Locomotive, 1930, No. 12 tender, Nos. 551, 558.   *$225–$250*

IV No. 39 Set, "Oswego" No. 26 Locomotive, 1930, Nos. 550, 551, 558 baggage, chair, and observation cars.   *$350–$375*

IV No. 42 Set, No. 40 Locomotive, 1904, No. 40 tender, No. 71 "St. Louis" buffet car.   *$1,000–$1,100*

IV No. 43 Set, 1904, same as above with additional No. 72 "San Francisco" dining car.   *$1,100–$1,250*

IV No. 44 Set, same as Set No. 42 with No. 70 baggage car.
$1,100–$1,300

IV No. 400 Set, No. 1100 Locomotive, 1917, No. 11 tender, Nos. 550, 551 baggage and chair cars.   *$225–$250*

IV No. 400R Set, No. 1122 Locomotive, 1921, No. 25 tender, Nos. 141, 141, 142 Pullman cars, "Seagrave Special Deluxe."
$600–$650

IV No. 400 Set, No. 1100 Locomotive, 1919, No. 11 tender, Nos. 550, 551 chair and baggage cars.   *$200–$225*

IV No. 401 Set, No. 1116 Locomotive, 1919, No. 11 tender, Nos. 550, 551, 552 baggage, chair, and parlor cars.   *$400–$425*

IV Set No. 401, No. 19 Locomotive, 1925, No. 17 tender, Nos. 60, 68 passenger and observation cars.   *$300–$350*

IV No. 402 Set, No. 19 Locomotive, 1925, No. 17 tender, Nos. 60, 61, 68 baggage, passenger, and observation cars.   *$330–$360*

IV No. 479 Set, No. 3260 Locomotive, 1928, Nos. 63, 70 "Suburban Freight," gravel and baggage cars.   *$175–$200*

IV No. 480 Set, "Blue Comet Express" No. 3260 Locomotive, 1928, Nos. 62, 68 parlor and observation cars.   *$175–$200*

IV No. 481 Set, "Oriole Limited" No. 3260 Locomotive, 1928, Nos. 133, 134 parlor and observation cars.   *$200–$250*

IV No. 482 Set, "Southern Special" No. 3261 Locomotive, 1928, Nos. 133, 133, 134 parlor and observation cars.   *$200–$250*

IV Set No. 483, "Commerce Freight" No. 3255 Locomotive, 1928, Nos. 63, 64, 69, 70 gravel, merchandise, lumber, and baggage cars.   *$300–$325*

IV No. 483R Set, 1928, same as above with automatic reverse.
$325–$350

IV No. 484 Set, "Red Hawk Special" No. 3255 Locomotive, 1928, Nos. 135, 135, 136 parlor and observation cars.   *$325–$350*

IV No. 484R Set, 1928, same as above with automatic reverse.
$350–$375

IV No. 485 Set, "Midwest Fast Freight" No. 1122 Locomotive, 1928, No. 25 tender, Nos. 125, 128, 67.   *$400–$450*

No. 485 Set, 1928, same as above with automatic reverse.
$450–$475

IV No. 486 Set, "Major H.O.D. Seagrave Special" No. 1122 Locomotive, No. 25 tender, Nos. 135, 135, 136 parlor cars.
$450–$475

IV No. 486R Set, 1928, same as above with automatic reverse.
$475–$500

IV No. 487 Set, "Dixie Flyer" No. 3257 Locomotive, 1928, Nos. 141, 141, 142 Pullmans.   *$550–$600*

IV No. 487R Set, 1928, same as above with automatic reverse.
$600–$625

IV No. 488 Set, "Cascade Limited" No. 1122 Locomotive, 1928, No. 25 tender, Nos. 141, 141, 142 Pullmans.   *$550–$600*

IV No. 488 Set, 1928, same as above with automatic reverse.
$600–$625

IV No. 489 Set, "Black Diamond Junior" No. 1122 Locomotive,
No. 25 tender, Nos. 141, 141, 142 Pullmans. $550–$600

IV No. 489R Set, 1928, same as above with automatic reverse.
$600–$625

*IV No. 490 Set, "Universal Fast Freight Junior" No. 1122 Loco-
motive*, No. 25 tender, Nos. 121, 122, 123, 124, 125, 127, 128
caboose, tanker, lumber car, refrigerator car, stock car, gravel car.
$550–$600

IV No. 490R Set, 1928, same as above with automatic reverse.
$575–$625

IV No. 500 Set, No. 3258 Locomotive, 1924, Nos. 551, 552 chair
and parlor cars. $175–$200

IV No. 500 Set, No. 3250 Locomotive, 1924, Nos. 551, 550 chair
and baggage cars. $100–$125

IV No. 500 Set, "Green Mountain Express" No. 3258 Locomotive,
1927, Nos. 551, 552 chair and parlor cars. $150–$175

IV No. 500 Set, No. 3250 Locomotive, 1919, Nos. 550, 551 chair
and baggage cars. $100–$125

IV No. 500 Set, No. 3251 Locomotive, 1925, Nos. 60, 62 parlor
cars. $175–$200

IV No. 501 Set, No. 3251 Locomotive, 1919, 1924, Nos. 550, 551,
552 baggage, chair, and parlor cars. $125–$150

IV No. 501 Set, No. 3252 Locomotive, 1925, Nos. 60, 68 baggage
and freight cars. $175–$200

IV No. 501 Set, "Red Arrow" No. 3251 Locomotive, 1926, Nos.
61, 68 baggage and freight cars. $175–$200

IV No. 502 Set, "Manager's Special" No. 3252 Locomotive, 1926, Nos. 60, 62-3, 68-3 baggage and freight cars. $200–$225

IV No. 502 Set, No. 3259 Locomotive, 1927, Nos. 551, 552, 568 "White Owl" chair, parlor cars, and caboose. $200–$250

IV No. 503 Set, "Ives Limited" No. 3255 Locomotive, 1927, Nos. 135, 135 illuminated parlor cars. $300–$325

IV No. 503 Set, 1926, same as above except No. 3254 locomotive.
        $200–$225

IV No. 504R Set, "Fort Orange" No. 3255 Locomotive, Nos. 129, 130, 132 Pullmans and observation car. $350–$375

IV No. 507 Set, "Greyhound" No. 3257 Locomotive, 1926, Nos. 140, 140, 141. $550–$600

IV No. 508 Set, "Green Mountain Express" No. 3255 Locomotive, 1926, Nos. 130, 132 Pullman, observation car. $250–$300

IV No. 510 Set, "Merchant's Dispatch" No. 3251 Locomotive, Nos. 63, 64, 67.   *Value Indeterminate*

IV No. 516 Set, "Fast Freight" No. 3255 Locomotive, 1926, Nos. 127, 125, 128, 67 stock, gravel and freight cars, and caboose.
        $400–$450

IV No. 570 Set, "Yankee Clipper" No. 3258 Locomotive, 1930, Nos. 552, 558 parlor and observation cars. $175–$200

IV No. 571 Set, "Country Freight" No. 3258 Locomotive, 1930, Nos. 564, 63, 562 baggage, parlor car, and caboose. $200–$225

Note: All of the following were available with an R designation to their catalog listing; signifies auto-reverse feature. Add $25 per set for auto reverse.

IV No. 572 Set, "Blue Vagabond" No. 1125 Locomotive, 1930, No. 17 tender, Nos. 550, 552, 558 chair, parlor, and observation cars. $450–$500

IV No. 572F Set, "Trader's Fast Freight" No. 1125 Locomotive,
1930, No. 17 tender, Nos. 554, 562, 63 caboose, parlor, and gravel
cars. $400–$500

IV No. 573 Set, "Knickerbocker" No. 3261 Locomotive, 1930,
Nos. 133, 133, 134 parlor and observation cars. $300–$350

IV No. 574 Set, "Patriot" No. 3255 Locomotive, 1930, Nos. 135,
135, 136 parlor and observation cars. $250–$300

IV No. 575 Set, "Midwest Fast Freight" No. 1122 Locomotive,
1930, No. 25 tender, Nos. 121, 125, 128 merchandise and gravel
cars, caboose. $500–$550

IV No. 576 Set, "Commodore Vanderbilt" No. 1122 Locomotive,
1930, No. 25 tender, Nos. 135, 135, 136 parlor and observation
cars. $600–$650

IV No. 577 Set, "Columbian" No. 3257 Locomotive, 1930, Nos.
141, 141, 142 Pullmans. $600–$650

IV No. 579 Set, "Black Diamond" No. 1122 Locomotive, No. 25
tender, Nos. 141, 141, 142 Pullmans. $650–$700

IV No. 590 Set, "Universal Fast Freight" No. 1122 Locomotive,
1930, No. 25 tender, Nos. 121, 122, 123, 124, 125, 127, 128 stock
car, gravel car, tanker, merchandise car, refrigerator car, caboose.
                                                   $550–$600

IV No. 61 Set, "Wonderville" No. 3252 Locomotive, 1927, Nos.
60, 62, 68, includes Nos. 201, 107D, 215, 111, 103 (six), 86 baggage car, parlor car, freight, caboose, passenger station, tunnels,
crossing gate, flag pole. $400–$450

IV No. 610 Set, "Joy Town" No. 3251 Locomotive, 1926, Nos.
550, 552 plus Nos. 201, 103, 107S baggage, parlor cars, with
passenger station and accessories. $200–$225

IV No. 620 Set, "Pleasantville" No. 1 Locomotive, 1927, No. 11
tender, Nos. 50, 51 plus Nos. 107S, 89, 201 baggage and chair
cars, passenger station, and accessories. $225–$250

IV No. 639 Set, "Tribal Village" No. 176 Locomotive, 1930, No. 12 tender, Nos. 551, 551 plus Nos. 201, 103, 107D, 215, 111 (five), 86 chair cars, passenger station, and accessories.   *$450–$500*

IV No. 691 Set, "Red Arrow" No. 3235 Locomotive, 1927, Nos. 184, 186 buffet and observation cars.   *$350–$400*

Standard Gauge

IV No. 691 Set, "Fifth Avenue Special" No. 3235 Locomotive, 1926, Nos. 184, 186 parlor and observation cars.   *$350–$400*

IV No. 692 Set, "Night Hawk" No. 3236 Locomotive, 1926, Nos. 184, 185, 186 buffet, parlor, and observation cars.   *$350–$400*

IV No. 701 Set, "New Yorker" No. 3242 Locomotive, 1926, Nos. 184, 185, 186 buffet, parlor, and observation cars.   *$450–$500*

IV No. 703 Set, "Transcontinental Limited" No. 3237 Locomotive, 1926, Nos. 187, 188, 189 club, parlor, and observation cars.
    $700–$750

IV No. 704 Set, "Deluxe Special" No. 3243 Locomotive, 1926, Nos. 180, 181, 182 club, parlor, and observation cars. *$750–$800*

Ives No. 3238 NYC locomotive, 1930s, with "Santa Fe" and Swift refrigerator cars, caboose, NY, NH & H box car, No. 1025 tanker and gondola, $650–$750.

IV No. 705 Set, "Ives Night Freight" No. *1132 Locomotive,* 1926, No. 40 tender, Nos. 191, 192, 195 coke, freight cars, and caboose.
$1,000–$1,200

IV No. 705 Set, "Capitol Limited" No. *1134 Locomotive,* 1927, No. 40 tender, Nos. 184, 185, 186 buffet, parlor, and observation cars.
$1,000–$1,200

IV No. 706 Set, "Banker's Special" No. *3243 Locomotive,* 1926, Nos. 187, 189 club, observation cars.
$600–$650

IV No. 707 Set, "Capitol City Special" No. *1134 Locomotive,* 1927, No. 40 tender, Nos. 187, 188, 189 club, parlor car, observation car.
$1,000–$1,200

IV No. 710 Set, "Cannonball Express" No. *1132 Locomotive,* 1926, No. 40 tender, Nos. 184, 185, 186 buffet, parlor, and observation cars.
$900–$1,100

IV No. 710 Set, "Capitol Limited," same as No. 705 Set.
$1,000–$1,200

IV No. 711 Set, "Number Seven Eleven" No. *3242 Locomotive,* 1926, Nos. 195, 196 flat car and caboose.
$450–$500

IV No. 712 Set, "Universal Fast Freight" No. *1134 Locomotive,* 1927, No. 40 tender, Nos. 190, 191, 192, 193, 194, 195, 196 tanker, coke, merchandise, stock, coal, flat cars, and caboose.
$1,500–$2,000

IV No. 714R Set, "Park City" No. *1134 Locomotive,* 1927, No. 40 tender, Nos. 190-196 tanker, coke, merchandise, stock, coal, flat cars, and caboose, plus Nos. 115, 116-3, 106, 216, 331, 332, 99-2-3, 307 (three), 86 (28) illuminated station and accessories.
$2,000 plus

IV No. 1000 Set, "Prosperity Special" No. *1134 Locomotive,* 1929, No. 40 tender, Nos. 241, 242, 243 club, parlor, and observation cars, copper plated, Ives' greatest train.
$8,000–$10,000

IV No. 1070 Set, "Ives Railway Circus" No. 1134 Locomotive, No. 40 tender, Nos. 192C, 193C, 196C, 196C, 171 circus cage cars and buffet car, plus pole wagons, animal set, and car runways.
$4,000–$5,000

IV No. 1072 Set, "Local Freight" No. 3236 Locomotive, 1930, Nos. 198, 195 gravel car and caboose. $500–$550

IV No. 1073 Set, "Skyliner" No. 3242 Locomotive, Nos. 184, 185, 186 buffet, parlor, and observation cars, illuminated. $550–$600

IV No. 1075 Set, "Merchant's Fast Freight" No. 1134 Locomotive, 1930, Nos. 192, 198, 195 merchandise, gravel cars, and caboose.
$1,200–$1,500

IV No. 1076 Set, "Westerner" No. 1134 Locomotive, 1930, No. 40 tender, Nos. 184, 185, 186 buffet, parlor, and observation cars.
$1,000–$1,200

IV No. 1078 Set, "Chief" No. 3245 Locomotive, 1930, Nos. 247, 248, 248, 249 club, chair, and observation cars, illuminated.
$4,000–$5,000

IV No. 1078 Set, "Olympian" No. 3245 Locomotive, 1930, Nos. 247, 248, 249 club, chair, and observation cars, illuminated.
$4,000–$5,000

IV No. 1079 Set, "National Limited" No. 1134 Locomotive, 1930, No. 40 tender, Nos. 247, 246, 249 dining, club, and observation cars, illuminated. $3,000–$4,000

IV No. 1080 Set, "Cadet Express" No. 3236 Locomotive, 1930, Nos. 185, 186 parlor and observation cars. $400–$500

IV No. 1081 Set, "Local Freight" No. 3236 Locomotive, 1928, Nos. 198, 195 gravel car and caboose, same as No. 1072.
$500–$550

IV No. 1082 Set, "Interstate Limited" No. 3236 Locomotive, 1928,
Nos. 184, 185, 186 buffet, parlor, and observation cars.

$450–$500

IV No. 1083 Set, "Lumberjack" No. 3242 Locomotive, 1928, Nos.
198, 192, 197, 195 merchandise, gravel, lumber car, and caboose.

$500–$600

IV No. 1084 Set, "Cardinal Special" No. 3242 Locomotive, 1928,
Nos. 184, 185, 186 buffet, parlor, and observation cars.

$500–$600

IV No. 1085 Set, "Merchant's Fast Freight" No. 1134 Locomotive,
1928, No. 40 tender, Nos. 192, 198, 195 freight cars.

$1,200–$1,500

IV No. 1086 Set, "Westerner" No. 1134 Locomotive, 1928, No.
40 tender, Nos. 184, 185, 186 buffet, parlor, and observation cars.

$1,000–$1,200

IV No. 1087 Set, "Northern Limited" No. 3237 Locomotive, 1928,
No. 244, 245, 246 parlor cars. $1,000–$1,200

IV No. 1088 Set, "Olympian" No. 3245 Locomotive, 1928, Nos.
241, 242, 243 club, parlor, and observation cars. $1,200–$1,500

Ives steam outline No. 1134 and tender, $1,200–$1,500.

IV No. 1089 Set, "Black Diamond Express" No. 1134 Locomotive, No. 40 tender, Nos. 241, 242, 243 passenger cars.

$3,000–$4,000

IV No. 1090 Set, "Universal Fast Freight" No. 1134 Locomotive, No. 40 tender, Nos. 190, 192, 193, 195, 196, 197, 198 tanker, merchandise, stock, freight, and gravel cars plus caboose.

$2,500–$3,000

IV No. 1091 Set, "Domestic Freight" No. 1134 Locomotive, 1930, No. 40 tender, Nos. 190, 192, 195, 197, 198 tanker, lumber, gravel, merchandise cars plus caboose.

$2,000–$2,500

IV No. 1114 Set, No. 1118 Locomotive, 1915, No. 17 tender, Nos. 60, 61 baggage and parlor cars.

$150–$200

IV No. 1114 Set, No. 17 Locomotive, 1910, No. 17 tender, Nos. 60, 61 baggage and parlor cars.

$200–$250

IV No. 1115 Set, No. 1118 Locomotive, 1912–1915, No. 25 tender, Nos. 129, 130, 131 Pullmans and baggage car.

$200–$250

IV No. 1115F Set, No. 1125 Locomotive, 1914, No. 25 tender, Nos. 125, 127, 67 merchandise, stock cars, caboose.

$350–$450

Trolleys

IV No. 800 Trolley, 1910–1913, yellow, red/black litho.

$725–$750

IV No. 805 Trail Car (1912–1915) for No. 809 Trolley, 1912–1915, red, blue, white, yellow, green.

$225–$250

IV No. 809 Trolley, 1912–1915, spoke wheels, electric, red, white, blue, green, yellow.

$750–$850

IV No. 810 Trolley, 1910–1912, spoke wheels, electric, yellow, green, red, white, blue.

$750–$850

IV No. 810 Trolley, 1910–1913, yellow, red, brown litho.
$725–$750

Rolling Stock

IV No. 20-192 Box Car, 1929, blue, red, green, yellow, brass plates.
$50–$75

IV No. 20-192 Freight Car, 1929, Standard gauge. $325–$350

IV No. 20-192 Box Car, 1929, Standard gauge. $200–$250

IV No. 20-193 Cattle Car, 1929, yellow, red, green. $50–$70

IV No. 20-193 Freight Car, Standard gauge. $310–$335

IV No. 20-194 Gondola, 1932, Standard gauge, American Flyer/Ives.
$50–$75

IV No. 20-194 Caboose, Standard gauge, American Flyer/Ives, brass plates.
$250–$275

IV No. 20-195 Gondola, Standard gauge, American Flyer/Ives.
$125–$150

IV No. 20-198 Gondola, Standard gauge, American Flyer/Ives, black.
$350–$400

IV No. 20-198 Gravel Car, Standard gauge, American Flyer/Ives.
$150–$160

IV No. 50 Baggage Car, 1901–1903, red, green, white.
$275–$300

IV No. 50 "Fast Express" Baggage Car, 1904–1905, white, black.
$275–$300

IV No. 50 "L.V.E." Baggage Car, 1906–1908, orange, yellow, red litho.
$250–$275

IV No. 50 "Ives Railway Lines" Baggage Car, 1915–1930, orange, yellow, black.   *$50–$75*

IV No. 50 "Express Mail" Baggage Car, 1928–1930, red, orange litho.   *$35–$50*

IV No. 50 "Express Mail" Baggage Car, 1930, black, yellow litho.
                                    $50–$75

IV No. 51 Chair Car, 1901–1903, cast-metal wheels, green, red, white.   *$275–$300*

IV No. 51 "Fast Express" Chair Car, 1901–1905, green, red, white.   *$275–$300*

IV No. 51 "Mohawk" Chair Car, 1905–1907, green litho, red, white.   *$275–$300*

IV No. 51 "Iroquois" Chair Car, 1906–1908, red litho.
                                    $275–$300

IV No. 51, same as above, "Hiawatha."   *$275–$300*

IV No. 51 "Brooklyn" Chair Car, 1909, red, white.   *$150–$175*

IV No. 51 "Newark" Chair Car, 1910–1914, "Ives Lines."
                                    $50–$75

IV No. 51, same as above, "Pennsylvania Lines."   *$50–$75*

IV No. 51 "Ives Railway Lines" Chair Car, 1915–1930, black, white.   *$50–$75*

IV No. 52 "Buffalo Parlor Car," 1909, black, white.   *$150–$175*

IV No. 52 "Washington" Parlor Car, 1910–1914, black, yellow, "Pennsylvania or Ives Lines."   *$100–$110*

IV No. 52 "Ives Railway Lines" Parlor Car, 1915–1928, black, orange, olive.   *$50–$75*

IV No. 52 "Ives Railway Lines," 1928–1930, yellow, red, orange.
$40–$50

IV No. 53 "Fast Freight" Merchandise Car, 1908–1909, litho-on-wood.
$175–$200

IV No. 53 "Pennsylvania Lines" Merchandising Car, 1910–1930, black, gray, white litho.
$100–$110

IV No. 53 Merchandise Car, 1910–1930, white, maroon, also several other color combinations.
$30–$40

IV No. 54 Gravel Car, 1901–1905, red, green.
$175–$200

IV No. 54 Gravel Car, 1906, red, white, black frame.
$50–$75

IV No. 54 Gravel Car, 1908, black, red wood-grain litho.
$50–$75

IV No. 54 Gravel Car, 1911–1930, green, white litho.
$35–$40

IV No. 54 Gravel Car, 1911–1930, red, gray, several other color combinations.
$25–$30

IV No. 55 "Livestock Transportation" Stock Car, 1910–1930, maroon, orange wood litho.
$35–$40

IV No. 55 Stock Car, 1910–1930, white, green, several other color combinations.
$25–$30

IV No. 56 Caboose, 1910–1915, gray, white, maroon, wood litho.
$75–$100

IV No. 56 Caboose, 1915–1930, white, maroon, black. *$100–$110*

IV No. 60 Baggage Car, 1901–1904, red, white.
$200–$225

IV No. 60 Baggage Car, 1905–1909, blue, tan, black or brown, red, yellow.
$200–$225

IV No. 61 Passenger Car, 1901–1904, red, green, white.
$200–$225

IV No. 61 "Empress" Passenger Car, 1905–1909, tan, blue, brown, black, yellow litho. $200–$225

IV No. 61 "Yale" Passenger Car, 1910–1915, blue, red, white wood litho. $100–$125

IV No. 62 Parlor Car, 1901–1904, red, green, white. $200–$225

IV No. 62 "Princess" Parlor Car, 1905–1909, red, yellow, blue, white litho. $200–$225

IV No. 62 "Harvard" Parlor Car, 1910–1915, tan, blue, white, red wood litho. $150–$175

IV No. 62 Parlor Car, 1915–1928, olive, red, green, maroon steel litho. $50–$75

IV No. 63 Gravel Car, 1901–1904, cast-metal wheels, black.
$250–$275

IV No. 63 Gravel Car, 1904–1906, blue, gray or tan with brown stripes litho. $250–$275

IV No. 63 Gravel Car, 1907–1909, tan, brown wood litho.
$135–$150

IV No. 64 Merchandise Car, 1906–1909, red, black body, dark green roof. $275–$300

IV No. 64 Merchandise Car, 1910–1930, at least 15 versions including eight- and four-wheel cars, wood litho. (This and the above No. 64 series cars featured road herald insignias, i.e., B & O, Rock Island, Illinois Central, among others.) $125–$175

IV No. 65 Stock Car, 1906–1907, gray, brown wood litho.
$200–$225

IV No. 65 Stock Car, 1908–1909, red, white litho.   *$100–$125*

IV No. 66 Chair Car, black, yellow, red.   *$125–$150*

IV No. 66 Tank Car, 1910–1915, red with green dome litho.
$125–$150

IV No. 66 Tank Car, 1929–1930, orange, black dome litho.
$35–$50

IV No. 67 Caboose, 1910–1916, red, black, white, wood litho.
$65–$75

IV No. 67 Caboose, 1917–1925, red, black, wood litho.   *$25–$35*

IV No. 68 Freight, 1911–1912, black, white wood litho.   *$50–$75*

IV No. 68 Freight, 1917–1930, black, white litho, refrigerated box car.   *$100–$125*

IV No. 68 Observation Car, 1926, orange, emerald.   *$75–$100*

IV No. 68 Observation Car, 1929–1930, blue/green litho.
$55–$75

IV No. 69 Lumber Car, 1910–1930, tan, brown, black, maroon, three log chains.   *$25–$35*

IV No. 70 Baggage Car, 1904–1914, yellow, black with green roof, wood litho, 1 gauge.   *$300–$325*

IV No. 70 Baggage Car, 1925, red, yellow, with black trim, O gauge.   *$35–$50*

IV No. 71 "St. Louis" Buffet Car, 1904–1910, black, yellow with green roof, wood litho, 1 gauge.   *$275–$300*

IV No. 71 Buffet Car, 1917–1920, gilt, brown, steel litho, 1 gauge.
$175–$200

IV No. 71 Buffet Car, 1911–1916, green, white, gray roof, wood litho, 1 gauge.   *$150–$175*

IV No. 72 Drawing Room Car, 1925, yellow, red, black with green trim, O gauge.   *$40–$50*

IV No. 72 "San Francisco" Parlor Car, 1904–1910, black, yellow wood litho, 1 gauge.   *$275–$325*

IV No. 72 "Chicago" Parlor Car, 1911–1916, brown, white wood litho, 1 gauge.   *$275–$325*

IV No. 72 "Washington" Parlor Car, 1917–1920, yellow, brown wood litho, 1 gauge.   *$275–$325*

IV No. 73 Observation Car, 1925, black, yellow, red with green trim, O gauge.   *$35–$50*

IV No. 73 Observation Car, 1917–1920, yellow, brown steel litho, 1 gauge.   *$275–$325*

IV No. 123 Lumber Car, 1925, green or black, eight wheels, O gauge.   *$25–$35*

IV No. 121 Caboose, 1930, brass plates (American Flyer No. 3211).   *$50–$75*

IV No. 121 Caboose, with red brass plates (Lionel No. 817).   *$50–$75*

IV No. 122 Tank Car, 1929–1930 (Lionel No. 815).   *$75–$100*

IV No. 124 Refrigerator Car, 1925–1930, black, white litho.   *$75–$100*

IV No. 125 Merchandise Car, 1904–1909, cream, red, with black roof, wood litho, O gauge.   *$25–$50*

IV No. 125 Merchandise Car, 1910–1917, red or gray, white, wood litho, O gauge.   *$65–$85*

IV No. 125 Merchandise Car, 1918–1930, with herald insignia, gray, black wood litho, O gauge.   *$150–$200*

IV No. 126 Caboose, 1904–1909, gray, red with black roof, wood litho, O gauge.   *$250–$275*

IV No. 126 Caboose, 1906–1909, tan, red with black roof, wood litho, O gauge.   *$250–$275*

IV No. 127 Stock Car, 1904–1909, red, gray, with black roof, wood litho, O gauge.   *$250–$275*

IV No. 127 Stock Car, 1910, gray, with green roof, wood litho, O gauge.   *$250–$275*

IV No. 127 Stock Car, 1912, gray, white with blue roof, wood litho.
$50–$75

IV No. 127 Stock Car, 1924, yellow with gray roof, wood litho, O gauge.   *$40–$50*

IV No. 128 Gravel Car, 1904–1909, gray, blue wood litho, O gauge.   *$40–$50*

IV No. 128 Gravel Car, 1918–1930, gray, maroon, black steel litho, O gauge.   *$25–$35*

IV No. 129 "Philadelphia" Pullman, 1904–1910, yellow, red, green, gray litho.   *$75–$100*

IV No. 129 "Saratoga" Pullman, 1910–1917, green, red with yellow trim litho.   *$50–$75*

IV No. 129 Pullman, 1919–1925, olive, green, black, red, O gauge.
$50–$75

IV No. 129 "Saratoga" Pullman, 1926–1930, orange, brown litho.
$50–$75

IV No. 130 Pullman, 1904–1910, green, red, yellow, gray, O gauge.
$175–$200

IV No. 130 Pullman, 1910–1917, green, red, yellow trim, wood litho, O gauge.
$175–$200

IV No. 130 "Ives Railway" Pullman, 1919–1925, olive, black, with red trim, steel litho.
$75–$100

IV No. 130 Pullman, 1926–1930, brown, orange litho, O gauge.
$25–$50

IV No. 131 Baggage Car, 1904–1910, green, yellow, gray, red litho, O gauge.
$175–$200

IV No. 131 Baggage Car, 1926–1930, brown, orange litho, O gauge.
$25–$50

IV No. 132 Observation Car, 1924–1925, red, olive, yellow, steel litho, O gauge.
$65–$85

IV No. 132 Observation Car, 1926–1930, green, blue with red roof, O gauge.
$35–$50

IV No. 133 Parlor Car, 1928–1930, green, blue with red roof, O gauge.
$75–$100

IV No. 135 Parlor Car, 1927, blue with brass trim, illuminated, O gauge.
$75–$100

IV No. 135 Parlor Car, 1928, orange, with brass trim, illuminated, O gauge.
$75–$100

IV No. 135 Parlor Car, 1929, red, black with brass trim, illuminated, O gauge.
$75–$100

IV No. 135 Parlor Car, 1930, orange, black, blue, red, brass trim, illuminated, O gauge.
$75–$100

IV No. 136 Observation Car, 1926, tan with brass trim, illuminated, O gauge. *$75–$100*

IV No. 136 Observation Car, 1927, blue, with brass trim, illuminated, O gauge. *$75–$100*

IV No. 136 Observation Car, 1930, orange, black, blue, red with brass trim, illuminated, O gauge. *$75–$100*

IV No. 140 Pullman, 1926–1927, gray with brass trim, illuminated, O gauge. *$85–$110*

IV No. 140 "Black Diamond" Pullman, 1928, black, red with brass trim, illuminated, O gauge. *$85–$110*

IV No. 140 "Seagrave Special" Pullman, 1929, green, orange with brass trim, illuminated, O gauge. *$85–$110*

IV No. 140 Passenger Car, 1926, illuminated, Standard gauge.
$125–$150

IV No. 141 Pullman, 1926–1927, gray with brass trim, illuminated, O gauge. *$100–$125*

IV No. 141 Passenger Car, 1926, illuminated, Standard gauge.
$125–$150

IV No. 141 "Black Diamond" Pullman, 1928, black, red with brass trim, illuminated, O gauge. *$100–$125*

IV No. 141 "Seagrave Special" Pullman, 1929, green, orange, black, brass trim, illuminated, O gauge. *$100–$125*

IV No. 142 Pullman, 1926–1927, gray with brass trim, illuminated, O gauge. *$125–$150*

IV No. 142 Passenger Car, 1926, black, red with brass trim, Standard gauge. *$125–$150*

IV No. 142 "Black Diamond" Pullman, 1928, black, red with brass trim, illuminated, O gauge. *$100–$125*

IV No. 142 "Seagrave Special" Pullman, 1929, green, orange, black with brass trim, illuminated, O gauge. *$100–$125*

IV No. 171 Buffet, 1925, rubber-stamped letters, 13 in., Standard gauge. *$110–$135*

IV No. 172 Parlor Car, 1925, rubber-stamped letters, Standard gauge. *$110–$135*

IV No. 173 Observation Car, 1925, rubber-stamped letters, 13 in., Standard gauge. *$110–$135*

IV No. 180 Club Car, 1926–1927, orange, red, Standard gauge. *$135–$150*

IV No. 180 Club Car, 1927–1928, orange, red, green, Standard gauge. *$135–$150*

IV No. 181 Parlor Car, 1926–1927, orange, red, green, Standard gauge. *$135–$150*

IV No. 181 Parlor Car, 1927–1928, orange, red, green, Standard gauge. *$135–$150*

IV No. 181 Buffet Car, 1912–1920, dark green, gray roof, steel litho, 1 gauge. *$225–$250*

IV No. 182 Drawing Room Car, 1912–1920, dark green, with gray roof, Standard gauge. *$225–$250*

IV No. 182 Observation Car, 1926–1927, orange, red, green, Standard gauge. *$135–$150*

IV No. 183 Observation Car, 1912–1920, dark green with gray roof, steel litho, 1 gauge. *$225–$250*

IV No. 184 Buffet Car, 1921–1930, green, red, brown, illuminated, Standard gauge.   *$100–$125*

IV No. 184-3 Buffet Car, 1925–1930, green, brown, red, gray, illuminated, Standard gauge.   ***Value Indeterminate***

IV No. 185 Parlor Car, 1921–1930, blue, tan, orange, maroon, Standard gauge.   *$100–$125*

IV No. 186 Observation Car, 1925–1930, green, red, brown, illuminated, Standard gauge.   *$100–$125*

IV No. 187 Truck Car, 1925, green, 12 wheels, Standard gauge.
$450–$500

IV No. 187-3 Passenger Car, 1925, white, Standard gauge.
$275–$300

IV No. 187 Club Car, 1921–1928, green, gray or red, blue, Standard gauge.   *$100–$125*

IV No. 187-1 Club Car, 1921–1922, green, gray or red, blue, Standard gauge.   *$100–$125*

IV No. 187-3 Club Car, 1923–1925, green, gray or red, blue, Standard gauge.   *$275–$300*

IV No. 188 Parlor Car, 1921–1926, gray or green, Standard gauge.
$100–$125

IV No. 188 Parlor Car, 1926–1928, gray or green with brass plates, illuminated, Standard gauge.   *$135–$150*

IV No. 188-1 Parlor Car, 1921–1922, gray, green, Standard gauge.
$100–$125

IV No. 188 Truck Car, green, 12 wheels, Standard gauge.
$425–$450

IV No. 188-3 Passenger Car, 1926, white, Standard gauge.
$250–$275

IV No. 189 Truck Car, 1926, white, Standard gauge. $425–$450

IV No. 189 Observation Car, 1926–1927, red, green, gray, blue, Standard gauge. $135–$150

IV No. 189-1 Observation Car, 1921–1922, red, green, gray, blue, Standard gauge. $125–$150

IV No. 189-3 Observation Car, 1923–1925, red, green, blue, gray, Standard gauge. $250–$275

IV No. 191 Tank Car, 1921–1928, green, orange, yellow, Standard gauge. $125–$150

IV No. 190-20 Tank Car, 1929, orange, green, brass plates, American Flyer/Ives, Standard gauge. $125-$150

IV No. 190 Tank Car, 1930, orange, green with brass plates, Lionel/Ives, Standard gauge. $425–$450

IV No. 191 Coke Car, 1921–1930, maroon, black, blue, brown, Standard gauge. $150–$175

IV No. 192 Merchandise Car, 1921–1923, blue, green, litho, Standard gauge. $75–$100

IV No. 192-20 Merchandise Car, 1929, blue, yellow, red, green, litho, American Flyer/Ives, Standard gauge. $275–$300

IV No. 192 Merchandise Car, 1930, blue, yellow litho, Standard gauge. $100–$125

IV No. 193 Stock Car, 1921–1923, orange, gray, Standard gauge.
$125–$150

IV No. 193 Stock Car, 1924–1928, brown, Standard gauge.
$100–$125

IV No. 193 Stock Car, 1930, brown, with brass plates, Lionel/Ives, Standard gauge.   *$275–$300*

IV No. 193-20 Stock Car, 1929, brown, brass plates, American Flyer/Ives, Standard gauge.   *$100–$125*

IV No. 194 Coal Car, 1921–1930, black, gray, maroon litho, Standard gauge.   *$225–$250*

IV No. 195-20 Freight Car, 1930, brown, brass plates, Lionel/Ives, Standard gauge.   *$300–$350*

IV No. 195 Caboose, 1921–1923, maroon litho, Standard gauge.
$150–$200

IV No. 195 Caboose, 1924–1928, red litho, Standard gauge.
$175–$200

IV No. 195-20 Caboose, 1929, red with brass plates, litho, American Flyer/Ives, Standard gauge.   *$175–$200*

IV No. 195 Caboose, 1930, red with brass plates litho, Lionel/Ives, Standard gauge.   *$125–$150*

IV No. 196 Flat Car, 1921–1925, dark green, olive, Standard gauge.
$75–$100

IV No. 196 Flat Car, 1926, orange, Standard gauge.   *$75–$100*

IV No. 196 "Harmony Creamery" Special Flat Car, 1922, Standard gauge.   *$450–$500*

IV No. 196 Freight Car, Standard Gauge.   *$400–$450*

IV No. 196 Cage Flat Car (Circus), 1928, with hippos in cage, Standard gauge.   *$500–$550*

IV No. 197 Lumber Car, 1928–1929, orange, green, Standard gauge.   *$175–$200*

IV No. 197 Lumber Car, 1930, green, Lionel/Ives No. 211, Standard gauge. *$325–$350*

IV No. 198-20 Gravel Car, 1929, black with brass plates, American Flyer/Ives, Standard gauge. *$225–$250*

IV No. 198 Gravel Car, 1930, maroon, black, with brass plates, Lionel/Ives, Standard gauge. *$325–$350*

IV No. 199 Derrick Car, 1929–1930, blue, with maroon brass plates, Standard gauge. *$350–$400*

IV No. 241 Club Car, 1928–1929, illuminated, with brass plates, Standard gauge. *$1,100–$1,200*

IV No. 242 Parlor Car, 1928–1929, illuminated with brass plates. *$1,100–$1,200*

IV No. 243 Observation Car, 1928–1929, with brass plates, illuminated, Standard gauge. *$1,100–$1,200*

IV No. 246 Dining Car, 1930, brass plates, illuminated, 12 wheels, Standard gauge. *$1,100–$1,200*

IV No. 247 Club Car, 1930, brass plates, illuminated, Standard gauge. *$800–$900*

IV No. 248 Chair Car, 1930, brass plates, 12 wheels, illuminated, Standard gauge. *$1,100–$1,200*

IV No. 249 Observation Car, 1930, brass plates, illuminated, 12 wheels, Standard gauge. *$1,100–$1,200*

IV No. 332 Baggage Car, 1932, orange, peacock, brass plates, illuminated, Standard gauge. *$100–$125*

IV No. 339 Pullman, 1932, orange, peacock, brass plates, illuminated, Standard gauge. *$100–$125*

IV No. 341 Observation Car, 1932, orange, peacock, brass plates, illuminated, Standard gauge.   *$100–$125*

IV No. 550 Baggage Car, 1915, black, yellow, red, wood litho, O gauge.   *$50–$75*

IV No. 550 Baggage Car, 1915, red, white, black, O gauge.
$50–$75

IV No. 550 Baggage Car, 1926–1928, orange, olive litho, O gauge.
$50–$75

IV No. 550 Baggage Car, 1929, green, black litho, O gauge.
$35–$50

IV No. 550 Baggage Car, 1930, tan, blue litho, O gauge.
$50–$75

IV No. 551 Chair Car, 1915, black, yellow, red, wood litho, O gauge.   *$35–$50*

IV No. 551 Chair Car, 1916–1925, orange, olive, black steel litho, O gauge.   *$25–$35*

IV No. 551 Chair Car, 1926–1928, orange, olive litho, O gauge.
$25–$50

IV No. 551 Chair Car, 1928, black, white, red, gilt litho, O gauge.
$50–$75

IV No. 551 Chair Car, 1930, black, tan, blue, white litho, O gauge.
$50–$75

IV No. 552 Parlor Car, 1916–1925, orange, olive, yellow steel litho, O gauge.   *$50–$75*

IV No. 552 Parlor Car, 1926–1928, red, gilt, white and black litho, O gauge.   *$25–$50*

IV No. 552 Parlor Car, 1928, black, white, gilt, red litho, O gauge.
$50–$75

IV No. 552 Parlor Car, 1929, black, green litho, O gauge.
$25–$50

IV No. 552 Parlor Car, 1930, tan, black, green litho, O gauge.
$50–$75

IV No. 558 Observation Car, 1928, red, white, black, gilt litho, O gauge.
$50–$75

IV No. 558 Observation Car, 1929, black, green litho, O gauge.
$35–$50

IV No. 558 Observation Car, 1930, tan, blue, white litho, O gauge.
$35–$50

IV No. 558 Observation Car, 1930, black, green, tan litho, O gauge.
$35–$50

IV No. 562 Caboose, 1930, red with brass trim, O gauge.
$50–$75

IV No. 563 Gondola, 1915–1916, gray, green steel litho, O gauge.
$35–$50

IV No. 563 Gondola, 1917–1930, maroon, gray steel litho, O gauge.
$30–$45

IV No. 564 Box Car, 1915–1930, red, orange, yellow, wood litho, O gauge.
$30–$45

IV No. 565 Stock Car, 1915–1917, orange, silver litho, O gauge.
$35–$45

IV No. 566 Tank Car, 1915–1917, gray, gilt litho, O gauge.
$25–$35

IV No. 566 Tank Car, 1917–1928, gray, orange, black litho, O gauge.   *$20–$30*

IV No. 567 Caboose, 1915–1928, red, white, black wood litho, O gauge.   *$35–$45*

IV No. 567 Caboose, 1929–1930, black, white, red litho, O gauge.
                                                                         $20–$30

IV No. 569 Lumber Car, 1915–1928, black, O gauge.   *$25–$30*

IV No. 610 Pullman, 1931–1932, olive, punched window inserts, illuminated, O gauge.   *$65–$75*

IV No. 1504 Coach, 1931–1932, red, black, yellow, green, steel, O gauge.   *$50–$60*

IV No. 1512 Gondola, 1931–1932, blue litho, O gauge.
                                                                         $25–$30

IV No. 1513 Cattle Car, 1931–1932, numerous color versions, litho, O gauge.   *$35–$45*

IV No. 1514 Merchandise Car, 1931–1932, blue, yellow litho, O gauge.   *$20–$25*

IV No. 1515 Tank Car, 1931–1932, aluminum, brass, copper trim, litho, O gauge.   *$15–$20*

IV No. 1517 Caboose, 1931–1932, brown, red litho, O gauge.
                                                                         $15–$20

IV No. 1677 Gondola, 1931–1932, blue, tan, yellow litho, O gauge.
                                                                         $15–$20

IV No. 1678 Cattle Car, 1931–1932, yellow litho, O gauge.
                                                                         $15–$20

IV No. 1679 Box Car, 1931–1932, tan, yellow, blue litho, eight wheels, O gauge. $15–$20

IV No. 1680 Tank Car, 1931–1932, aluminum litho, eight wheels, O gauge. $15–$20

IV No. 1682 Caboose, 1931–1932, brown, red litho, eight wheels, O gauge. $15–$20

IV No. 1690 Coach, 1932, cream, red litho, eight wheels, O gauge. $20–$25

IV No. 1691 Observation Car, 1932, cream, red, eight wheels, litho, O gauge. *Value Indeterminate*

IV No. 1695 Pullman, 1932, maroon, beige, illuminated, O gauge. *Value Indeterminate*

IV No. 1696 Baggage Car, 1932, beige, maroon, illuminated, 12 wheels. *Value Indeterminate*

IV No. 1697 Observation Car, 1932, beige, maroon, 12 wheels, illuminated, O gauge. (This and the above two cars in the No. 1690s series surface so infrequently that it is difficult to give it a proper value rating; our nearest estimate would be in the $4,500 to $5,000 range for the three.) *Value Indeterminate*

IV No. 1707 Gondola, 1932, eight wheels, O gauge. $45–$55

IV No. 1708 Cattle Car, 1932, eight wheels, front and rear ladders. $45–$55

IV No. 1709 Box Car, 1932, eight wheels, O gauge. $45–$55

IV No. 1712 Caboose, 1932, red litho, front and rear ladders, O gauge. $45–$55

IV No. 1767 Coach, 1932, brown, yellow, maroon, Standard gauge. $100–$125

IV No. 1767 Baggage Car, yellow, brown, maroon, Standard gauge.
$100–$125

IV No. 1768 Observation Car, 1932, brown, yellow, maroon, Standard gauge.
$100–$125

IV No. 1771 Lumber Car, 1932, with nickel stakes, brakes, Standard gauge.
$150–$175

IV No. 1772 Gondola, 1932, brakes, peacock, Standard gauge.
$150–$175

IV No. 1773 Cattle Car, 1932, with sliding doors, yellow, Standard gauge.
$160–$180

IV No. 1774 Box Car, 1932, orange, yellow, Standard gauge.
$160–$180

IV No. 1775 Tank Car, 1932, black, white, Standard gauge.
$160–$180

IV No. 1776 Coal Car, 1932, red, coal load with adjustable bottom, Standard gauge.
$160–$180

IV No. 1777 Caboose, 1932, green, red with brass trim, illuminated, Standard gauge.
$150–$175

IV No. 1778 Refrigerator Car, 1932, green, white with swinging doors, Standard gauge.
$150–$175

IV No. 1779 Derrick Car, 1932, automatic, Standard gauge.
$225–$250

IV No. 1811 Pullman, 1931–1932, orange, blue, O gauge.
$25–$30

IV No. 1812 Observation Car, 1931–1932, orange, blue litho, O gauge.
$25–$30

IV No. 1813 Baggage Car, 1931–1932, orange, blue litho, O gauge.
$25–$30

IV No. 7345 Merchandise Car, 1915, steel spring doors, 1 gauge.
$175–$200

IV No. 7446 Stock Car, 1915–1920, 1 gauge.   *$200–$225*

IV No. 7546 Caboose, 1915–1920, red, silver litho, 1 gauge.
$100–$125

IV No. 7648 Hopper, 1915–1920, black, maroon litho, 1 gauge.
$200–$225

IV No. 7849 Tank Car, 1915–1920, black litho, 1 gauge.
$200–$225

IV No. 7950 Coke Car, 1915–1920, maroon, black litho, 1 gauge.
$150–$175

IV No. 17882 Cattle Car, "D & L Transportation," red, black, green litho.   *$200–$225*

Accessories/Lineside Equipment

IV No. 75 Circus Set Car Runways, 1930–1932, Standard gauge.
$65–$75

IV No. 80 Scenery, 1906–1907, six sections displaying pastoral scene, sections 20 in. × 15 in.   *Value Indeterminate*

IV No. 86 Telegraph Poles, 1912–1930, 12 poles with connection wire ($7 each).   *$65–$75*

IV No. 87 American Flag, 1923–1930, on pole, square base, flag can be raised or lowered.   *$25–$35*

IV No. 89 Water Tank, 1930, spill spout, steel construction and cross beams, 11 in. h.   *$175–$225*

IV No. 90 Bridge, 1912–1927, brick work design, two sections, O gauge, mechanical train, 31 in. l. *$35–$45*

IV No. 90-3 Bridge, 1929, brick work, two sections, 1 gauge, electric, 21 in. l. *$35–$45*

IV No. 91 Bridge, 1912–1930, brick work, double arch, three sections, O gauge, mechanical, 31 in. l. *Value Indeterminate*

IV No. 91-2 Bridge, 1912–1930, brick work, double arch, three sections, O gauge, electrical, 31 in. l. *$45–$55*

IV No. 92 Bridge, 1912–1930, brick work, triple arches, four sections, O gauge, for mechanical, 42 in. l. *$45–$55*

IV No. 92-3 Bridge, 1912–1930, brick work, triple arches, four sections, O gauge, for electrical, 42 in. l. *Value Indeterminate*

IV No. 97 Swing Drawbridge, 1910–1912, opens side-to-side, three sections, Standard gauge, 31 in. l. *$100–$125*

IV No. 98 Single-Trestle Bridge, three sections, O gauge, 31 in. l. *$50–$75*

IV No. 98-3 Single-Trestle Bridge, 1912–1930, three sections, electric, O gauge, 31 in. l. *$50–$75*

IV No. 98-1-3 Single-Trestle Bridge, 1912–1921, three sections, electric, O gauge, 31 in. l. *$75–$100*

IV No. 99 Double-Trestle Bridge, four sections, O gauge, mechanical, 41 in. l. *$100–$110*

IV No. 99-1 Double-Trestle Bridge, 1912–1916, four sections, 1 gauge, mechanical, 51 in. l. *$100–$111*

IV No. 99-3 Double-Trestle Bridge, 1912–1929, four sections, electric, 41 in. l. *$75–$100*

IV No. 99-1-3 Double-Trestle Bridge, 1912–1916, four sections, electric, 56 in. l. *$75–$100*

IV No. 100 Bridge, 1912–1918, arch base, two sections, O gauge, 21 in. l.   *$35–$50*

IV No. 100-2 Bridge, 1912–1918, arch base, two sections, 1 gauge, 28 in. l.   *$35–$50*

IV No. 101 Bridge, 1912–1928, three sections, aquaduct base, O gauge, 31 in. l.   *$50–$75*

IV No. 101-1 Bridge, 1912–1928, three sections, aquaduct base, 1 gauge, 42 in l.   *$50–$75*

IV No. 102 Bridge, 1910–1912, roller lift, drops as train approaches, 31 in. l.   *$75–$100*

IV No. 103 Tunnel, 1910–1930, mountain style, papier-mâché, 6½ in. l.   *$20–$25*

IV No. 105 Tunnel, 1910–1929, mountain style, 11 in l.   *$20–$25*

IV No. 106 Tunnel, 1931–1932, mountain formation, 14 in. l.
                                                                   $25–$30

IV No. 106E Tunnel, 1931–1932, mountain style, 16 in. l.
                                                                   $30–$35

IV No. 107 Signal, 1905–1919, single arm, with track check, O gauge.   *$30–$35*

IV No. 107D Signal, 1908–1930, two arms, pedestal base.
                                                                   $35–$40

IV No. 107S Signal, one arm, pedestal base. *Value Indeterminate*

IV No. 108 Signal, 1911–1916, single arm, with track check, 1 gauge.   *$20–$25*

IV No. 109 Semaphore, 1905–1922, double arm, 11½ in. h.
                                                                   $50–$75

IV No. 110 Bumper, 1904–1928, O gauge.   *$5–$10*

IV No. 110-1 Bumper, 1912–1917, 1 gauge.   *$5–$10*

IV No. 111 Elevating Post, 1904–1907, pedestal base, rectangular top.   *$15–$20*

IV No. 112 Danger Sign, 1906–1930, for railroad crossing gates.
                    $15–$20

IV No. 113 Passenger Station, 1910–1928, sidewalk base, windows and doors, 13½ in. × 9¾ in.   *$75–$100*

IV No. 114 Station, 1904–1923, doors and windows, passenger, 13½ in. × 6 in.   *$125–$150*

IV No. 115 Station, 1904–1928, one door, freight dock, 10 in. × 5½ in.   *$125–$150*

IV No. 116 Passenger Station, 1901–1908, one side of the track, windows and doors, 18½ in. × 8 in.   *$150–$175*

IV No. 117 Covered Platform, 1904–1916, eight posts, two facing benches, 19 in. × 7½ in.   *$75–$100*

IV No. 118 Covered Platform, 1910–1912, one post.   *$25–$35*

IV No. 119 Covered Platform, 1910–1914, two posts on sidewalk with roof, 11½ in. × 3½ in.   *$75–$85*

IV No. 120 Covered Platform, 1904–1916, four posts, trellis fence, 18½ in. × 4 in.   *$75–$85*

IV No. 121 Glass Dome Station, 1910–1924, canopy supported by two posts, brickwork sidewalk, 18½ in. × 9½ in.   *$125–$150*

IV No. 122 Glass Dome Station, 1910–1924, one building, glass dome supported on other side by four posts, 18½ in. × 16½ in.
                    $450–$500

IV No. 123 Glass Dome Station, 1910–1924, two buildings connected over the track by glass canopy, 18½ in. × 22¼ in.
$650–$700

IV No. 140 Crossing Gates, 1910–1916, automatic, with guard house, O gauge, length 20½ in.
$35–$40

IV No. 140-3 Crossing Gates, 1910–1916, with guard house and sign, for 2¼ in. track.
$45–$50

IV No. 145 Turntable, 1910–1930, handturned, diameter 10¼ in.
$50–$75

IV No. 146 Turntable, 1910–1930, mechanical, O gauge.
$100–$125

IV No. 215 Crossing Gate, 1923–1930, no guard house, O gauge.
$20–$25

IV No. 220 Freight Station, 1929–1930, lithographed sides, 9 in. l.
$65–$75

IV No. 221 Passenger Station, 1929–1930, lithographed and painted, 9 in. l.
$65–$75

IV No. 225 Way Station, 1929–1930, lighted, arched windows, 8½ in. l.
$75–$100

IV No. 226 Suburban Station, 1929–1930, lighted, double chimney, 8½ in. l.
$75–$100

IV No. 226 Suburban Station, 1929–1930, lighted, double chimney, 10¼ in. l.
$85–$110

IV No. 228 Covered Platform, 1929–1930, four benches facing, six posts supporting roof, open air.
$45–$55

IV No. 230 Town Station, lighted, working doors and windows, steel construction, Lionel No. 124, 14 in. l.
$100–$125

IV No. 349 Crossing Signal, flashes, cross design, wrought iron base.   *$65–$75*

IV No. 350 Traffic Signal, blinks, small and globular, used in city-scapes.   *$75–$85*

IV No. 601-4 Lamp Post, 1926, double bulb, 3½ volts, scroll design.   *$25–$30*

IV No. 601-8 Lamp Post, double bulb, 8 volts, scroll design.
                                                                                                                   $35–$40

Lionel Trains

Lionel Corporation, New York City, New York
1900–present day (1900–1908, Lionel Manufacturing Co.; 1987, Lionel Trains, Inc.)
Founder: Joshua Lionel Cowen
Specialty: Lionel ranks as the pre-eminent name in U.S. model trains.

A LIFETIME INVESTMENT IN HAPPINESS

Milestones:

- In 1901, Lionel produced an ungainly looking battery-powered flat car in 2⅞-in. gauge, the first of a long, extensive model train line. Today, Lionel remains as the last surviving member of the U.S. "Big Four."
- Published its first catalog (in black and white) in 1902, featuring the "City Hall Park" trolley.

- Successfully marketed the innovative Standard-gauge line in 1906, carving its own special niche in the hobby. Lionel adopted O gauge in 1915, but also featured Standard-gauge versions until 1939.
- By 1912, Lionel, using a lustrous enamel decorated with rubber-stamped lettering and smatterings of bright brass trim, avoided litho costs and was able to achieve a highly competitive price structure. Their 2⅛-in. track size meant that Lionel trains appeared wider, taller, and sturdier than any gauge-1 models by rivals Bing, Märklin or Ives.
- Automatic train control, the only device to automatically control a model train's operation, was a Lionel "first" in 1917.
- Inserted panels in locomotive doors and windows were added in 1918 for greater strength and finer detail. Also, etched brass plates were inserted in locomotive bodies as another patented feature.
- Lionel brought the latch coupler to its O-gauge cars in 1924.
- In 1926, the firm scooped the industry with remote-control switches; the nonderailing feature was not added until 1931.
- In 1928, another innovation: Lionel introduced remote-control electrically operated couplers.

Lionel's clever way of announcing three-rail track in 1906 catalog.

- In 1925, Lionel patented a perfect die-cast wheel with nickeled steel rim over tread for improved performance and reliability. Also, insulated fiber frogs were added on Lionel switches. Headlights with individual switches and red and green transparent side panels were further improvements.
- The "Chugger"-imitating sound of a steam-driven locomotive provided added realism in 1933, as well as a locomotive whistle sparked by DC current in 1935.
- *Other Lionel "Firsts":*
  Automatic block signals.
  Automatic warning signals.
  All-steel electrically lit miniature villas and bungalows.
  Roller contact shoes on locomotives.
  Three bearing armature shafts on miniature motors.
  Automatic crossing gates.
  All-steel locomotive and car bodies.
  Reinforced phosphor-bronze bearings for wheel axles; armature shaft.
  Trucks with nickeled journals.
- The years 1930–1942 have been hailed as Lionel's "Golden Years." Standard gauge reached its zenith with huge steamers and splendid terminals, bridges, and other accessories. The mid-1930s heralded the arrival of sleek Torpedos such as the "Hiawathas" and "Zephyrs" in O gauge. The trend toward realism peaked in the scale model "Hudson."
- From 1928–1930, Lionel and American Flyer held joint control of the failing Ives firm. In 1930 Lionel assumed full command of Ives and continued the Ives line and name through 1932. Still feeling the effects of the 1929 crash, Lionel, too, was on the brink of financial disaster in the early 1930s. Actually, the Lionel No. 1101 "Mickey Mouse Hand Car" from 1934 is credited with turning the company around.
- From 1942–1946, Lionel went to war, shutting down its model train production to make changeovers to meet the demands of military contracts.
- In 1946, Lionel and American Flyer dominated the U.S. market with Lionel continuing with O gauge, introducing a large

6-8-6 "Pennsylvania" steam turbine plus the "Pennsylvania" GG1.

- By 1952, Lionel had eclipsed the production of America's real-life railroads by producing 622,209 engines and 2,460,764 freight and passenger sets (with freight outselling passengers by 20 to 1); by 1953, Lionel had become the largest model train maker in the world. In 1957, the firm belatedly converted to HO gauge.

- In 1966, American Flyer, hurt (as was Lionel) by their failure to convert to the burgeoning HO gauge, closed its doors, with Lionel purchasing existing inventory.

- In 1969, as a failing corporation, Lionel was purchased by General Mills. (From 1953 to 1959, Lionel's sales had dropped by 50%, coinciding with the postwar decline of America's real-life railroads.)

- From 1969 to 1987, General Mills, as an exclusive Lionel licensee, produced trains through a subsidiary in Mt. Clemons, Michigan, under the name "Fundimensions," which even purists admitted had many of the best features of the oldies.

- In 1987, General Mills spun off its toy interests to a new independent corporation—Kenner-Parker. This firm subsequently offered the Lionel division to real-estate developer Richard Kughn. The new company was renamed "Lionel Trains, Inc."

- In 1988, Lionel enjoyed its best year since the banner year of 1953, and all signs point to a groundswell revival of interest in Lionel model trains.

Trolleys, Trailers, Gondolas: 1901–1910

LI No. 10 Interurban Motor Car, "N.Y.C. Lines," Standard gauge, 1910. *$1,200–$1,500*

LI No. 100 Locomotive, 2⅞ in., 1901. *$3,000 plus*

LI No. 200 Gondola, motorized, 2⅛ in.   *$3,000 plus*

LI No. 300 "City Hall Park Trolley No. 17," 2⅛ in., 1901.
$3,000 plus

LI No. 303 Summer Trolley Motor Car, Standard gauge, 1910.
$3,000 plus

LI No. 309 Trolley Trailer, 1901.   *$3,000 plus*

LI No. 400 Gondola Trailer, 1901.   *$1,500–$1,700*

LI No. 500 Motorized Derrick, 1903.   *$5,000 plus*

LI No. 600 Derrick Trailer, 2⅛ in., 1903.   *$5,000 plus*

LI No. 700 Window Display Set, 2⅛ in., 1904.
Value Indeterminate

LI No. 800 Express Motor Car (Box Car), 2⅛ in., 1904.
$3,000–$3,500

LI No. 900 Express Trail Car, 2⅛ in., 1904.   *$3,000–$3,500*

LI No. 1000 Passenger Car, motorized, 2⅛ in., 1905.
$4,000–$5,000

LI No. 1010 Interurban Trolley Trailer, Standard gauge, 1910.
(Matches No. 10 Interurban "New York Central Lines.")
$2,000–$2,500

LI No. 1050 Passenger Car, Trailer, 2⅛ in., 1905.
$4,500–$5,500

LI 1012 Interurban Trolley Trailer, 1910.   *$2,000–$2,500*

LI No. 2200 Summer Trolley Trailer, "2200 Rapid Transit 2200,"
nonpowered, gold rubber-stamped letters, 1910.   *$2,000–$2,500*

"Name" Train Sets and Passenger Cars

Train Sets

LI No. 250E "Hiawatha" Set, with No. 250WX tender, No. 782 coach, No. 783 coach, No. 784 observation car, 1935.

$650–$700

LI No. 263T "Blue Comet" Set, Nos. 263W or 2263W tender, Nos. 615 or 2615 baggage car, Nos. 613 or 2613 Pullman, Nos. 614 or 2614 observation car, 1936–1939.   *$1,300–$1,500*

LI No. 264E "Red Comet" Set, 2-4-2, O gauge, No. 265T tender, No. 603 Pullmans (two), No. 604 observation car (red matching set), 1935.   *$500–$550*

Catalog from 1930 features the classic "State" set; 1913 catalog brings a girl into the scene (but only as onlooker, while boy operates his Standard-gauge sets).

Lionel "Blue Comet" five-piece passenger train set, $2,090 at Bidonde Sale.
(Courtesy of Sotheby's, New York)

LI No. 265E "Blue Streak" Set, 2-4-2, O gauge, No. 265WX tender, No. 619 combine, No. 617 coach, No. 618 observation car, 1935.   *$500–$550*

LI No. 367E "Flying Yankee" Set, Standard gauge, Nos. 385E, 384 tender, gunmetal, Connecticut; Nos. 1767, 1766, 1768, terra cotta, maroon cars, 1934.   *$2,500–$3,000*

LI No. 367W "Washington Special" Set, Standard gauge, Nos. 1767, 1766, 1768, red, maroon cars, 1935–1939. *$1,500–$2,000*

LI No. 381E "Olympian" State Set, No. 381E locomotive, 12 wheels, Standard gauge, Pullmans: No. 412 "California," No. 413 "Colorado," No. 414 "Illinois," No. 416 "New York" observation car, 1928.   *$7,000–$7,500*

LI No. 396E "Blue Comet" Set, Standard gauge, No. 400 engine, No. 400 tender, Nos. 421, 422 Pullmans, light blue body, dark blue roof, 1931.   *$5,500–$6,000*

LI No. 396E, same as above, with cast journals, 1933.
                                                        $6,000–$6,500

LI No. 409E "The Olympian" Set, Standard gauge, "State" green, No. 381 engine, Nos. 412, 413, 416 "State" Pullmans, observation car, "State" green with pale green ventilators, ivory windows, brass journals, rivet detail, 1933.   *$8,000–$8,500*

LI No. 409E, same as above, apple green windows (Black Dot), 1930. *$8,500–$9,000*

LI No. 411E "Transcontinental Limited" Set, Standard gauge, 1929, 408E, Nos. 412, 413, 414, 416 Pullmans and observation car, two-tone brown with light brown ventilators, cast journals, 1930–1931. *$12,000–$15,000*

LI No. 411E, same as above, 381E, "State" green with lighter green ventilators, apple green windows (Red Dot), 1929.
$10,000–$12,000

LI No. 433E "Twentieth Century Limited" Set, 400E, No. 400 tender, Nos. 412, 414, 416 "State" green cars with dark ventilators, black locomotive, 1931–1940. *$5,000–$5,500*

LI No. 616E or 616W "Flying Yankee" Set, power unit with No. 617 coaches (two), No. 618 observation car, black frame, chrome shells, 1935. *$250–$300*

LI No. 636W "City of Denver" Power Unit, No. 637 coaches (two), No. 638 observation car, Union Pacific R.R., yellow, brown, 1936.
$275–$350

LI No. 636W Special Set of "City of Denver," with No. 637 coach, No. 630 observation car, two-tone green. *$525–$575*

Lionel "City of Denver" Union Pacific Locomotive, 1936; streamliner set was one of the most desireable of Lionel's smaller entries. (Courtesy of Phillips, New York)

LI No. 752E or 752W "Union Pacific" Power Unit, No. 753 coaches (two), No. 754 observation car, O gauge, 1934–1941.

$175–$250

Passenger Cars: 1929–1941

LI No. 412 "California" Pullman, Standard gauge, light green, 1929. (Part of "State" Set) $1,100–$1,150

LI No. 412, same as above, light brown. $1,150–$2,000

LI No. 413 "Colorado" Pullman, Standard gauge, light green, 1929. ("State" Set) $1,100–$1,150

LI No. 413, same as above, light brown. $1,150–$2,000

LI No. 414 "Illinois" Pullman, Standard gauge, light green, 1930. ("State" Set) $1,100–$1,150

LI No. 414, same as above, light brown. $1,150–$2,000

LI No. 416 "New York" Observation Car, Standard gauge, light green, 1929–1935. ("State" Set) $1,100–$1,150

LI No. 420 "Faye" Pullman, Standard gauge, light blue shell, dark blue roof, 1930. ("Blue Comet" Set) $850–$900

LI No. 421 "Westphal" Pullman, light blue shell, dark blue roof, 1930. ("Blue Comet" Set) $850–$900

LI No. 422 "Tempel" Observation Car, light blue shell, dark blue roof, 1930–1940. ("Blue Comet" Set) $850–$900

LI No. 424 "Liberty Bell" Pullman, light green, 1931–1940. ("Stephen Girard" Set) $550–$600

LI No. 425 "Stephen Girard" Pullman, light green, 1931–1940. ("Stephen Girard" Set) $550–$600

LI No. 426 "Coral Isle" Observation Car, light green, 1931–1940. ("Stephen Girard" Set)   *$550–$600*

LI No. 607 "Macy" Pullman, O gauge, 1926–1937.   *$75–$85*

LI No. 608 "Macy" Observation Car, O gauge, 1926–1937.
$75–$85

LI No. 610 "Macy" Pullman, 1926–1930.   *$85–$95*

LI No. 612 "Macy" Observation Car, O gauge, 1915–1925.
$75–$85

LI No. 630 "Macy" Observation Car, O gauge, 1926–1931.
$40–$50

LI No. 637 "City of Denver" Streamliner Coach, 1936–1939.
$100–$125

LI No. 638 "City of Denver" Observation Car, yellow, brown, 1936–1939.   *$100–$125*

LI No. 782 "The Milwaukee Road" Streamliner Front Coach, "072," gray roof, orange sides, maroon underframe, 1935–1941. (Articulated "Hiawatha" Set)   *$325–$375*

LI No. 783, same as above, "072."   *$325–$375*

LI No. 784, same as above, observation car. *Value Indeterminate*

LI No. "792 Lionel Lines 792" Streamliner Front Coach, "072," maroon roof, red sides and underframe, 1937–1941. (Combines with 700E locomotive as part of "Rail Chief" Set)   *$375–$425*

*LI No. "793 Lionel Lines 793," same as above.   *$375–$425*

*LI No. "794 Lionel Lines 794," same as above, observation car, 1927–1941.   *$375–$425*

Torpedo Streamliners, O Gauge: 1936–1940

LI No. 238/238-E Locomotive (4-4-2), "238-E" plates, nickel journal, gunmetal gray, with No. 265W tender, bolted weight in cab, type 1 box coupler, 1936.   *$250–$300*

1937: No weight in cab.   *$250–$300*

1938: No. 225-W or 2265-W tender, no weight in cab.
$250–$300

1939: Same tender combination, black, no weight in cab, "238" plates.   *$250–$300*

1940: Same tender combination, "238" plates, Type II box, automatic, solenoid operated.   *$250–$300*

LI No. 1588 Locomotive Mechanical (0-4-0), no firebox doors, semigloss black, with No. 1588 tender, hook coupler, 1936.
$175–$225

1937: Thin with no firebox doors or thick with firebox doors, with No. 1588 tender, also available with No. 1516 tender.
$175–$225

LI No. 1668/1668-E Locomotive (2-6-2), "1668 E" plates, No. 1689 tender, nickel journals, latch coupler, gunmetal gray, 1937.
$150–$200

1938.   *$150–$200*

1939: But also known with "1668" plates, nickel or black journals.   *$150–$200*

1940: With "1668" plates, black.   *$150–$200*

1941: Type II box coupler, black.   *$150–$200*

Note: A first run of the 1668-E with forward-facing cab windows is highly uncommon, the only one of the nine major variations of Torpedos that commands big prices. Because of the ever-increasing popularity of these Art Deco-styled Streamliners, one can expect to pay considerably more for examples in top condition at auction.

Value Indeterminate

LI No. 1688/1688-E Locomotives (2-4-2), no firebox doors, 8-spoke drivers, ''1688-E'' plates, No. 1689 tender, nickel journal, latch coupler, gunmetal gray, also in semigloss black, 1936.

$75–$100

1937: Thick casting, 8 or 12 spokes.   *$75–$100*

1938: 12-spoke drivers, ''1688-E'' plates, latch or type I box coupler, Nos. 1689 or 2689 tender.   *$75–$100*

1939: ''1688-E'' or ''1688'' plates, above two tender options, nickel or black journals, type 1 box or latch coupler.

$75–$100

1940: Black, type II box automatic coupler.   *$75–$100*

Train Sets, Locomotives, and Tenders: Prewar

LI No. 2 Build-A-Motor, O gauge, 1928–1931.   *$120–$150*

LI No. 00-2 Steam Locomotive, OO gauge, ''Hudson'' 4-6-4, three-rail with No. 002T tender (with or without whistle), black, 1939–1942.   *$150–$250*

LI No. 00-3 Steam Locomotive, OO gauge, two-rail with No. 003T tender (with or without whistle), black, 1939–1942.

With whistle.   *$150–$250*

Without whistle.   *$175–$275*

LI No. 004 Electric Locomotive, OO gauge, two color variations, 1928–1932.

Orange.   *$500–$700*

Gray.   *$550–$750*

Lionel No. 5 Standard-gauge loco-motive, 1906–1926, B & O, based on electric prototype, $3,500–$4,500. Derrick trailer, 1903, a Joshua Cowen "original," $5,000-plus.

LI No. 00-4, OO-Gauge Locomotive (only), 0-4-0, 1939–1942, steam, 4-6-4, two-rail, No. 004 tender, with or without whistle, black.

> With whistle. $150–$225

> Without whistle. $175–$250

LI No. 5 Electric Locomotive (only), Standard gauge, black, 1906–1926. $3,500–$4,500

LI No. 6 Steam Locomotive, Standard gauge, 4-4-0, sheet brass and nickeled steel, 1910–1923. $2,000–$3,000

LI No. 7 Steam Locomotive, brass, red solid pilot wheels, nickeled bell, 1908–1914. $3,000–$3,500

LI No. 8 Electric Outline Locomotive, 0-4-0, Standard gauge, in maroon, olive, red, mojave or peacock (the latter being the rarer), 1925–1932. $125–$150

LI No. 8E, same as above, in red, olive, pea green (with cream stripe, ''Macy''), mojave.   *$150–$225*

LI No. 33 Electric Locomotive, Standard gauge, 0-6-0, engine only, dark green, 1912 (early version).   *$300–$350*

LI No. 33, same as above, dark olive or black, 0-4-0, 1913–1924 (late version).   *$150–$200*

LI No. 42 Electric Locomotive, Standard gauge, 0-4-4-0, square hood, dark green, 1912.   *$1,000–$1,500*

LI No. 42, same as above with round hood, in dark green, gray, black, peacock or mojave, maroon finish, 1913–1923.

$500–$700

LI No. 54 Electric Locomotive, 0-4-4-0, ''NYC,'' brass, red pilots, wheel spokes, 1913–1923.   *$2,500–$3,000*

LI No. 100 Locomotive, 2⁷/₈ in., 1901.   *$4,000–$5,000*

LI No. 150 Electric Locomotive, O gauge, 0-4-0, dark green, 1917 (early version).   *$50–$100*

LI No. 150, same as above, 1918–1925 (late version).   *$50–$100*

LI No. 152 Electric Locomotive, O gauge, 0-4-0, dark green, steel gray, 1917–1927.   *$125–$150*

  2nd Version: Light gray.   *$150–$175*

  3rd Version: Mojave or peacock blue.   *$175–$200*

LI No. 153 Electric Locomotive, O gauge, 0-4-0, dark green, 1924–1925.   *$125–$150*

  2nd Version: Gray.   *$150–$175*

  3rd Version: Mojave.   *$200–$275*

LI No. 154 Electric Locomotive, O gauge, 0-4-0, dark green, 1917–1923.   *$125–$150*

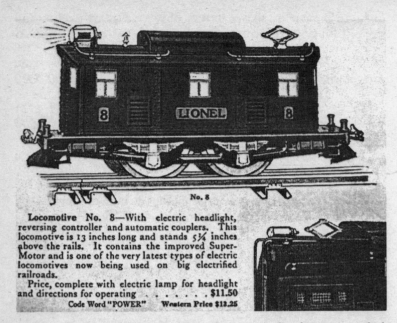

No. 8

Locomotive No. 8—With electric headlight, reversing controller and automatic couplers. This locomotive is 13 inches long and stands 5¼ inches above the rails. It contains the improved Super-Motor and is one of the very latest types of electric locomotives now being used on big electrified railroads.

Price, complete with electric lamp for headlight and directions for operating $11.50

Code Word "POWER"   Western Price $13.25

Catalog page from 1925 for Lionel No. 8 electric outline locomotive, which is very similar to their O-gauge No. 256, minus roof-mounted air tanks; replaced by monitor roof, $125–$150.

Lionel No. 54 locomotive, 0-4-4-0, ca. 1913, brass finish with red trim on wheels, ventilators, pilots, 14 in. 1.; one of Lionel's showpieces, $3,000–$3,500.

LI No. 156 Electric Locomotive, O gauge, 4-4-4, olive, maroon, gray, 1917–1923.   *$500–$600*

LI No. 156, same as above, in 0-4-0.   *$475–$575*

LI No. 158 Electric Locomotive, O gauge, gray, 1923–1924.
                                                               $200–$300

  2nd Version: Black.   *$250–$350*

LI No. 201 Steam Locomotive, O gauge, 0-6-0, switcher with No. 2201B tender with bell, 1917.   *$300–$350*

  2nd Version: Without bell on tender.   *$250–$325*

LI No. 202 "Alco" A Diesel, "Union Pacific" 027, orange with black lettering, 1957.   *$35–$50*

LI No. 203 Armored Locomotive, O gauge, 0-4-0, cannon, only World War I military-type train produced by Lionel, 1917–1921.
                                                             $2,500–$3,500

LI No. 222/224E Steam Locomotive, O gauge, 2-6-2, 1938–1942.
                                                               $100–$150

LI No. 225/225E Steam Locomotive, O gauge, 2-6-2, tender, black, 1938–1942.   *$175–$225*

LI No. 226/226E Steam Locomotive, O gauge, 2-6-4, No. 226 tender, 1938–1941.   *$400–$500*

One of Lionel's scarcest train sets: the "Armored Set," 1917–1921, with ammunition cars, several variations, $2,500–$3,500.

LI No. 238/238EW Steam Locomotive, 4-4-2, O gauge, Pennsylvania R.R. "Torpedo" and tender with whistle, gunmetal gray, Nos. 2225T, 2225W or 265W tenders, 1936–1938. *$225–$250*

LI No. 248 Electric Locomotive, O gauge, dark green, red, orange, olive, 1926–1932. *$100–$150*

LI No. 249/249E Steam Locomotive, O gauge, gunmetal gray, 1936–1937. *$200–$225*

LI No. 250E "Hiawatha" Steam Locomotive, 0-4-0, with Nos. 250W, 250WX, 2250W tenders, 1935–1942. *$600–$700*

LI No. 250 Electric Locomotive, O gauge, "New York Central," peacock, orange, dark green, 1926 (early version). *$150–$200*

2nd Version: terra cotta, orange, 1934 (late version).
$150–$200

LI No. 255E Steam Locomotive, O gauge, 2-4-2, No. 263W tender, gunmetal gray, 1935–1936. *$450–$550*

LI No. 256 Electric Locomotive, O gauge, 0-4-4-0, 1924–1930.
$500–$600

LI No. 257 Steam Locomotive, O gauge, 0-4-0, with Nos. 257T or 259T tender, 1930. *$150–$200*

LI No. 258 Steam Locomotive, 2-4-0, 1930 (early version).
$150–$200

LI No. 258, same as above, 2-4-2, with No. 1689T tender, 1941 (late version). *$75–$125*

LI No. 259 Steam Locomotive, O gauge, 2-4-2, black, 1932.
$75–$100

LI No. 259E Steam Locomotive, O gauge, 1936-8 black or gunmetal gray, 1933–1934. *$75–$100*

LI No. 260E Steam Locomotive, O gauge, 2-4-2, with No. 260T tender, black, 1930–1935.   *$400–$500*

LI No. 260E, same as above in gunmetal gray, 263T tender.
                                                    $425–$525

LI No. 261 Steam Locomotive, O gauge, 2-4-2, with No. 257T tender, 1931.   *$200–$250*

LI No. 261E Steam Locomotive, O gauge, 2-4-2, No. 261T tender, 1935.   *$200–$250*

LI No. 263E Steam Locomotive, O gauge, 2-4-2, gunmetal gray, 1936–1939.   *$450–$500*

LI No. 265E Steam Locomotive, O gauge, 2-4-2, "Torpedo" Streamliner, black, 1935–1939.   *$200–$250*

  2nd Version: Gunmetal gray.   *$175–$225*

  3rd Version: Blue, "Blue Streak."   *$250–$300*

LI No. 380E Electric Locomotive, Standard gauge, maroon, 1926–1928.   *$350–$400*

LI No. 381 Electric Locomotive, Standard gauge, 4-4-4, green, 1928–1929. ("State" Set)   *$3,500–$4,000*

LI No. 381E Electric Locomotive, Standard gauge, "State" green, 1928–1936.   *$2,000–$2,500*

  2nd Version: Green body with red frame.   *$2,250–$2,750*

Lionel PRR, 0-6-0, 1939, switcher, O-gauge, $1,300–$1,500.

LI No. 381U Electric Locomotive, Standard gauge, includes kit with engine track, original box, 1928–1929.   *$3,500–$4,000*

LI No. 385E Steam Locomotive, Standard gauge, 2-4-2, with Nos. 384T, 385T, 385TW or 385W tenders, gunmetal gray, 1933–1939.
$650–$750

LI No. 390 Steam Locomotive, Standard gauge, 2-4-2, with No. 390T tender, black, 1929.   *$650–$750*

LI No. 390E Steam Locomotive, Standard gauge, 2-4-2, black, 1932–1939.   *$600–$700*

LI No. 392E Steam Locomotive, Standard gauge, 4-4-2, black, 1932–1939.   *$1,000–$1,200*

2nd Version: Gunmetal gray.   *$1,200–$1,400*

LI No. 400E Steam Locomotive, Standard gauge, 4-4-4, with No. 400T tender, black, 1931–1940.   *$2,000–$2,200*

2nd Version: Gunmetal gray.   *$2,200–$2,500*

3rd Version: Blue.   *$2,500–$2,700*

LI No. 408E Electric Locomotive, Standard gauge, 0-4-4-0, apple green or mojave, 1927–1936.   *$1,000–$1,500*

2nd Version: "State" brown.   *$1,500–$2,000*

3rd Version: "State" green.   *$2,000–$2,500*

LI No. 450 Electric Locomotive, O gauge, 0-4-0, "Macy Special," red with black frame, 1930.   *$500–$600*

LI No. 616E/616W Diesel Locomotive, O gauge, 1935–1941.
$75–$100

LI No. 636W Diesel Locomotive, O gauge, Union Pacific "City of Denver," yellow, brown, 1936–1941.   *$100–$150*

Lionel No. 402 locomotive, No. 215 tanker, No. 212 gondola with containers, No. 218 dump car, No. 211 flat car, No. 219 crane, No. 200 series freight cars were largest ever offered by Lionel. $1,500-plus. (Courtesy of Sotheby's, New York)

LI No. 700 Electric Locomotive, O gauge, 0-4-0, "New York Central," dark green, 1913–1916.   *$300–$350*

LI No. 700E Steam Locomotive, "Hudson 5344," black, Nos. 700/700W 12-wheel tender, 1937–1942.   *$2,500–$3,000*

LI No. 701 Electric Locomotive, O gauge, 0-4-0, dark green, 1913–1916.   *$500–$600*

LI No. 703 Electric Locomotive, O gauge, 4-4-4, dark green, 1913–1916.   *$1,000–$1,500*

LI No. 706 Electric Locomotive, O gauge, 0-4-0, dark green, 1913–1916.   *$400–$500*

LI No. 708 Steam Locomotive, "8796" appears on boiler front, 0-6-0, 1939–1942.   *$1,200–$1,500*

LI No. 736E Steam Locomotive, O gauge, 4-6-4, black, 1937–1942.   *$1,200–$1,500*

Lionel 1942, patriotic wartime catalog highlights 4-6-4 "Hudson" locomotive No. 5344 and updated version of No. 700E, $2,500–$3,000.

LI No. 1010 Electric Locomotive, "Winner," 0-4-0, 1931–1932.
$75–$100

LI No. 1015 Steam Locomotive, O gauge, "027 Winner," 0-4-0, with No. 1016 tender, black, 1931–1932. *$75–$100*

LI No. 1030 Steam Locomotive, O gauge, 0-4-0, "027 Winner," orange body, green roof, 1932. *$100–$125*

LI No. 1506L Steam Locomotive, O gauge, 0-4-0, with No. 1502T tender, 1933–1934. *$100–$125*

LI No. 1506M Steam Locomotive, O gauge, 0-4-0, black, 1935.
$400–$450

LI No. 1511 Steam Locomotive, with No. 1509T tender, "Commodore Vanderbilt"-type, black, 1936–1937. *$75–$100*

2nd Version: Red. *$100–$150*

LI No. 1588 Steam Locomotive, O gauge, 0-4-0, "Torpedo"-type, with No. 1588T tender, 1936–1937. *$150–$175*

LI No. 1651E Electric Locomotive, O gauge, 0-4-0, red body, brown roof, 1933. *$150–$200*

LI No. 1910 Electric Locomotive, Standard gauge, 0-6-0, "New York, New Haven & Hartford" gilt on side of cab, deep olive green, 1910–1911 (early version). *$1,500–$2,000*

LI No. 1910, same as above, 1912 (late version). *$1,000–$1,500*

LI No. 1911 Electric Locomotive, Standard gauge, 0-4-0, deep olive, 1910–1912 (early version). *$2,000–$2,500*

LI No. 1911, same as above, 0-4-4-0, maroon or deep olive, 1913 (late version). *$1,000–$1,500*

LI No. 1911 Special Electric Locomotive, Standard gauge, 0-4-4-0, "New Haven & Hartford" or "New York Central Lines" rubber-stamped in gilt over maroon finish, 1911–1912. *$2,000–$2,500*

LIONEL/IVES TRAINS PRODUCTION: 1931–1932

Number	Wheels	Item	Years	Motor	Comments	Price Range
257	2-4-0	Steam Loco	1931	Elec	w/ Tender #257T	$125–$175
258	2-4-0	Steam Loco	1931–32	Elec	w/Tenders #257T, 1663T	$125–$175
610	8	Pullman	1931–32			$75–$100
612	8	Observation	1931–32			$75–$100
1501	0-4-0	Steam Loco	1932	Windup	w/Tender #1502	$135–$150
1504	4	Pullman	1931–32			$25–$30
1506	0-4-0	Steam Loco	1931–32	Windup	w/Tender #1507 (includes #1515 Tank Car and #1517 Caboose)	$375–$425
1512	4	Gondola	1931–32			$25–$35
1513	4	Stock Car	1931–32			$25–$35
1514	4	Box Car	1931–32			$25–$35
1515	4	Tank Car	1932			$25–$35
1517	4	Caboose	1931–32			$25–$35
1651	0-4-0	Elec Loco	1932	Elec		$150–$175
1654	0-4-0	Elec Loco	1931	Elec		$150–$175
1661	2-4-0	Steam Loco	1932	Elec	w/Tender #1661T	$50–$75
1663	2-4-2	Steam Loco	1931	Elec	w/Tender #1663T	$100–$125
1677	8	Gondola	1931–32			$20–$30
1678	8	Stock Car	1931–32			$20–$30
1679	8	Box Car	1931–32			$20–$30
1680	8	Tank Car	1931–32			$20–$30
1682	8	Caboose	1931–32			$20–$30
1690	8	Pullman	1931–32			$25–$35
1691	8	Observation	1931–32			$25–$35
1694	4-4-4	Elec Loco	1932	Elec		$100–$110

1695	12	Pullman	1932		$30–$40
1696	12	Baggage Car	1932		$30–$40
1697	12	Observation	1932		$30–$40
1707	8	Gondola	1932		$30–$40
1708	8	Stock Car	1932		$20–$30
1709	8	Box Car	1932		$20–$30
1712	8	Caboose	1932		$20–$30
1810	0-4-0	Electric Loco	1931–32	Elec	$100–$120
1811	4	Pullman	1931–32		$20–$30
1812	4	Observation	1931–32		$20–$30
1813	4	Baggage Car	1931–32		$20–$30
1815	0-4-0	Steam Loco	1931–32	Elec w/Tender #1507	$75–$100

TOP 20 LIONEL POSTWAR TRAIN SETS AND CONSISTS

	Year	Engine No.	Tender/Trailer	Cars						Price Range
1.	1945	224	2466WX	2452	2458	2555	2457			$200–$225
2.	1946	726	2426W	2625	2625	2625	2625			$425–$475
3.	1948	671	4671W	4452	4454	5459	4357			$450–$500
4.	1948	671	2671W	3451	3462	2456	2357			$200–$225
5.	1950	2023P	2023T	2481	2482	2483				$475–$500
6.	1950	773	2426W	2625	2627	2628				$1,300–$1,500
7.	1954	2353P	2353T	2530	2532	2533	2531			$400–$450
8.	1955/56	2340(55)	2360(56)	2541	2542	2543	2544			$1,000–$1,500
9.	1956	2328		2444	2442	2442	2446			$300–$350
10.	1956	2341		2533	2532	2531				$800–$850
11.	1957	2037	1130T	6462	6464	6436	6464	6427		$200–$250
12.	1957	2373P	2373T	2552	2552	2552	2551			$1,200–$1,400
13.	1958	1625	1625T	6804	6808	6806	6017			$400–$450
14.	1958	400		2559	2550					$1,800–$2,000
15.	1958	2329		6556	6425	6414	6434	3359	6427-60	$750–$800
16.	1960	1882	1882T	1887	1866	1885				$775–$825
17.	1960	45		3429	3820	6640	6824			$300–$350
18.	1961	2383P	2383T	2563	2562	2562	2561			$900–$1,000
19.	1962	2383P	2383T	2523	2522	2522	2521			$600–$650
20.	1964	240	1130T	3666	F/C tank	6470	6814			$500–$550

Note: These are the author's value guides and not those of Joe Algozzini, who compiled the list.

The 20 "Most Wanted" Postwar Lionel Train Sets

Joe Algozzini, writing in the Summer 1989 issue of *Classic Toy Trains*, rates the following 1945–1980s Lionel train sets as his favorites.

1. The No. 224 Lionel steamer—the first and only set offered in Lionel's catalog for 1945, the year the war ended.
2. The 1946 No. 726 "Berkshire," with many nice trimmings; 2-8-4 locomotive pulled three "Irvington" passenger cars.
3. The 1948 Lionel O-gauge "Sante Fe" diesel scale model of the General Motors prototype. Set sold at a whopping $199.95.
4. The No. 2745WS Deluxe Passenger Set, 1948. Set sold at $58.75 and was a sentimental pick, having been Algozzini's first set.
5. In 1950, two Union Pacific "Alco" Diesel No. 027 Series, "The Anniversary Set" in Lionel's Golden Anniversary year. Bright orange and black locomotives—one pulled three passenger coaches, the other pulled freight car, tanker, coal car, and caboose; $55 and $47.50 respectively.
6. The No. 773 "Hudson" classic from the 1950 Anniversary year; $85 for passenger set; $79.50 for freight set.
7. The 1954 "Sante Fe" No. 2234W four-car Super Streamliner, with the No. 2530 "American Express" baggage car. Locomotive sold at $89.50; silver finish cars sold at $10.95 each for deluxe cars, $9.95 for standard cars.
8. The 1955 Pennsylvania R.R. "Congressional," with No. 2340 Tuscan red GG1, and "Molly Pitcher," "William Penn," "Betsy Ross," and "Alexander Hamilton" passenger cars. Sold at $49.95.
9. The 1956 "Burlington" No. 2328, a four-car set with distinctive red stripes. Models of General Motors or Fairbanks Morse prototypes.
10. The 1956 No. 2341 "Jersey Central Train Master" with wide channel passenger cars. One of the most coveted of the postwar engines, the No. 2341 is often replicated.
11. From 1957, "The Lady Lionel" or "Girl's Train," which

featured a pink No. 2037-500LT engine and rainbow-colored cars. While the concept derailed, limited production run makes the set very desirable to collectors. "Boy's Set" issued same year.

12. The 1957 "Canadian Pacific" Super "O" Luxury Liner Set, "The Hudson" with five cars, with two additional Pullmans—"Blair Manor" and "Craig" sold separately. Algozzini writes that this "has to be one of the most striking Lionels made."

13. The 1958 U.S. Marines No. 1625 military 0-4-0 set includes three flat cars with toy military vehicles (made for Lionel by Pyro). Gray No. 6017-85 caboose is a tough car to find.

14. The 1958 No. 400 locomotive with Budd cars comprising a commuter car and baggage/mail car. Minneapolis & St. Louis R.R.

15. The 1958 "Virginian" and "Owl" rectifier freight set features the always elusive No. 6556 Katy stock car and No. 6427-60 "Virginian" caboose.

16. From 1960, an uncataloged No. 1882, known as the "Halloween Set." Speculation has it that it was made for either Sears, Macy's or Wards, depending on who you talk to; at any rate, it's a classic.

16½. From 1960, the set that's variously known as the "Over & Under" or "Father & Son" set; an HO-layout at ground level; O gauge above. The O-gauge set includes the uncommon No. 6357-50 "Santa Fe" caboose.

17. The 1960 "New Salute to the Future: Land, Sea, & Air Gift Pack" Set with No. 5 engine. All cars have U.S. Marine Corps khaki markings; includes U.S.M.C. helicopter and rocket launcher. Sold for $33.00.

18. From 1961, another red-striped "Sante Fe Super Chief," the first of which appeared in 1959. Has one of the all-time favorite paint schemes with a classy four-car passenger set.

19. The 1962 silver-with-gold-striped "Presidential" passenger set. Includes a "Garfield" Pullman, "Harrison" Vista Domes (two), and "McKinley" observation car.

20. The 1964, No. 9820 uncataloged "Military Train Set" Lionel made for Sears; includes rare flat car with tank, No. 3666 cannon box car and No. 347 cannon firing range set and toy soldiers.

Honorable Mention: No. 2338 "Milwaukee Road" orange-stripe geep from 1955; also the B & O and "Milwaukee Road" F3s. Author Algozzini left off the highly touted "Boys Train," considering it "nothing more than a pre-production sample/project at best." Another uncataloged Sears set barely missed out—the classic No. 2347 Chesapeake & Ohio geep.

Not surprisingly, Algozzini's "Top Twenty" (see Table) triggered considerable *Classic Toy Trains* reader response from Lionel loyalists. One wrote, "Lionel's great (postwar) years were 1946, 1950, and 1955. Almost every good item is a variation of items available in those years. After 1958, most Lionel trains were poor matches for what had been made earlier."

In tallying votes from a *Classic Toy Trains* readership poll on the "Top Twenty," editor Dick Christianson observed that all the "Santa Fe" sets received notes; also that "many of the favorites came from 1950, The Golden Anniversary year, and 1957, the year of the CP passenger set and the Lady Lionel. Also, from the comments accompanying cards, favorites were often the first set each reader got as a child, or the first set they *didn't* get as a child.

Locomotives and Tenders, Postwar: 1945–1980s

LI No. 1862 "General," Civil War classic prototype, steam outline, 4-4-0, No. 1862 tender, black, 1959–1962.   *$175–$225*

LI No. 1872 "General," with Nos. 1872, 1875W tender, Super O gauge, 1959.   *$225–$275*

LI No. 1882 "General," with No. 1881 tender, Sears & Roebuck edition, 1959–1962.   *$425–$475*

LI No. 2016 Locomotive, steam outline, 2-6-4, No. 6026W tender, 1955–1956.   *$50–$75*

Lionel's 1955 advance catalog shows fledgling engineer with new "Virginian" diesel with magnetraction.

LI No. 2020 Locomotive, with Nos. 2020W, 2466WX or 6020W tender, 6-8-6, 1946–1947.   *$125–$150*

LI No. 2028 Pennsylvania R.R. Diesel Locomotive, GP-7, 1955.
$225–$275

LI No. 2031 Rock Island "Alco" AA Diesel Locomotive, black shell with red midstripe, 1952–1954.   *$200–$225*

LI No. 2032 Erie "Alco" AA Diesel Locomotive, black shell, yellow mid-stripe, 1952–1954.   *$125–$150*

LI No. 2033 Union Pacific "Alco" AA Diesel, silver shell, 1952–1954.   *$125–$175*

LI No. 2037/500 "Girl's Set" Steam Engine, 2-6-4, pink, 1957.
$600–$700

LI No. 2240 Wabash R.R. F-3 AB Diesel, gray and blue shell, 1956.   *$300–$350*

LI No. 2242 New Haven R.R. F-3 AB Diesel, checkerboard design, silver and black, 1958–1959.   *$300–$350*

LI No. 2243 Santa Fe R.R. F-3AB Diesel, silver shell, red nose, 1955–1957.   *$175–$200*

LI No. 2245 "Texas Special" F-3 AB Diesel, red, 1954–1955.
                                                    $250–$275

LI No. 2321 "Lackawanna Trainmaster" Diesel FM, double engine, gray roof, 1954–1956.   *$275–$325*

LI No. 2321, same as above, maroon roof.   *$375–$425*

LI No. 2322 "Virginian Trainmaster," with double engine, yellow with blue roof, 1965–1966.   *$350–$400*

LI No. 2340 Pennsylvania GG-1 Locomotive, double motor, Tuscan, five gold stripes, 1955.   *$600–$650*

LI No. 2340-25, same as above, green with silver stripes.
                                                    $425–$475

"Toy Fair" box car by Fundimensions (General Mills subsidiary which marketed Lionel trains beginning in the 1960s); red, white, blue (oval portrait of Joshua Lionel Cowen), $150–$200.

LI No. 2341 "Jersey Central (Diesel) Trainmaster," double motor, orange with blue stripe, 1956. $725–$775

LI No. 2345 Western Pacific F-3 AA, double motor, silver, orange, screen roof, 1952. $500–$550

LI No. 2345, same as above, louvered roof. $475–$500

LI No. 2347 Chesapeake & Ohio GP-7, Sears edition, blue with yellow lettering. $1,000–$1,500

LI No. 2355 Western Pacific F-3 AA, double motor, silver, orange, 1953. $450–$500

LI No. 2356 Southern R.R. F-3 AA Diesel,. green, 1954–1956. $400–$450

LI No. 2358 Great Northern EP-5, orange, green with yellow stripes, 1959–1960. $400–$450

LI No. 2360 Pennsylvania GG-1, Tuscan, letters and numbers plus stripe are rubber-stamped, 1956–1958, 1961–1963. $550–$650

LI No. 2360, same as above, with heat-stamped letters, numbers. $650–$700

LI No. 2373 Canadian Pacific F# AA; Super O, gray, maroon with yellow trim, 1957. $675–$725

LI No. 2378 Milwaukee Road F-3 AB, gray with orange stripe, 1956. $575–$625

LI No. 2379 Rio Grande F-3 AB, yellow shell, silver roof and stripe, 1957–1958. $350–$400

LI No. 2383 Rio Grande F-3 AA, silver, red nose, 1958–1966. $200–$250

Rolling Stock

Standard Gauge Rolling Stock

LI No. 112 Gondola, "Rock Island" with black trucks, gray body, 1910–1926.   *$30–$35*

LI No. 113 Cattle Car, pea green with black trucks, 1912–1926.
$35–$50

LI No. 114 Box Car, orange with black trucks, 1912–1926.
$35–$50

LI No. 117 Caboose, with trucks, black and maroon, 1912–1926.
$50–$65

LI No. 164 Log Loader, chain drive, with roof, silver, 1940–1942.
$150–$175

LI No. 460 Transport Set, piggyback style, flat car with two green vans, 1930–1933.   *$100–$125*

LI No. 490 Observation Car, mojave, 1923.   *$250–$300*

LI No. 490, same as above, pale green.   *$300–$325*

LI No. 500 Motorized Derrick Car, $2^{7}/_{8}$ in. l., 1903–1904.
$4,000 plus

LI No. 511 Flat Car, dark green, 1927–1940.   *$50–$75*

LI No. 511, same as above, medium green.   *$50–$75*

LI No. 511 Lumber Car, stakes and load, dark green, 1927–1940.
$50–$75

LI No. 512 Gondola, deep green, 1927.   *$50–$75*

LI No. 512, same as above, peacock.   *$65–$85*

LI No. 513 Cattle Car, 1927.   *$85–$100*

LI No. 513, same as above, nickel trim.   *$250–$275*

LI No. 513 Cattle Car, olive drab and orange detail, 1927–1938.
$75–$100

LI No. 514 Box Car, says "Union Pacific," yellow and brown trim,
1929–1940.   *$100–$125*

LI No. 514 Reefer, with air vents, blue and silver, 1927–1928.
$300–$350

LI No. 514R Reefer, with air vents, red, 1929–1940.   *$150–$200*

LI No. 514 Box Car, ivory, brown, 1929.   *$100–$125*

LI No. 514, same as above, yellow, brown.   *$135–$160*

LI No. 514 Refrigerator Car, ventilated refrigerator, 1927.
$325–$350

LI No. 514R Refrigerator Car, 1929–1940.   *$150–$200*

LI No. 515 Tank Car, "Sunoco," silver, 1927–1940.   *$125–$150*

LI No. 515, same as above, ivory.   *$100–$125*

LI No. 515, same as above, no identification, terra cotta.
$100–$125

LI No. 515, same as above, "Shell," orange.   *$300–$350*

LI No. 515 Tank Car, terra cotta, 1927–1940.   *$125–$150*

LI No. 516 Hopper, with coal load, brass trim, 1928–1940.
$150–$200

LI No. 516 Hopper, 1928–1940.   *$125–$150*

LI No. 517 Caboose, red, nickel trim, 1927–1940.   *$60–$80*

LI No. 517 Caboose, with working windows, pea green and orange, brass trim, 1927–1940.   *$50–$75*

LI No. 603 Pullman, red with black roof.   *$65–$75*

LI No. 604 Observation Car, orange, 1920–1925.   *$25–$35*

LI No. 1766 Coach, transition series, brass fittings, maroon and terra cotta, 1934–1940.   *$450–$550*

O-Gauge Rolling Stock: Prewar

LI No. 175 Rocket Launcher, with tower and rocket, spring action, 1940–1942.   *$100–$125*

LI No. 652 Gondola, burnt orange and white, rubber-stamped, 1935–1940.   *$50–$60*

LI No. 653 Hopper, "Minneapolis and St. Louis," quad type, 1934–1940.   *$25–$35*

LI No. 655 Box Car, cream and brown, 1934–1942.   *$15–$30*

LI No. 655 Box car, yellow and maroon.   *$15–$30*

LI No. 657 Caboose, red with Tuscan roof, 1934–1942.   *$30–$35*

LI No. 657 Caboose, red with yellow roof, 1934–1942.   *$15–$20*

LI No. 657 Caboose, 1934–1942.   *$20–$25*

LI No. 804 Tank Car, four wheels, silver, 1923–1928.   *$25–$35*

LI No. 804 Tank Car, says "Shell," ladders decal, red and yellow.
        $35–$40

LI No. 804 Tank Car, says "Sunoco," silver with red and yellow detail.   *$25–$35*

LI No. 805 Box Car, pea green and orange.   *$20–$30*

LI No. 806 Stock Car, orange and maroon, 1927.   *$20–$30*

LI No. 807 Caboose, nickel-plated, red, 1927–1934.   *$20–$25*

LI No. 810 Crane Car, with cab and swivel base, 1930–1942.
                                                                                            $75–$100

LI No. 812 Gondola, giraud style, green, 1926–1942.   *$55–$65*

LI No. 812 Gondola, mojave green.   *$55–$65*

LI No. 813 Cattle Car, orange and brass trim, 1926–1942.
                                                                                            $75–$100

LI No. 814 Box Car, yellow and orange, automobile furniture, 1926–1942.   *$75–$100*

LI No. 815 Tank Car, says "Sunoco," silver.   *$75–$100*

LI No. 816 Hopper, red with nickel trim, 1927–1942.   *$90–$110*

LI No. 817 Caboose, two-tone green, 1926–1942.   *$50–$75*

LI No. 820 Searchlight Car, orange and black, rubber-stamped, says "Illinois Central & Missouri Valley Route R.R.," 1931–1942.
                                                                                            $100–$125

LI No. 831 Lumber Car, giraud green.   *$25–$50*

LI No. 831 Log Car, with load, stakes, and rail, green, 1927–1934.
                                                                                            $25–$50

LI No. 1004 Box Car, says "Baby Ruth," orange and blue.
                                                                                            $25–$50

LI No. 1005 Tank Car, says "Sunoco," gray. $25–$50

LI No. 1514 Box Car, says "Baby Ruth," windup series, tile red, 1931–1937. $35–$50

LI No. 1615 Tender, black with red lettering. $15–$20

LI No. 1679 Box Car, says "Baby Ruth," cream and blue, 1933–1942. $15–$20

LI No. 1680 Tank Car, lithographed, gray. $10–$15

LI No. 1682 Caboose, red. $10–$15

LI No. 1690 Pullman, dark red and brown, 1933–1934. $25–$30

LI No. 1691 Observation Car, dark red and brown, 1939.
$30–$35

LI No. 1717 Gondola, 1933–1940. $20–$25

LI No. 1719 Box Car, 1933–1940. $30–$40

LI No. 1722 Caboose, 1933–1942. $25–$30

LI No. 1722 Caboose, lithographed, 1939–1940. $25–$30

LI No. 1777 Gondola, lithographed. $50–$75

LI No. 2651 Lumber Car, with load, 1938. $25–$30

LI No. 2652 Gondola, burnt orange, 1938. $15–$25

LI No. 2654 Tank Car, "Shell," 1938. $15–$25

LI No. 2655 Box Car, rubber-stamped, cream and brown, 1938.
$15–$25

LI No. 2657 Caboose, 1938. $20–$25

LI No. 2657 Caboose, Tuscan roof, 1938.   *$20–$25*

LI No. 2675 Tank Car, "DuPont," single dome, 1940.   *$20–$25*

LI No. 2677 Gondola, red, black, "027," 1938.   *$20–$25*

LI No. 2679 Box Car, says "Baby Ruth," maroon and red lettering, "027," 1938.   *$20–$25*

LI No. 2682 Caboose, "027," 1938.   *$20–$25*

LI No. 2812 Gondola, burnt orange, 1938.   *$25–$30*

LI No. 2812 Gondola, deep green, 1938.   *$25–$30*

LI No. 2812 Gondola, pea green, nickel trim.   *$25–$30*

LI No. 2814 Box Car, cream and maroon.   *$25–$30*

LI No. 2817 Caboose, red, 1938.   *$70–$80*

LI No. 2817 Caboose, Tuscan roof.   *$125–$130*

Postwar Rolling Stock

LI No. 44 U.S. Mobile Missile Launcher, 1959–1962.   *$75–$125*

LI No. 45 U.S. Mobile Launcher Switcher, 1960–1962.
                                                        $125–$175

LI No. 56 Minneapolis & St. Louis Mine Transport, 1958.
                                                        $275–$325

LI No. 58 Great Northern Snowplow Locomotive, green shell, white cab, 1959–1961.   *$350–$400*

LI No. 60 "Lionelville" Trolley, yellow with red roof, blue lettering, 1955–1958.   *$225–$250*

LI No. 60, same as above, with black lettering. $250–$260

LI No. 60, same as above, with motorman silhouette in front.
$260–$275

LI No. 69 Maintenance Car, motorized, gray, black, blue man with red danger sign, 1960–1962. $200–$250

LI No. 2257 Caboose, ''Southern Pacific,'' red. $10–$20

LI No. 2357 Caboose, deluxe with tools, ladders, silver and blue.
$25–$35

LI No. 2400 Passenger Car, ''Maplewood,'' green and gray.
$35–$50

LI Nos. 2404–2410, ''Santa Fe'' Pullmans, Vista Domes, and observation cars, aluminum with blue lettering, 1964–1965. Each
$20–$30

LI Nos. 2412–2414, 2416, Vista Dome, Pullman, observation car, ''Santa Fe,'' same colors as above, 1959–1963. Each $35–$40

LI No. 2420 DL & W Work Cab, with light, gray, 1946–1949.
$50–$75

LI No. 2421 ''Maplewood'' Pullman, aluminum with gray roof, black stripe, 1950, 1952–1953. $35–$50

LI No. 2422 ''Chatham'' Pullman, same colors as above, 1950, 1952–1953. $35–$50

LI No. 2423 ''Hillside'' Observation Car, same colors as above, 1950, 1952–1953. $35–$50

LI No. 2429 ''Livingston'' Pullman, 1950, same colors as above, no stripe, 1950, 1952–1953. $45–$55

LI No. 2432 Vista Dome, says ''Clifton,'' silver and red, 1954–1958. $35–$50

LI No. 2436 Observation Car, "Summit," silver and red, 1954–1958. *$35–$45*

LI No. 2442 "Chatham" Pullman, with lights, brown with gray trim, 1955–1956. *$40–$50*

LI No. 2442 Vista Dome, "Clifton," double-dome, 1955–1956. *$45–$50*

LI No. 2443 Observation Car, with lights, brown with gray trim, 1946–1947. *$35–$45*

LI No. 2444 Pullman, "Newark," window stripe, red, 1955–1956. *$45–$50*

LI No. 2445 Pullman, "Elizabeth," window stripe, red, 1955–1956. *$50–$75*

LI No. 2452 Gondola, Pennsylvania R.R., 1945–1947. *$10–$15*

LI No. 2454 Box Car, Pennsylvania R.R., "Baby Ruth," 1946. *$15–$20*

LI No. 2456 Hopper, "Lehigh Valley," black. *$20–$25*

LI No. 2458 Box Car, black metal, 1947. *$5–$10*

LI No. 2458X Box Car, "Pennsylvania," Tuscan and maroon, 1947. *$35–$55*

LI No. 2460 Erie Crane, 12 wheels, black, 1946–1950. *$75–$100*

LI No. 2460 Tank Car, "Sunoco," double-dome, silver, 1946–1948. *$10–$15*

LI No. 2472 Caboose, Pennsylvania R.R., without light, die-cast, 1945–1947. *$25–$30*

LI No. 2555 Tank Car, "Sunoco," with decal, 1946–1948. *$35–$40*

LI No. 2434 "Newark" Pullman, silver with red lettering, 1954–1958.   *$35–$50*

LI No. 2435 "Elizabeth" Pullman, silver, red lettering, 1954–1958.
$35–$50

LI No. 2446 "Summit" Observation Car, silver, red lettering, 1954–1958.   *$40–$60*

LI No. 2454 Pennsylvania Box Car, 1945–1946.   *$50–$75*

LI No. 2454, same as above, "Baby Ruth" with Pennsylvania R.R. logo, 1946.   *$20–$25*

LI No. 2460 "Bucyrus" Erie Crane Car, 12 wheels, 1946–1960.
$65–$85

LI No. 2481 "Plainfield" Pullman, yellow, gray with red stripes, illuminated, 1950. (Anniversary Set)   *$125–$150*

LI No. 2482 "Westfield" Pullman, same colors as above, 1950. (Anniversary Set)   *$125–$150*

LI No. 2483 "Livingston" Observation Car, same colors as above, 1950. (Anniversary Set)   *$125–$150*

LI No. 2521 "President McKinley" Observation Car, aluminum shell, gold stripe with McKinley's name, Super O gauge, illuminated, 1962–1966.   *$100–$125*

LI No. 2522 "President Harrison" Vista Dome, aluminum with gold stripe, lettering, 1962–1966.   *$100–$125*

LI No. 2523 "President Garfield" Pullman, same as above.
$100–$125

LI No. 2541 "Alexander Hamilton" Observation Car, aluminum with brown stripes, illuminated, 1955–1956.   *$110–$135*

LI No. 2542 "Betsy Ross" Vista Dome, same as above, 1955–1956.   *$110–$135*

LI No. 2543 "William Penn," same as above, 1955–1956.
$110–$135

LI No. 2544 "Molly Pitcher" Pullman, same as above, 1955–1956.
$110–$135

LI No. 2550 B & O Diesel-Powered Baggage Mail Car, Budd prototype, matches motorized Budd No. 404, silver with blue lettering, 1957–1958.
$250–$275

LI No. 2551 "Banff Park" Observation Car, aluminum, pair of brown stripes, Canadian Pacific, illuminated, 1957.
$150–$200

LI No. 2552 "Skyline 500" Vista Dome, Super O gauge, 1957.
$150–$160

LI No. 2553 "Blair Manor" Pullman, Super O gauge, 1957.
$175–$200

LI No. 2554 "Craig Manor" Pullman, same as above, 1957.
$200–$235

LI No. 2559 B & O Diesel-Powered Passenger Car, silver with blue lettering, 1957–1958.
$225–$250

LI No. 2625 "Madison," "Manhattan" or "Irvington" Pullman, Tuscan, 12 wheels, 1946–1947. Each
$150–$175

LI Nos. 2627, 2628, "Madison" and "Manhattan" Pullmans, 12 wheels, Tuscan Bakelite, 1946–1947. Each
$150–$175

LI No. X2758 Pennsylvania R.R. Box Car, Tuscan, 1945-1946.
$35–$40

LI No. X2954 Pennsylvania Scale Box Car, Tuscan, 1941–1942.
$250–$300

LI No. 2955 "Sunoco" 1-D Tank Car, black, 1940–1942, 1946.
$275–$300

LI No. 2956 B & O Scale Hopper Car, black, 1946.   *$300–$350*

LI No. 2957 "NYC" Scale Caboose, Tuscan, 1946.   *$225–$250*

LI No. 3309 Turbo Missile Launch Car, 1960.   *$35–$45*

LI No. 3330 Flat Car With Submarine Kit, 1960–1962. *$50–$60*

LI No. 3349 Turbo Missile Launching Car, blue, O gauge, 1960.
$35–$45

LI No. 3349 Jet Cat, with turbo rocket, spring mechanism on deck, 1960.   *$20–$25*

LI No. 3356 Horse Car Set, with corral, horses, and ramp, 1956.
$50–$60

LI No. 3357 Maintenance Car, hydraulic platform and figures, 1962.   *$40–$50*

LI No. 3360 Burro Crane Car, black, 1956.   *$175–$200*

LI No. 3360 Operating Burro Crane, yellow cab and boom, motorized, 1956–1957.   *$200–$225*

LI No. 3366 Circus Car Corral Set, 1959–1962.   *$150–$175*

LI No. 3366 Circus Car, white, nine horses and corral, 1959–1962.
Value Indeterminate

LI No. 3370 Western & Atlantic Outlaw Car, green, 1961–1964.
$50–$75

LI No. 3376 Zoo Car, "Bronx Zoo," 1960.   *$35–$40*

LI No. 3376 Zoo Car, "Bronx Zoo," operating giraffe activator unit, blue, includes track trips, poles, etc., 1960–1969. *$75–$100*

LI No. 3376, same as above, in green stock car.   *$85–$110*

LI No. 3386 Zoo Car, "Bronx Zoo," 1960.   *$45–$50*

LI No. 3413 Mercury Capsule Car (Launching Car), red flat with gray helicopter, 1962–1964. $50–$75

LI No. 3419 Helicopter Car With Helicopter, with windup wheel, 1959. $30–$35

LI No. 3428 U.S. Mail Operating Box Car, red, white, blue, man figure with mail bag, 1959. $25–$35

LI No. 3429 U.S.M.C. Helicopter Car, olive, 1960. $75–$85

LI No. 3434 Poultry Dispatch Car, brown, man figure sweeps at stock car door, 1959–1960, 1965–1966. $75–$100

LI No. 3435 Traveling Aquarium Car, green with four clear windows, fish revolve on pair of spindles, 1959–1962. $80–$100

LI No. 3435, same as above, with green box marked "Tank 1" and "Tank 2" in gilt. $100–$125

LI No. 3444 Erie Animated Gondola, red, railroad cop pursues hobo around freight load, 1957–1959. $50–$75

LI No. 3451 Operating Lumber Car, with log stakes, black platform, 1946–1947. $25–$35

LI No. 3454 Pennsylvania R.R. Operating Merchandise Car, silver, releases five brown cubes, 1946–1947. $75–$85

LI No. 3462 Milk Car, automatic, white, man figure with five milk cans, 1947–1948. $50–$75

LI No. 3494/550 Monon Operating Box Car, maroon with white stripe, plunger mechanism, 1957. $175–$225

LI No. 3494/625 Soo Operating Box Car, Tuscan, plunger mechanism, 1957. $175–$225

LI No. 3512 Fireman Ladder Car, red frame and structure, black ladders, 1959–1961. $65–$75

LI No. 3512, same as above, with silver ladders.   *$75–$85*

LI No. 3530 General Motors Electro Mobile Generator Car, blue with white trim, 1956–1958.   *$50–$75*

LI No. 3530 Searchlight Car, with base and pole, gray, orange.
          $50–$75

LI No. 3535 A.E.C. Security Car, red with white lettering, gray gun and rotating searchlight, 1960–1961.   *$50–$75*

LI No. 3540 Operating Radar Car, red flat, gray structure, yellow radar scope, silver revolving antenna, 1959–1960.   *$75–$100*

LI No. 3545 TV Monitor Car, black base, blue structure, yellow camera and monitor, two figures.   *$75–$100*

LI No. 3562-1 AT & SF Operating Barrel Car, black, wooden barrels (six), 1954.   *$50–$60*

LI No. 6014 Box Car, "Chung King," plastic and die-cast.
          $25–$35

LI No. 6014 Box Car, says "Ship It on Frisco," white and red, 1957.   *$5–$10*

LI No. 6017 Caboose, "Boston and Maine," blue and white.
          $10–$15

LI No. 6017 Caboose, "A.T.S.F.," gray.   *$25–$30*

LI No. 6024 Box Car, "Nabisco Shredded Wheat," 1957.
          $25–$30

LI No. 6025 Box Car, "Gulf Lines," with catwalk, black.
          $15–$20

LI No. 6025 Tank Car, "Gulf Oil," double tank, orange, 1956.
          $15–$20

LI No. 6032 Gondola, black, 1952.   *$5–$10*

LI No. 6035 Tank Car, says "Sunoco," gray, 1950.   *$5–$10*

LI No. 6037 Caboose, brown, 1952.   *$5–$10*

LI No. 6042 Gondola, blue.   *$10–$15*

LI No. 6042 Gondola, blue and white.   *$10–$15*

LI No. 6044 Box Car, "Airex," with catwalk and rails. *$10–$15*

LI No. 6045 Tank Car, "Cities Services," double-dome with catwalk.   *$12–$15*

LI No. 6047 Caboose, red, 1962.   *$10–$15*

LI No. 6050 Savings Bank Car, savings bank with teller window,
white, green, 1961.   *$20–$25*

LI No. 6050 Box Car, "Libby's Tomato Juice," Savings Bank Car,
1961.   *$20–$25*

LI No. 6057 Caboose, "Long Island Railway," red, 1959.
                                                       $5–$10

LI No. 6059 Caboose, "Minneapolis and St. Louis," maroon
plastic, 1961.   *$10–$15*

LI No. 6062 Gondola, with cable reels, black and white, 1959.
                                                       $20–$25

LI No. 6111 Flat Car, with log load, stamped steel gray, 1955.
                                                       $5–$10

LI No. 6112 Gondola, black, with containers, 1956.   *$5–$10*

LI No. 6112–86 Gondola, blue.   *$5–$10*

LI No. 6119 DL & W Work Caboose, red and gray, 1957.

$15–$20

LI No. 6119 Work Caboose, 1955.   *$10–$15*

LI No. 6141 Gondola, green and white.   *$10–$15*

LI No. 6162 Gondola, "New York Central," with three canisters, red, 1963.   *$5–$10*

LI No. 6176 L.V. Hopper, light yellow and black lettering, 1964.

$10–$15

LI No. 6257 Caboose, light brown.   *$5–$10*

LI No. 6257 Caboose, tile red.   *$5–$10*

LI No. 6282 Wheel Car, red.   *$20–$25*

LI No. 6315 Tank Car, "T.C.A. 18th Convention Car," orange and yellow, 1972.

$100–$110

LI No. 6343 Flat Car, barrel-type with manually operated ramp, red, gray ramp, 1961.   *$10–$12*

LI No. 6346 Covered Hopper, "Alcoa Aluminum," silver, 1956.

$25–$30

LI No. 6357 Caboose, with light, maroon, 1948.   *$5–$10*

LI No. 6357 Caboose, Tuscan and red, 1948.   *$5–$10*

LI No. 6404 Flat Car, with load of boats, gray and blue, 1961.

$40–$45

LI No. 6405 Flat Car, with piggyback yellow van, brown.

$20–$25

LI No. 6405 Horse Car, "Lionel Lines."   *$20–$25*

LI No. 6413 Mercury Capsule Car, metal platforms, silver, blue, 1962.   *$20–$25*

LI No. 6414 Evans Auto Loader, four super cars, special paint, 1955.   *$25–$30*

LI No. 6414 Auto Car, with four cars, blue and white, 1955.
$20–$25

LI No. 6414 Auto Loader, with four cars, red and gray.   *$15–$20*

LI No. 6414 Auto Loader, with four cars, yellow and turquoise.
$25–$30

LI No. 6414 Auto Loader, with red and black cars, yellow body.
$30–$35

LI No. 6415 Tank Car, "Sunoco," silver, three-dome, 1953.
$25–$30

LI No. 6417 Caboose, Pennsylvania R.R., Tuscan, 1953.
$35–$45

LI No. 6418 Girder Car, with U.S. steel girder load, straps and rails, gray, 1955.   *$45–$50*

LI No. 6424 Flat Car, with cars, red and white, 1956.   *$20–$25*

LI No. 6425 "Gulf" Tank Car, triple-dome, 1956.   *$25–$30*

LI No. 6427 Caboose, N5C-type, 1956.   *$20–$25*

LI No. 6428 Mail Car, "U.S. Mail," red, white, blue, 1960.
$25–$30

LI No. 6434 Poultry Dispatch Car, red, gray, illuminated, 1958.
$25–$30

LI No. 6436-25 L. V. Hopper, maroon, 1956.   *$20–$25*

LI No. 6436-100 L. V. Hopper, 1957.   *$20–$25*

LI No. 6437 Caboose, "Pennsylvania" with herald, Tuscan, 1961.
                                                         $20–$25

LI No. 6446 Hopper, new, gray, 1956.   *$20–$25*

LI No. 6446 Hopper, "Jack Frost Cane Sugar," 1956.   *$30–$35*

LI No. 6446-54 Covered Cement Hopper, covers and latches, new,
black, 1954.   *$30–$35*

LI No. 6446-25 Hopper, new, covered, gray, 1925.   *$25–$30*

LI No. 6448 Target Range Car, red and white, 1961.   *$10–$15*

LI No. 6452 Gondola, black.   *$5–$10*

LI No. 6454 Box Car, "New York Central," terra-cotta with Tuscan doors, 1949.   *$20–$25*

LI No. 6454 Box Car, "Erie," brown, 1950.   *$20–$25*

LI No. 6454 Box Car, "Southern Pacific," No. 027, with decal,
1950.   *$20–$25*

LI No. 6456 Hopper, "Lehigh Valley," maroon, black, gray, 1948.
                                                         $10–$15

LI No. 6457 Caboose, deluxe model, with smoke stack, tools,
ladders, maroon, 1949.   *$15–$20*

LI No. 6460 Crane Car, red cab, 1952.   *$25–$30*

LI No. 6460 Crane Car, swivel base, hook and wire, gray, 1952.
                                                         $30–$35

LI No. 6462 Gondola, "New York Central" Girl's Train, pink,
1957.   *$125–$150*

LI No. 6462-25 Gondola, red, 1954.   *$20–$25*

LI No. 6464 Great Northern Box Car.   *$45–$50*

O Gauge

LI No. 6464-1 Western Pacific Box Car, silver, 1953.   *$30–$35*

LI No. 6464-50 M & SL Box Car, maroon, 1953.   *$25–$30*

LI No. 6464-75 Rock Island Box Car, green, 1953.   *$45–$50*

LI No. 6464-225 Southern Pacific Box Car, black, red, yellow, 1954.   *$30–$35*

LI No. 6464-275 State of Maine Box Car, red, white, blue, 1955.
                                                       $30–$35

LI No. 6464-375 Central of Georgia Box Car, silver and maroon, 1956.   *$45–$55*

LI No. 6464-400 B & O Box Car, "Time Saver," orange, blue, 1956.   *$35–$40*

LI No. 6464-425 New Hampshire Box Car, black, 1956. *$25–$30*

LI No. 6464-450 Great Northern Box Car, orange, olive, 1956.
                                                       $45–$50

LI No. 6464-475 B & M Box Car, blue, black, 1957.   *$25–$30*

LI No. 6464-525 M & SL Box Car, red, 1957.   *$30–$35*

LI No. 6464-725 New Haven R.R. Box Car, black, 1962.
                                                       $25–$30

LI No. 6465 Tank Car, "Sunoco," double-dome, "027," silver, 1958.   *$5–$10*

LI No. 6465 Tank Car, "Lionel Lines," two-dome, orange, 1958.
$10–$15

LI No. 6468 New Hampshire Box Car, working doors and ramp, orange, 1956. $30–$35

LI No. 6468, same as above, B & O, blue. $25–$30

LI No. 6473 Horse Transport, with two horse figures, yellow, 1963.
$25–$30

LI No. 6476 Hopper, "Lehigh Valley," red, white letters, 1963.
$10–$15

LI No. 6511 Flat Car, with load of four pipes, red with aluminum pipes, 1953. $15–$20

LI No. 6517 Erie Caboose, with bay window, insulators, 16 wheels, red. $225–$250

LI No. 6517, same as above, "Lionel Lines," 1955. $50–$60

LI No. 6518 Transformer Car, with insulators, 16 wheels, four sets of trucks, gray frame, black transformer, 1956. $50–$60

LI No. 6519 "Allis Chalmers" Coach, orange car, 1956.
$30–$35

LI No. 6560 Crane Car, with plastic frame, black cab, gray frame, 1955. $30–$35

LI No. 6560, same as above, red cab. $25–$30

LI No. 6561 Cable Reel Car, with two spools, gray, 1953.
$25–$30

LI No. 6572 Refrigerator Car, "REA," white shell, brown roof, black lettering, 1954. $25–$30

LI No. 6572, same as above, blue lettering, "Santa Fe."

$20–$25

LI No. 6650 Missile Launch, spring action, white missiles, red, blue, black, 1959. $30–$35

LI No. 6656 Stock Car, yellow, black, 1950. $10–$15

LI No. 6801 Flat Car, with boat, red with white boat, 1957.

$20–$25

LI No. 6801, same as above, with cradle and blue boat. $20–$25

LI No. 6802 Girder Car, red flat, black bridge, 1958. $10–$15

LI No. 6803 Flat Car, with military load (tank and sound truck), red frame, two gray vehicles, 1958. $30–$40

LI No. 6805 Atomic Waste Car, "Caution: Radioactive," red frame, pari gray containers, lights under containers, 1958.

$35–$40

LI No. 6812 Track Maintenance Car, red, gray, blue or yellow platform, two figures, 1959. $25–$30

LI No. 6814 Caboose-First Aid "Rescue Unit," stretchers, oxygen tank, two figures, white, 1959. $60–$70

LI No. 6819 Flat Car, with gray helicopter, red frame, 1959.

$15–$20

LI No. 6821 Flat Car, with load of crates, red frame, tan crates, 1959. $15–$20

LI No. 6822 Searchlight Car, swivel base, red frame, gray light, blue figure, 1961. $25–$30

LI No. 6825 Trestle Car, flat with arched bridge, red frame, black or gray bridge, 1959. $15–$20

LI No. 6826 Flat Car, with load of Yule trees, red frame, green trees, 1959.   *$25–$30*

LI No. 9161 Caboose, "Canadian National NSC," black trucks, 1971–1972.   *$30–$40*

Accessories/Lineside Equipment

Prewar

LI No. 025 Bumper, 1925–1942.   *$5–$10*

LI No. 068 Railroad Crossing Sign.   *$5–$10*

LI No. 069 Railroad Crossing Signal, 1921–1942.   *$20–$30*

LI No. 45 Gateman, automatic, with signal, 1935–1942. *$20–$30*

LI No. 65 Whistle, 1935.   *$5–$10*

LI No. 67 Whistle Controller, 1936–1939.   *$10–$15*

LI No. 78 Train Control, automatic, with lights.   *$35–$50*

LI No. 81 Rheostat, 1927–1933.   *$5–$10*

LI No. 91 Circuit Breaker, 1930–1942.   *$10–$15*

LI No. 97 Coal Loader, with scoop and drawer, 1938–1942.
                    $125–$150

LI No. 99N Train Control, automatic, 1939–1942.   *$75–$100*

LI No. 122 Station, chimney lit, benches, dome.   *$100–$125*

LI No. 126 "Lionelsville" Station, one chimney, base, 1923–1936.
                    $75–$100

"Lionel City Station," 1930s, $100-$125.

LI No. 140 Swinging Banjo Signal, 1954–1966.   *$10–$15*

LI No. 145 Gateman, automatic action.   *$15–$20*

LI No. 153 Block Signal, 1940–1942.   *$15–$20*

LI No. 153C Contractor, 1940.   *$5–$10*

LI No. 175 Rocket Launcher, spring action, 1958–1960.

$110–$125

LI No. 191 Villa, lighted, 1923.   *$100–$125*

LI No. 196 Accessory Set, Standard O gauge, station, telegraph, semaphore, warning signal, two lamp posts (individual Nos. 127, 60, 62, 68, 58 in that order), 1927.   *$200–$225*

LI No. 200 Turntable, Standard gauge, green, tan, 17 in. dia., 1928.   *$125–$150*

LI No. 270 Single-Span Bridge, Standard gauge, red or maroon, 1931.   *$25–$30*

LI No. 271 Two-Span Bridge, Standard gauge, 1931.   *$35–$40*

Lionel Standard-gauge No. 300 ''Hell Gate'' bridge, orange, cream, green, lotted with miscellaneous accessories, $1,100 at Sotheby's 1986 Bidonde Sale. (Courtesy of Sotheby's, New York)

LI No. 272 Three-Span Bridge, Standard gauge, 1931.   *$60–$70*

LI No. 915 Curved Mountain Tunnel, O gauge, 1932, 1934–1935.
                                                    $250–$275

Uncataloged

LI Trestle Bridge, gauge 2⁷/₈, cast iron, with strip steel track, wood ties, 24 in. 1., 1903.   *$2,000–$2,500*

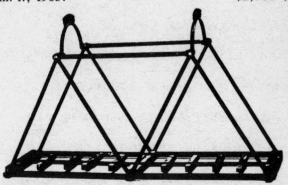

Scarce Lionel 2⁷/₈-gauge cast-iron bridge, ca. 1903, steel strip track and wood ties, 24 in. 1., $2,000-plus. (Courtesy of Sotheby's, New York)

Postwar

LI No. 199 Microwave Tower, 1958–1959.   *$30–$35*

LI No. 282 Gantry Crane, O gauge, 1954.   *$100–$110*

LI No. 300 "Hell Gate" Bridge, ivory green, with orange base, 1928.   *$900–$1,000*

LI No. 300, same as above, with white, silver, and red base. (Lionel's largest, most elaborate single-span bridge.) *$1,100–$1,300*

LI No. 310 Billboard Set, with five separate inserts, O gauge, 1950–1968.   *$5–$10*

LI No. 364 Log Loader, with crane and hook, gray, O gauge, 1948–1967.   *$50–$60*

LI No. 394 Rotary Beacon, aluminum, tower frame in green or red, 1949–1953.   *$15–$20*

LI No. 440C Panel Board.   *$75–$100*

LI No. 455 Oil Derrick, red base, 1950–1954.   *$75–$85*

LI No. 455, same as above, green base.   *$85–$95*

LI No. 456 Coal Ramp, with hopper car, 1950–1955. *$100–$125*

LI No. 460 Piggyback Terminal, 1955–1957.   *$50–$60*

LI No. 462 Derrick Platform Set, 1961–1962.   *$90–$100*

LI No. 464 Lumber Mill, 1956–1960.   *$90–$100*

LI No. 465 Dispatching Station, with whistle, 1956–1957.   *$75–$85*

LI No. 497 Coaling Station, 1953–1958.   *$110–$120*

Standard Gauge: Prewar

LI No. 440N Signal Bridge, 1936.   *$250–$275*

LI No. 444 Roundhouse Section, 1932–1935.   *$1,500–$2,000*

LI No. 550 Set of Miniature Figures, six figures, 1932–1936.
                                                     $150–$160

LI No. 551 Miniature Engineer, 1932.   *$25–$30*

LI No. 552 Miniature Conductor, 1932.   *$25–$30*

LI No. 553 Miniature Porter, 1932.   *$25–$30*

LI No. 554 Miniature Passenger (Male), 1932.   *$25–$30*

LI No. 555 Miniature Passenger (Female), 1932.   *$25–$30*

LI No. 731 R.C. Switches, T-rail, "072," pair, 1935. *$150–$200*

LI No. 760 16-Piece Pack of Curved Track, 1935.
                                                      $60–$70

LI No. 771 Curved Track, T-rail, "072."   *$10–$12*

LI No. 772 Straight Track, T-rail, "072."   *$10–$12*

LI No. 773 Fish Plate Set, "072," bolts, nuts, wrench, 50 fish
plates.   *$35–$40*

LI No. 910 Grove of 11 Trees, 1932.   *$150–$160*

LI No. 911 Country Estate, No. 191 Villa with shrubs, trees, 1932.
                                                    $350–$400

LI No. 913 Bungalow and Garden, includes flowers, trees, 1940–
1942.   *$250–$300*

LI No. 914 Formal Garden Park, cream base, grass plots, flowers,
1932–1935.   *$225–$250*

LI No. 916 Tunnel, curved, 29¼ in. l., 1935.   *$135–$165*

LI No. 917 Scenic Hillside, 1932–1936.   *$175–$200*

LI No. 918, same as above.   *$175–$200*

LI No. 920 Scenic Village, 1932–1933.   *$1,000–$1,500*

LI No. 921 Scenic Park, three-piece set, small, 1932–1933.
                                                             $2,250–$2,500

LI No. 921C Center Section, Scenic Park, 1932–1933.
                                                             $1,000–$1,200

LI No. 922 Lamp Terrace, 1932–1936.   *$125–$150*

LI No. 923 Tunnel, 40¼ in. l., 1933.   *$200–$225*

LI No. 924 Tunnel (Curved), 30 in. l., ''072,'' 1935–1942.
                                                                  $110–$135

LI No. 927 Flag Plot, 1937–1942.   *$100–$125*

O Gauge: Postwar

LI No. 974 Scenery Set, 1962.   *$10–$15*

LI No. 980 Ranch Set, plastic, 14 pieces, 1960.   *$10–$12*

LI No. 982 Suburban House, plastic, 1960.   *$10–$12*

LI No. 983 Farm Set, plastic, 1960.   *$10–$12*

LI No. 984 Railroad Set, plastic, 22 pieces, 1961.   *$10–$12*

LI No. 987 Town Set, plastic, 24 pieces, 1962.   *$10–$15*

LI No. 988 Railroad Setup, 16 pieces, 1962.   *$10–$12*

LI No. HO-990 Crossing, 90 degree-HO gauge, 1958.   *$5–$10*

Lionel accessories, 1930s–1940s, lot including cross-buck highway signal, crossing gates, and water tower. Automatic gateman sold at $110 at Skinner's June 1989 Toys & Dolls Auction. (Courtesy of Skinner)

Note: Uncoupling track sets in the No. 1000 series are valued in the $5–$10 range. This also applies to transformers, with the exception of the *No. 1012 Lionel/Ives Station Transformer* at $35–$50 and *Winner Transformer Station No. 1017,* 1931, at $50–$60.

LI No. 1023 Tunnel, straight, 19 in. l., O gauge, 1934–1942.
$20–$25

Note: the *LI No. 1229–1241 220 Volt Transformers,* from 1938–1941, are all priced as follows; each $20–$25

LI/IV No. 1550 Mechanical Ives/Lionel Switches, pair, 1933.
$25–$30

Miscellaneous Transformers, Motors, and Switches: Prewar

LI T-020 90 Degree Crossing, 1962. $5–$10

LI T-022 Remote-Control Switches, O gauge, 1962. $35–$40

LI TW Transformer, 115 Watts, 1953.   *$10–$15*

LI VW Transformer, 150 Watts, 1948.   *$20–$25*

LI Z Transformer, 250 Watts, 1939–1942.   *$70–$80*

LI ZW Transformer, 275 Watts, 1939–1942.   *$75–$85*

LI A Miniature Motor, 1904.   *$110–$125*

LI B New Departure Motor, 1906–1916.   *$110–$125*

LI B, same as above, 50–75 Watts transformer, 1916–1938.
                                                         $5–$10

LI C New Departure Motor, 1906–1916.   *$110–$120*

LI D New Departure Motor, 1906–1914.   *$110–$120*

LI E New departure Motor, 1906–1914.   *$110–$120*

LI F New Departure Motor, 1906–1914.   *$110–$120*

LI G Battery Fan Motor, 1906–1914.   *$110–$120*

LI K Power Motor, 1904–1906.   *$110–$120*

LI L Power Motor, 1905.   *$110–$120*

LI M Battery Motor, 1915–1920.   *$85–$100*

LI R Battery Motor, 1915–1920.   *$85–$100*

LI R Transformer, 100 Watts, 1938–1942.   *$25–$35*

LI S Transformer, 50 Watts, 1915.   *$5–$10*

LI S Transformer, 80 Watts, 1915.   *$10–$15*

Marx Trains

Louis Marx & Company,
New York City, New
York 1919–1979
Founder: Louis Marx
(formerly with the toy
firm of Ferdinand
Strauss)
Specialty: Originally
placed orders for toys and trains with Girard Model Works,
Strauss, and C.G. Wood, who produced them under the Marx
trademark. Marx's first trains, ''The Joy Line,'' were produced
under a commission sales arrangement with Girard.

Milestones:

- ''Joy Line'' introduced in 1927 and was marketed through
  the mid-1930s.
- Mid-1930s: Marx acquired Girard and began producing its
  famous line of 6-in., tin lithographed trains.
- 1930s: Girard used a heavier stamped steel frame for ''Joy
  Line'' cars and cast-iron locomotives, both clockwork and
  electric.

- "Joy Line" stamped steel locomotives were introduced in 1932.
- The first true Marx trains after the Girard acquisition were the "Commodore Vanderbilt" locomotive and the 6-in. cars in various colors. These would continue in production into the 1970s.
- Late 1930s to 1941—Marx's finest era: Lithograph Marx tinplate trains were produced in a variety of colors, in four-wheel and eight-wheel models. This era also witnessed the introduction of the most popular of all Marx trains, the "Marx Army Train."
- Early 1940s: Marx introduced a line of 3/16-in.-scale freight cars, competing directly with American Flyer. This line was continued after World War II and well into the 1950s.
- The successful 3/16-in. passenger cars were resumed into the 1950s with a New York Central, two-tone gray, die-cast "Pacific" No. 333 locomotive and tender leading the consist.
- Marx provides a "mix" of both freight and passenger cars in a single set—a cost-cutting coup since modelers were spared the expense of additional track, transformer, etc.
- In World War II, Marx switched from toy and train production to defense work.
- At the close of the war, Marx was one of the first manufacturers to enter the plastic toy/train field. His 1948 toys proved not to be durable, and Marx quickly switched to polyethylene for added strength.
- In 1972, Louis Marx was sold to the giant Quaker Oats conglomerate for $51.3 million and the name was changed to Marx Toys. The firm produced Marx trains up to 1975. By 1976, Quaker Oats had sold out to Dunbee-Combex-Marx Ltd. Marx trains were never again to reach the market following the 1976 acquisition.

Summary: Louis Marx used mass-production techniques to aim at a broad market with low-priced toy trains, concentrating on major accounts such as Woolworths. Some of Marx's most memorable and highly coveted toy trains are the specialty variety, such as the Marx "Bunny Train," and the numerous "Mickey Mouse" variations.

"Joy Line" Trains

These mechanical or windup trains were produced for Marx by Girard Model Works in Albion, Pennsylvania, from 1927–1936. Several later models in the line were electrified.

"Joy Line" Locomotives

MX No. 101 Locomotive, cast-iron electric, headlight, model of an electric prototype 0-4-0, black, 1930–1931.   *$100–$125*

MX No. 102 Locomotive, black cast-iron with screw-on key, 1930–1931.   *$50–$60*

   2nd Version: With slip key on square shaft, 1930.   *$50–$60*

MX No. 103 Locomotive, red finish, 1933–1935.   *$55–$65*

MX No. 104 Locomotive, with sparkler, minus bell, dummy headlight, black, 1933–1935.   *$50–$60*

   2nd Version: With battery-powered headlight, 1934–1935.
                                                        $60–$70

   3rd Version: Battery powered but with bullet-shaped boiler front.   *$70–$80*

MX No. 105 Locomotive, red body, black frame, 1932–1935.
                                                        $50–$60

MX No. 106 Locomotive, electrical model, black body, red frame, 1935–1936.   *$50–$60*

MX No. 350 Locomotive, black, yellow, red, blue, mechanical, 1927–1930.   *$300–$350*

Marx "Joy Line" set made for Sears-Roebuck in 1933–1934, $75–$100.

"Joy Line" Rolling Stock

MX No. 351 Tender, "Koal Kar" and "351," yellow body, black and gilt lettering, 1927–1933. (This and the two other versions below accompany No. 350 locomotive.)   *$60–$75*

  2nd Version: Black, short body, minus numerals, 1931–1933.
                                                        $25–$30

  3rd Version: Black, long body, minus numerals, 1934–1935.
                                                        $50–$60

MX No. 352 "Venice Gondola," pale blue, 1927–1930. *$60–$70*

  2nd Version: Black frame, 1930–1934.   *$50–$60*

  3rd Version: "Bunny Express," pale green frame, 1935–1936.
                                                        $100–$125

  4th Version: "Bunny Express," pale blue frame, 1935–1936.
                                                        $100–$125

  5th Version: "Bunny Express," lavender frame, 1935–1936.
                                                        $100–$125

6th Version: Orange body, blue frame, ca. 1934.   *$75–$100*

7th Version: Red body, blue frame, ca. 1934.   *$65–$75*

MX No. 353 "Everful Tank" Tanker, gold body, red ends, blue frame, lettering and rivets in black, 1927–1930.   *$50–$75*

2nd Version: Black ends, blue frame, 1927–1930.   *$50–$75*

3rd Version: Red ends, black frame, 1930–1934.   *$50–$75*

MX No. 354 "Contractor Dump" Side Dump Car, yellow body, blue ends, blue frame, 1927–1930.   *$60–$75*

2nd Version: Black frame, 1930.   *$60–$75*

3rd Version: Blue frame but with sturdier gauge metal couplers.
    $60–$75

MX No. 355 "Hobo Rest" Box Car, blue frame, red body, lettering in gold, blue roof, 1927–1934.   *$60–$75*

2nd Version: Yellow roof, 1927–1930.   *$45–$55*

3rd Version: Black roof, 1927–1930.   *$45–$55*

4th Version: Orange roof, 1930–1934.   *$45–$55*

5th Version: Yellow roof, black frame, 1930–1934.   *$45–$55*

6th Version: Blue roof and black frame, 1930–1934.   *$44–$55*

MX No. 356 "Eagle Eye" Caboose, red body, yellow roof, black frame, 1926–1928.   *$40–$50*

2nd Version: Yellow cupola, black roof, blue frame, short frame, 1927–1930.   *$40–$50*

3rd Version: Black frame, orange roof, red body, 1930–1934.
    $35–$40

4th Version: Black frame and roof.   *$35–$40*

MX No. 357 "The Joy Line Coach," green and black frame, short blue front, black print, yellow roof, 1931.   *$80–$100*

2nd Version: Black print and rivets, red roof, 1930.   *$35–$50*

3rd Version: Black and gilt print and trim, 1931.   *$35–$50*

4th Version: Orange roof, black and gilt decoration, 1932–1934.
$25–$35

5th Version: Black print, orange roof.   *$25–$35*

MX No. 458 "The Joy Line" Observation Car, green lithograph, black detail, red roof, 1931.   *$40–$45*

2nd Version: Gold detail, red roof, 1932.   *$40–$45*

3rd Version: Same as first except for orange roof, 1932–1933.
$35–$40

4th Version: Same as third but lighted rear drumhead with "Joy Line" logo, 1934.   *$60–$75*

Locomotives and Tenders

MX No. 897 Locomotive, 0-4-0, black, gray, and white lithography, 1939.   *$30–$35*

2nd Version: Olive, black, and white lithography.   *$110–$125*

Marx No. 400 locomotive, 1953–1954, steam outline, 0-4-0, one-piece plastic injection molded boiler and cab shell, black, $10–$15.

MX No. 999 Locomotive, steam-type, die-cast construction, with tender, 2-4-2, black, 1941–1942, 1947 open-spoke pilot. *$20–$25*

2nd Version: Embossed, spoke pilot.   *$30–$40*

MX No. 1666 Locomotive, steam-type, tender, 2-4-2, plastic, black lettering on red cab.   *$35–$45*

MX No. 1666 Locomotive, steam-type, front and rear trucks, head-lights, smokes, white numbers on red cab.   *$30–$35*

MX No. 3000 Locomotive, steam-type, black or nickel cab, run-ning board, red, silver, back boiler, 1938–1941, 1946–1952.

$20–$25

2nd Version: Blue and yellow sideboards.   *$80–$90*

Articulated Streamliners

Articulated streamliners were introduced in the mid–1930s (1934–1938). Marx later brought back the M10005 locomotives and pas-senger sets, and a few Mercury versions, following World War II.

MX 100000 No. 732 "Union Pacific" Diesel, four-wheels, brown top, yellow sides, 1934–1937.   *$35–$40*

2nd Version: Green top, cream sides.   *$30–$35*

3rd Version: Maroon top, silver sides.   *$30–$35*

4th Version: Olive top, yellow sides.   *$45–$50*

5th Version: Tan top, lighter tan sides.   *$40–$45*

6th Version: Tan top, yellow sides.   *$45–$50*

MX 100005 Mechanical or Electric Locomotive, cream with green and orange trim, orange cowcatcher, green grille, mechanical, 1936–1940.   *$25–$30*

2nd Version: Orange grille, green cowcatcher, electric, 1940.

$25–$30

1954 Marx accessory catalog features No. 1895E locomotive with No. 4551 "Santa Fe" tender.

3rd Version: *MX No. 735 Mechanical Locomotive,* brown and yellow, red trim and grille, 1948–1950.   *$30–$35*

4th Version: Orange trim and grille.   *$30–$35*

MX No. 791 Mechanical or Electric Locomotive, silver and red with blue trim, electric two-wheel motor, 1940, 1948–1952.

$25–$30

2nd Version: Electric, four-wheel motor.   *$25–$30*

3rd Version: Mechanical, 1948–1952.   *$25–$30*

MX No. 735D Mechanical Locomotive, with dummy, yellow with brown and orange trim, 1951–1953.   *$60–$70*

MX No. 732 GM Mechanical Locomotive, cream with green and orange trim, green grille, orange cowcatcher, 1937–1940, 1948.

$25–$30

2nd Version: Orange grille with green cowcatcher, 1948.

$25–$30

MX No. 732 GMD Union Pacific, electric, white with green and orange trim, green cowcatcher, streamliner coupler, 1948.

$25–$30

2nd Version: Freight coupler. $25–$30

Passenger Coaches for M100000 Power Car Sets

MX No. 657 Union Pacific Coach, four-wheel, brown roof, yellow body, 1934–1937. $30–$35

2nd Version: Green roof, cream body. $20–$25

3rd Version: Maroon roof, silver body, two- or four-wheel.

$20–$25

4th Version: Olive roof, yellow body. $35–$40

5th Version: Tan roof, lighter tan body. $25–$30

6th Version: Tan roof, yellow body. $35–$40

Long Articulated Versions

MX No. 658 Union Pacific Coach Buffet Observation Car, illuminated or nonilluminated jewels, brown roof, yellow body, 1934–1937. $30–$35

2nd Version: Green roof, cream sides. $20–$25

3rd Version: Maroon roof, silver body. $20–$25

4th Version: Olive roof, yellow body. $35–$40

5th Version: Two-tone tan. $25–$30

6th Version: Tan roof, yellow body. $35–$40

Short Articulated Versions, Two-Wheeled

MX No. 657G Union Pacific Passenger Coach, cream with green roof, orange trim, marked "RPO-REA" or "RPO-UP," 1936–1940. $15–$20

2nd Version: "Denver" coach.   *$15–$20*

3rd Version: "Los Angeles" coach.   *$15–$20*

4th Version: "Omaha" coach.   *$15–$20*

Short Articulated Passenger Coaches for M10005 Power Car and Mercury Sets

MX No. 658G Union Pacific "Squaw Bonnet" Observation Car, cream body, green roof, orange trim.   *$15–$20*

MX No. 757 M10005 Union Pacific Coach, marked "RPO-REA" or "RPO-UP," yellow body, brown roof, orange trim, 1937–1940.
$15–$20

2nd Version: "Denver."   *$15–$20*

3rd Version: "Los Angeles."   *$15–$20*

4th Version: "Omaha."   *$15–$20*

5th Version: "Diner" (uncommon).   *$100–$125*

MX No. 757A Coach, with numerous variations similar to No. 757, 1948–1950.   *$10–$15*

MX Nos. 657, 657CQ, 657RA, 658, 658CQ, 658RA Passenger Coaches for Marx Mercury Sets.   *$15–$20*

Rolling Stock, Six-Inch, Four-Wheel

Baggage/Express/Mail Cars

MX No. 547 New York Central Baggage Car, red body with black lettering, red runners, 1936.   *$50–$60*

2nd Version: Silver lettering, black runners.   *$35–$40*

Note: There are several other variations, all in the $35–$40 range.

MX No. 1935 "U.S. Mail Car," New York Central, green body and runners.   *$50-$60*

2nd Version: Same as above, but red runners, 1937. *$60-$70*

3rd Version: Red body, yellow lettering, red runners.

$40-$50

MX No. 1011-5026 New York Central, blue/gray body, 1957.

$40-$50

Box Cars

Note: All with black runners and sliding doors except when noted.

MX No. 4485-45, Bangor & Aroostook R.R. "State of Maine Products," red, white, blue, solid doors, ca. 1960.   *$15-$20*

MX No. 37960-37975 Pennsylvania R.R. "Merchandise Service," gray/red, solid doors, 1954.   *$10-$15*

MX No. 46010 St. Louis Southwestern "Cotton Belt Route," seven variations in color, 1940. Each   *$40-$50*

MX No. 51998 Canadian & Northwest "400 Streamliners," 1939–1940, 1955; seven variations in color, 1939–1940, 1955. Each   *$30-$40*

MX No. 90171 Bessemer & Lake Erie, solid or sliding lithographed doors, 11 variations in color. Each   *$20-$30*

Exception: Orange with white lettering.   *$40-$50*

MX No. 174580-1744595 New York Central "Pacemaker," red/gray, white and black trim, sliding doors.   *$30-$35*

MX No. 384299 Baltimore & Ohio, seven variations in color, 1940, 1954–1955, 1957. Each   *$25-$40*

Uncataloged

MX *Pennsylvania R.R. "Merchandise Service,"* same as No. 37960, 1965.   *$10–$15*

Cabooses

MX *No. 556 New York Central*, red with white lettering, numerous variations. Most   *$5–$10*

  Illuminated versions.   *$35–$40*

MX *No. 694 New York Central*, dark red, with variations.
                                                     $10–$15

MX *No. 956 Seaboard Air Lines*, green and yellow.   *$30–$35*

MX *No. 3824 Union Pacific*, yellow and brown body, orange lettering, brown frame.   *$20–$25*

  2nd Version: Black frame.   *$10–$15*

MX *No. 5563 Kansas City Southern*, yellow, red, black. *$60–$70*

MX *No. 20102 New York Central*, gray and red, illuminated.
                                                     $30–$35

  2nd Version: Nonilluminated.   *$5–$10*

MX *No. 31055 Monon*, gray and red, red cupola.   *$40–$50*

Work Cars and Flat Cars

MX *No. 550B New York Central Wrecker*, orange cab and frame, red platform (pivoting) and boom.   *$25–$30*

  Several variations of above.   *$15–$30*

MX No. 559 Double Floodlight Car, five versions on a value scale.
$15–$50

MX No. 562B Flat Car, with dump and stake trucks in a number of variations. $15–$50

MX No. 563 Lumber Car, U-stakes, load of four pieces of square lumber. $20–$25

MX No. 566B Cable Car, wood reel with rope simulating cable, black car. $30–$35

MX No. 563B Airplane Car, including plane, black car with red plane. $90–$100

2nd Version: Blue airplane. $110–$125

3rd Version: Yellow airplane. $110–$125

MX No. 574 Barrel Car, wire rail, seven wooden barrels, black car. $30–$40

MX No. 663B Pole Car, U-stakes, 15 sticks of dowel (lumber).
$20–$25

MX No. 2561 Searchlight Car, with single large red light, red deck.
$15–$20

2nd Version: Plastic light. $15–$20

3rd Version: Same as first but black deck. $30–$35

4th Version: Copper light/deck. $35–$40

Uncataloged

MX Rail Cars (Pair), U-stake, load of rails, black cars.
$110–$120

MX Wheel Car, with load of wheels, red over black embossed frame, several other variations. $45–$50

Gondolas

MX No. 548 Chicago, Rhode Island & Pacific "Guernsey Milk" Car, turquoise, cream wood cans in pasteboard insert, 1935–1940.
$55–$60

MX No. 552 CRI & P, with a number of decorative and color variations. $5–$10

Exception: A black litho, detailed and lettered version with green exterior. $25–$30

MX No. 552G CRI & P, "Groceries & Sundries," with box load, yellow, brown. $50–$60

MX No. 91257 Seaboard Air Lines, black interior, brown exterior, 1957. $12–$15

2nd Version: Red exterior. $8–$10

3rd Version: Dark blue exterior. $30–$35

MX No. 241708 B & O, yellow exterior, red interior, also gray or black interior color variations, 1953. Each $5–$10

High-Sided Gondolas

MX No. 554 Northern Pacific "General Coal Company," yellow/red, color variations, 1938–1940, 1946, 1950. Each $10–$15

MX No. 28500 Lehigh Valley, green and silver, 1953, 1960.
$5–$10

MX No. 86000 Delaware Lackawanna & Western, iridescent red, blue, 1956. $30–$35

MX No. 738701 Pennsylvania R.R., Tuscan with several color variations, 1940, 1952. Each $8–$12

Hopper Cars

MX No. 554 Northern Pacific "General Coal Co.," blue, red with white lettering, six variations, 1937–3938. Each   *$10–$15*

   Exception: Same as first but silver frame.   *$15–$20*

MX No. 1678 Northern Pacific "General Coal Co.," olive, bronze, and red, 1936.   *$10–$15*

MX No. 8600 DLW "Lackawanna," red interior, blue iridescent exterior, 1953.   *$8–$10*

   2nd Version: Pale iridescent blue.   *$8–$10*

MX No. 738701 PRR "Pennsylvania," Tuscan throughout, several variations, 1940. Each   *$5–$10*

Military

   Note: All models below feature olive drab frames.

MX No. 552M "Ordinance Dept." Gondola, olive lithograph body, 1939–1941.   *$35–$40*

   2nd Version: With load of bullets.   *$100–$110*

   3rd Version: With large and small ammo in cardboard insert.   *$110–$115*

MX No. 557M Army Supply Train Coach: "Radio Car," olive litho body with roof antennae.   *$25–$35*

   2nd Version: Minus antennae.   *$35–$40*

MX No. 558M Army Supply Train: "Official Car" Observation Car, olive litho, illuminated with brass end railing.   *$30–$35*

   Several variations. Each   *$30–$35*

Marx military tender No. 500, 1940, olive, gold, $25–$35.

MX No. 561M Searchlight Car, olive, numerous variations, 1939–1941. Each   *$30–$35*

MX No. 572 Field Gun Car.   *$30–$35*

MX No. 572A Flat Car, with olive or red airplane.   *$80–$100*

MX No. 572A Flat Car, dump truck or canopy truck, olive.   *$70–$80*

MX No. 572G Seige Gun (Cannon) Car.   *$50–$60*

MX No. 572M Flat Car, six gray plastic loads, 1940 and 1957.   *$40–$50*

MX No. 572AA Anti-Aircraft Gun Car, olive.   *$50–$60*

MX No. 572MG Machine Gun Car.   *$50–$60*

MX No. 572ST Flat Car With Tank, Rollover No. 5 Version, olive, red, and yellow lithography.   *$110–$120*

    Sparking tank variations (three).   *$50–$75*

Passenger Cars

MX No. 201 ''Observation'' Pullman, red.   *$35–$40*

MX No. 245 "Bogota" Pullman, red.   *$25–$30*

MX No. 246 "Montclair" Pullman, red.   *$25–$30*

MX No. 247 Canadian Pacific R.R. "Montreal" Coach, plus Nos. 248 "Quebec," 249 "Ottawa," 250 "Winnipeg," 251 "Vancouver," 252 "Calgary," and 253 "Hamilton," all in wine/maroon. Each   *$60–$80*

MX No. 2071 New York Central Coach, silver.   *$35–$40*

MX No. 2072 New York Central Observation Car, silver.
                                                        $35–$40

Refrigerator Cars

MX No. 555 Colorado & Southern Refrigerator Car, cream door and body, variations, 1937–1942, 1953–1954.

  Man in door, red roof, and man in door, red roof, silver frame (both uncommon). Each   *$160–$180*

  Man in door, blue roof, and man in door, blue roof, silver frame. Each   *$85–$100*

  Sliding-door versions without men. Each   *$15–$25*

MX Nos. 10961–10976 "Fruit Grower's Express," with yellow sliding doors, gray roof, 1940–1949, 1954–1956.   *$40–$50*

MX No. 91453 Colorado & Southern Refrigerator Car, yellow sliding doors, black or yellow runners, 1936–1938. Each   *$10–$15*

Side Dump Cars

MX No. 567 New York Central Side Dumping Car, yellow and dark brown, copper deck.   *$10–$12*

  2nd Version: Tan interior, copper deck.   *$10–$12*

3rd Version: Brown throughout. *$35–$40*

4th Version: Same as second with red litho frame. *$30–$35*

Stock Cars

MX No. 59 Union Pacific Stock Car, Tuscan, red or black guides, red and white lettering. *$10–$15*

2nd Version: Same as above, but with slotted car sides.

$25–$30

Tank Cars

MX No. 553 Santa Fe, with black lettering, flat or dome ends, yellow or silver tanks, numerous variations. Each *$10–$12*

MX No. 553 "Sinclair," tin dome and ends or black dome and ends. *$15–$20*

MX No. 19847 "Sinclair," black tank and dome ends. *$15–$20*

2nd Version: Green tank, green dome and ends. *$35–$40*

Note: Marx 6-in., 8-wheel cars tend to run 15 to 20% higher than the four-wheel rolling stock. With a few minor exceptions, for example, the No. 1476 Mickey Mouse Train (see "Cartoon/Character Novelty Train Sets"), we are not listing the 7-in., four-wheel Marx rolling stock, most of which is priced under $10.

Rolling Stock, Other

MX "Allstate Motor Oil" Tank Car, trucks, dome tank, blue (uncataloged). *$15–$20*

MX "Allstate Motor Oil" Tank Car, triple dome, die-cast wheels, blue (uncataloged). *$15–$20*

MX No. 4427 ATSF Caboose, die-cast wheels, red. *$10–$12*

MX No. 4427 ATSF Caboose, stamped steel, Tuscan. *$10–$12*

MX ATSF Caboose, working style, die-cast wheels. *$10–$12*

MX No. 467110 Baltimore and Ohio Box Car, simulated trucks, red and silver. *$10–$12*

MX No. 467110 Baltimore and Ohio Box Car, simulated four-wheel, red with white lettering. *$5–$10*

MX No. 241708 Baltimore and Ohio Gondola, four-wheel, red and green. *$5–$10*

MX No. 241708 Baltimore and Ohio Gondola, metal, lithographed, yellow and red. *$5–$10*

MX No. 241708 Baltimore and Ohio Gondola, steel, red. *$5–$10*

MX No. 4581 B.K.X. Car, with searchlight, working with generated red light. *$20–$25*

MX "Bogata" Pullman, die-cast, blue with white windows. *$15–$20*

MX No. 77003 Boston and Maine Car, die-cast wheels, plastic body, blue with silver trim. *$10–$12*

MX No. 4566 Cable Reel Car, die-cast wheels, single gray spool, blue. *$12–$15*

MX No. 956 Caboose, nickel plate, four-wheel, red "C.B. and Q" flat car, No. 5545, die-cast wheels, frame, blue. *$5–$10*

MX No. 552 "Lehigh Valley" Gondola, four-wheel, green and silver. *$5–$10*

MX No. 249319 (Marlines) Box Car, die-cast trucks, sliding doors. *$8–$10*

MX No. 553 "Middle States" Oil Tanker, four-wheel, red and silver. $5–$10

MX "Middle States" Tanker, four-wheel, with coupler, silver. $5–$10

MX "Missouri Pacific" Cattle Car, die-cast wheels, operating type, red. $10–$15

MX No. 540999 "Missouri Pacific" Stock Car, tin wheels, red. $5–$10

MX No. 350 "Monon" Caboose, with smokestack, die-cast frame, red. $15–$20

MX No. 5014 New York Central Baggage Car, lithographed, blue and gray. $25–$30

MX No. 694 New York Central Caboose, black frame, lithographed. $10–$15

MX New York Central Caboose, plastic, four-wheel, red. $5–$10

MX No. 20102 New York Central Caboose, four-wheel, red and gray. $5–$10

MX No. 20102 New York Central Caboose, red and blue. $5–$10

MX No. 556 New York Central Caboose, "Marx" logo with herald, red and black. $5–$10

MX No. 18326 New York Central Caboose, "Pacemaker," white. $5–$10

MX No. 556 New York Central Caboose, silver and blue. $5–$10

MX New York Central Caboose, with smokestack, stamped steel, white. $5–$10

MX No. 20102 New York Central Caboose, steel, forked couplers.
$5–$10

MX No. 18326 New York Central Caboose, with smokestack, metal and tin wheels, brown. $5–$10

MX No. 18326 New York Central Caboose, Tuscan red. $5–$10

MX No. 18326 New York Central Caboose, Tuscan. $5–$10

MX No. 18326 New York Central Caboose, with smokestack.
$5–$10

MX New York Central Caboose, with smokestack, four-wheel, simulated eight-wheel, magenta. $5–$10

MX New York Central Coffin Tender, four-wheel, gray with silver band. $5–$10

MX New York Central Coffin Tender, four wheels, lithographed.
$5–$10

MX No. 2532 "Cities Services" Tank, light wheel type, die-cast wheels, blue and white. $5–$7

MX No. 2532 "Cities Services" Tank Car, stamped steel. $5–$10

MX No. 91453 Colorado and Southern Box Car, yellow crane car.
$5–$7

MX Revolving Cab, gears, die-cast frame and wheels. $15–$20

MX No. 5526 C.R.I.P. Box Car, "Groceries and Sundries," yellow. $10–$15

MX No. 552 CRI&P Gondola, four-wheel, red, green. $5–$7

MX CSOX Tanker, single-dome, says "Cities Services," stamped-steel trucks. $5–$10

MX No. 4528 Erie Flat Car, with two wheels, 10 wheels. *$5–$7*

MX No. 51170 Erie Gondola, fold-down ends, black. *$10–$15*

MX No. 51170 Erie Gondola, fold-down ends, dark blue.
$15–$20

MX No. 51170 Erie Gondola, fold-down ends, die-cast wheels.
$5–$10

MX No. 51170 Erie Gondola, no ends, die-cast wheels, black.
$5–$10

MX No. 51170 Erie Gondola, removable ends, blue. *$5–$10*

MX No. 51170 Erie Gondola, stamped steel. *$5–$10*

MX No. 333 "Hudson" Steam-Type, with "Santa Fe" tender, electric motor. *$30–$50*

MX Illinois Central Switcher, "Gulf States," electric motor, red and white. *$20–$30*

MX "Los Angeles" Coach, cream and green. *$10–$15*

MX No. 21913 "Lehigh Valley" Hopper, simulated four-wheel, black with yellow letters. *$5–$10*

MX No. 21913 "Lehigh Valley" Hopper, simulated four-wheel, white with yellow lettering. *$10–$15*

MX No. 715100 New York Central Gondola, plastic, blue. *$5–$10*

MX No. 715100 New York Central Gondola, simulated four-wheel, blue with white lettering. *$5–$10*

MX No. 20120 "New York Central Pacemaker" Caboose, simulated wheels, school bus yellow. *$5–$10*

MX No. 20120 New York Central "Pacemaker" Caboose, steel, four-wheel, yellow and white.   *$5–$10*

MX New York Central Tender, with coal load, four-wheel, black.
$5–$10

MX New York Central Tender, plastic, four-wheel.   *$5–$10*

MX New York Central Tender, slope-back, with load, black.
$5–$10

MX New York Central Tender, tin construction, lithographed, silver, blue.   *$5–$10*

MX Northern Pacific Hopper, "General Coal Co.," blue, red.
$10–$12

MX No. 554 Northern Pacific Tender, "General Coal," red, yellow.   *$5–$10*

MX Observation Car, opening doors, lithographed, red. *$30–$35*

MX "Pacemaker" Caboose, smokestack, four-wheel, orange.
$5–$10

MX "Pacemaker" Caboose, smokestack, simulated eight-wheel, lithographed.   *$5–$10*

MX No. 43461 "Pacific Fruit" Express Box Car, catwalks, lithographed.   *$5–$10*

MX No. 43463 "Pacific Fruit" Express Closed Car, doors and catwalk.   *$5–$10*

MX "Pacific Fruit" Express Flat Car, doors, rails, red, white.
$5–$10

MX No. 18326 "Penn Central" Caboose, smokestack, jade green.
$5–$10

MX No. 347100 Pennsylvania Gondola, steel, gray. $5–$10

MX No. 34170 Pennsylvania Gondola, light gray, white. $5–$10

MX No. 347100 Pennsylvania Gondola, silver. $5–$10

MX No. 37956 Pennsylvania Merchandise Service Box Car, four-wheel, barn red. $5–$10

MX No. 92812 Reading Caboose, simulated wheels. $5–$10

MX No. 246 Rocket Fuel Tank Car, simulated four-wheel, white.
$5–$10

MX No. 147815 Rock Island Box Car, doors and railings, catwalk.
$5–$10

MX No. 17858 Rock Island Caboose, die-cast wheels, maroon.
$5–$10

MX No. 3280 Santa Fe Box Car, catwalk and railing, orange, white.
$5–$10

MX No. 13975 Santa Fe Cattle Car, catwalk, fence frame, brown.
$5–$10

MX No. 1998 Santa Fe 4 Switcher, die-cast frame, electric motor.
$15–$20

MX No. 13975 Santa Fe Stock Car, high side, brown. $10–$12

MX No. 13975 Santa Fe Stock Car, die-cast, Tuscan. $5–$10

MX Santa Fe Tanker, "Middle States Oil." $5–$10

MX No. 91257 Seaboard Gondola, red, black. $7–$10

MX No. 1998 Union Pacific Switcher, die-cast frame, motor, head-lights, white and gray. $25–$30

MX Union Pacific Switcher, horns, handrails, electric, die-cast frame, wheels.   *$30–$35*

MX No. 6000 Southern AA, snub nose, "ALCO," orange, silver.
$20–$25

MX No. 51100 Southern Auto Carrier, carload, die-cast wheels, rack.   *$10–$15*

MX No. 51100 Southern Flat Car, die-cast wheels, maroon.
$5–$10

MX No. 51100 Southern Flat Car, die-cast wheels, white.   *$5–$10*

MX Southern Pacific Caboose, die-cast wheels, Tuscan.   *$5–$10*

MX No. 1235 Southern Pacific Caboose, blue, red.   *$5–$10*

MX No. 9100 Union Pacific Box Car, "Challenger," die-cast frame, wheels, black, red.   *$15–$20*

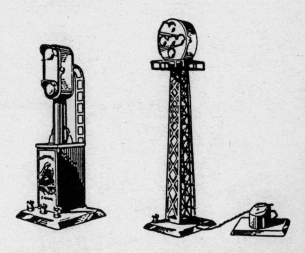

Marx No. 1402 block signal with remote control, No. 1404 position light block sign with chrome face, $10–$15 and $15–$20 respectively.

Marx No. 1600 "Glendale Depot" and No. 1430 Union Station with battery-operated crossing gates, $25–$35 and $10–$15 respectively.

Marx No. 2940 Grand Central Station, ca. 1939, yellow, buff litho with swinging doors, illuminated interior, 10¾ in. h. × 17 in. l., $75–$100.

MX No. 3900 Union Pacific Caboose, black, orange.   *$5–$10*

MX No. 3824 Union Pacific Caboose, with bay window, die-cast wheels, Tuscan.   *$15–$20*

MX No. 3900 Union Pacific Caboose, smokestack, orange, red.
$10–$12

MX No. 4586 Union Pacific Caboose, working type, overhung roof.
$5–$10

MX No. 3824 Union Pacific Caboose, yellow, brown.   *$5–$10*

MX No. 3824 Union Pacific Caboose, yellow, black.   *$5–$10*

MX Union Pacific Cattle Car, sliding door, lithographed on brown body.   *$10–$12*

MX Union Pacific Coffin Tender, black.   *$5–$10*

Specialty
Trains

Cartoon/Character Novelty Train Sets and Hand Cars

Novelty Train Sets

This category is one of the most highly coveted and valued in the hobby. They may be frowned upon by certain rail purists as bearing no resemblance to reality, but Disneyana and comic toy collectors place them high on their "want lists." The Marx versions, for example, rank as the most expensive trains in their line by far. This includes the infamous "Easter Rabbit Train" of 1936, which was such a resounding flop that production was halted by Marx and very few survived. The following section includes only the novelty train sets. (See also *Trolley Cars* for further examples of cartoon/character whimsey.)

"Bunny Express" Easter Rabbit Train Set, Mechanical, Marx, 1936, figural rabbit locomotive and three hopper cars (originally filled with jelly beans), appeared in several color variations: pink and blue or orange and green, hopper cars with lithographed images of pair of chicks emerging from shell. (Sold for $1,210 at Christie's Charles Gasque Collection Sale in 1986.)

$1,000–$1,500

"Mickey Mouse" Circus Train, Lionel Locomotive No. 1536, 1935, lithographed tin and steel, 7 in. 1., No. 1508 "Commodore Vanderbilt" engine, Mickey sits in No. 1509 tender, five cars in all, 30 in. 1. overall, 84 in. of track in set, locomotive: 7 in. 1.

$1,000–$1,500*

Note: Included in Circus Train Set: four-panel cardboard circus tent, "Sunoco" service station, circus truck, billboard, popout showing Mickey and Minnie running to circus, 12 circus tickets, Mickey Mouse statue (composition). Add $500–$600 if Circus Set is complete.

"Mickey Mouse" Circus Train Set, Wells O'London, England, Brimtoy, 1935, silver link engine No. 2509, "Mickey the Stoker" composition figure in coal car with swivel action for Mickey to shovel coal, circus car, band car, circus dining car, engine: 7½ in. 1., tender: 4 in. 1., cars: 6 in. 1., runs on O-gauge track.

$1,000–$1,500

"Mickey Mouse" Circus Tent (to accompany Train Set), 1935, lithographed tin, 5½ in. h., 8 in. dia. *$800–$900*

"Mickey Mouse Express," Marx, early 1940s, litho tin mechanical, Disneyland Depot included, small streamliner circles track while Mickey soars above in airplane (variation of "Popeye Express"), 9½ in. dia. *$900–$1,100*

"Mickey Mouse Liberty Special" Locomotive With "Mickey Mouse" Box Car, Lionel, 1976, four other cars. *$100–$125*

"Popeye Airplane Car," Marx, 1936, airplane with Popeye figure mounted on wire above standard "Montclair" coach No. 246, red, black, blue. *$1,000–$1,100*

"Popeye Express" With Airplane, Marx, 1937, litho tin windup, Popeye soars overhead in tiny airplane on wire, Wimpy, Olive, Sappo, and Swee' Pea circle around 9 in. dia. track in Union Pacific train. *$1,300–$1,600*

---

*A circus train set with original box, including tent (minus one flap) and missing truck, service station, sold at $5,125 at Ron Lashway's Auctions, Hadley, MA, March 4, 1990.

"Toonerville Trolley," Nifty, 1922, litho tin mechanical.

$650–$700

"Toonerville Trolley," Dent, 1929, cast iron, color variations: green with orange, red with blue, gilt-trimmed, 4 in. 1., 6 in. h.

$450–$550

"Toonerville Trolley," Kenton, 1938, HO-gauge electric, brass finish, tiny working headlight, 2½ in. h. $500–$550

"Walt Disney's Mickey Mouse Meteor Train Set," Marx, mid-1930s, litho tin mechanical, five cars, locomotive features Donald Duck and three nephews, Donald is running on the tender, multicolor, keywind, 43 in. 1. overall. $700–$800

2nd Version: Same as above but illustrates Mickey, Minnie, Goofy, and Doc (from the Seven Dwarfs). $900–$1,100

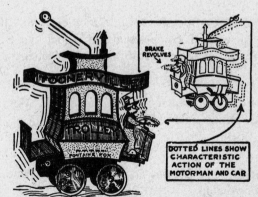

2F7010—"Toonerville Trolley," 6¾ in. high, bright colored. When wound the "Skipper" motor man starts and stops car in life-like manner and car moves with character- istic action, strong spring. ½ doz. in box. Doz **$8.00**

Catalog page for "Toonerville Trolley" tin mechanical, Nifty, 1922, $650–$700.

Hand Cars

"Barney Rubble and Fred Flintstone Bedrock" Hand Car, Marx No. 2028, 1964, windup, multicolor plastic. $50–$75

"Donald Duck and Pluto" Rail Car, Lionel No. 1107, 1936–1937, composition and steel windup, Pluto is emerging from his dog-house while Donald stands at rear, 10 in. l. $1,000–$1,200

"Easter Bunny" Hand Car, Marx (uncataloged), early 1930s, heavy pasteboard lithographed bunny and checkered basket, O-gauge flanged wheels. $300–$600

Girard Hand Car, Marx (made for Marx by Girard, uncataloged), 1933–1935, litho tin windup, two R.R. worker figures.
$150–$200

"Mickey Mouse Hand Car," English, mid-1930s, Mickey and Donald composition figures, car is litho tin with illustration of Pluto on side, comes with track and litho cardboard houses fea-turing other Disney characters, hand car: 7 in. l. $900–$1,000

"Mickey and Minnie Mouse" Hand Car, Lionel No. 1100, 1935–1937, litho tin windup, composition and rubber figures, 8 in. l., available in red, green, orange or maroon (the latter is rarest).
$800–$900

"Mickey Mouse and Donald Duck" Hand Car, Marx (uncatal-oged), 1962, plastic electrical. $50–$60

Also in tin layout. $75–$100

"Mickey Mouse and Donald Duck" Hand Car, same as above, 1964, plastic windup. $50–$60

Also in tin layout. $75–$100

"Moon Mullins and Kayo" Hand Car, Marx, early 1930s, litho tin windup, appeared in three versions:

Lionel "Mickey Mouse mechanical hand car, $800–$900. (Courtesy of Sotheby's, New York)

1st Version: Kayo sits on dynamite box, lightweight black frame, barrel spring, 6 in. 1. *$150–$200*

2nd Version: Same, but with heavy-gauge steel frame, 6 in. 1. *$200–$250*

3rd Version: Kayo stands on platform opposite Moon Mullins, heavy-gauge steel underframe, 6 in. 1. *$250–$300*

"Peter Rabbit Chick Mobile," Lionel No. 1103, 1935–1937, gauge O, cast metal and composition windup, Peter pumps hand car at one end, chick in basket on opposite end, 9 in. 1., green basket, yellow frame, white rabbit. *$900–$1,000*

"Popeye and Olive Oyl" Hand Car, Hercules Metal Line (made for Marx), 1935, tin windup with rubber figures, two versions:

1st Version: Large, tin gauge-O wheels, flanged.
$300–$400

2nd Version: Tin floor toy, flangeless. *$400–$500*

Santa Claus hand car, Lionel, 1935–1936, $1,500–$2,000. An example, with original box, sold for $3,850 at a Ron Lashway Auction in Hadley, MA, in March 1990.

Railroad Worker's Hand Car, Marx No. 2002, 1954–1974, electrical, plastic, red with blue and gray men (1955–1956).

$50–$100

Variation: Brown with blue and gray men, 1956–1974.

$35–$50

Variation: Red with yellow men. *$75–$125*

"Santa Claus" Hand Car, Lionel No. 1105, 1935–1936, gauge O, cast metal and composition windup, Santa with Mickey Mouse in sack, Christmas tree at opposite end, 9 in. 1.

$1,500–$2,000*

---

*When tree and figures are intact, original box is retained, and top condition prevails, price can go haywire, as was the case at Lashway's 1990 auction, when an example brought $3,850.

Cast-Iron Floor Trains

Cast-iron mechanical and pull toy trains first appeared in the 1880s as an almost exclusively American art form. These hefty examples brought with them a sense of realism, scale, and detail that tin forerunners lacked. Early U.S. makers included Carpenter, Ives, Wilkins, Kenton, Hubley, Secor, Dent, Stevens, Harris, and Pratt & Letchworth.

Cast-iron floor trains continued in popularity until the 1930s. Instead of replicating prototypes from the later period, most manufacturers persisted in turning out models patterned after late 19th-century classics and repeating these models year after year. For this reason, and because so many makers did not identify their trains, it is often difficult to properly place an example in time. Later models tend to reveal less care in production and lack of attention to detail. The practiced eye should be able to spot the differences.

Bay Window Switcher Locomotive, Wilkins, 1890s, painted black cast iron, 7½ in. l.   *$500–$550*

No. 6 Engine and Coal Car, Carpenter, known for its high stack, large cowcatcher, and bright red and green trim.   *$500–$550*

Cast-Iron Hand Car, articulated, possibly by Wilkins, 1890s; while unpretentious, it is an elusive toy to find; an example brought $3,000 at a Lloyd Ralston Auction several years ago.
                                                        $2,000–$3,000

First cast-iron clockwork locomotive, patented by Jerome Secor, June 8, 1980. Original model crank wound. Model shown is key wound, $1,500–$2,000.

"Clockwork Locomotive," Jerome Secor, patented 1880. (In a disputed patent rights case, Secor won out over Francis Carpenter with the first clockwork-powered cast-iron locomotive.) Patent date embossed in boiler front of black engine with gilt trim, original model was crank wound, later versions key wound.

$1,500–$2,000

"Double-Track Elevated Railway," Hubley, 1893, clockwork, circular track on platform with two train sets, one on each track, Hubley's finest toy (they also patented two versions of a single-track unit). Price indeterminate; an example brought $10,000 at the Perelman Museum Sale in 1988.   *Value Indeterminate*

"Gravity Railway," Hubley, 1893, three-section toy of irregularly curved malleable iron tracks, clockwork, two men in open gondola car, track: 4 ft. l., car: 4 in. l., 1½-gauge track.   *$2,000 plus*

"Excursion Train," Ives, 1895, 28 in. l. overall, includes engine, tender, and "President" coach with 16 passengers (early cast-iron trains rarely were made with passengers), latter car was available separately.   *$1,000–$1,500*

Camelback No. 600, Kenton 2-6-0 wheel alignment, replica of a New Jersey Central double-boiler locomotive (an unusual feature in toy trains).   *$500–$600*

The Hubley Manufacturing Company, Lancaster, Pa.

Double Track Elevated Railway.

MALLEABLE, HEAVY CAST IRON AND STEEL.

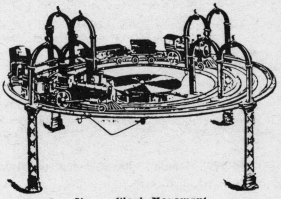

No. 4.   Clock Movement.
Pat. April 11, 1893.

Hubley "Double-Track Elevated Railway," 1893, cast iron. Price indeterminate.

Kenton "Camelback" locomotive, ca. 1912, $500–$600.

Cast-iron, five-piece parlor train set, maker unknown, 1890s, NYC & Hudson River Line, No. "154" locomotive, No. 185 baggage car and Smoking car, parlor car, metallic finish, locomotive: 12¼ in. l., $660 at Skinner's June 1989 Toys & Dolls Auction.

Locomotive No. 999, Kenton, circa 1890s, same as above except has M.C.R.R. name embossed, red, white, and blue gondolas, 48 in. l.   *$600–$650*

Locomotive No. 999,. Kenton, 1900s, tender, two stock cars, M.C.R.R. caboose, 43 in. l., cast iron.   *$650–$750*

Locomotive with No. 189 Tender and "Union Line" Freight Car, Ives, ca. 1893, 4-4-0 steam outline locomotive, black with gilt trim, whistle, bell, steam valve, jointed piston rods attached to drive wheels, black tender with numbers in relief, orange freight car with "Union Line" and "Capacity 50,000 Lbs" embossed in gilt, simulated wooden siding, 34¼ in. l. overall. *$900–$1,000*

Nickel-Plated Locomotive and "Santa Fe Railroad Granague" Passenger Train, Kenton, ca. 1923, 2-4-0 locomotive with short stack, whistle, steam valve, steel piston strips connecting rear wheels, pair of parlor cars with name embossed in relief, also observation car, 37 in. l. overall.   *$600–$700*

"999 Buffalo Express," Pratt & Letchworth, 1892, cataloged as "Vestibule Train #FFF," No. 880 locomotive with tender and two coaches, 60 in. l. overall.   *$700–$800*

"999" Railway Locomotive and "Fast Express" Passenger Train, maker unknown, ca. 1880–1920, steam outline 4-4-0, oval-cut window in cab front, ornate-cut windows on each side, "999" gilt

Ives, Blakeslee & Williams Co., 294 Broadway, New York. Factory, Bridgeport, Conn. **45**

LARGE IRON FREIGHT TRAIN.   Good Model, Fine Finish.

No. 182. Locomotive, Tender and two Freight Cars. In case. Gross weight of case. 192 lbs. 34 inches long. Measurement of case, 16 x 20 x 40 inches. Price per doz., **$12.00.**

EXTRA LARGE IRON FREIGHT TRAIN.   A Good, Salable Toy.

No. 187, EXTRA. Locomotive, Tender, three Freight Cars and three Brakemen. Three dozen in case. Gross of case, 187 lbs. 33 inches long. Measurement of case, 14 x 20 x 39 inches. Price per doz.. **$10.00.**

LARGE IRON FREIGHT TRAIN.   A Popular Toy.

No. 187. Locomotive, Tender, two Cars and two Brakemen. Three dozen in case. Gross weight of case, 210 lbs. 27 inches long. Measurement of case. 17 x 22 x 31 inches. Price per doz.. **$9.00.**

IRON FREIGHT TRAIN.

No. 185. Locomotive, Tender and one Freight Car. Three dozen in case. Gross weight of case, 152 lbs. 19 inches long. Measurement of case, 14 x 22 x 31 inches. Price per doz., **$5.00.**

THE "HERO" PASSENGER TRAIN.

No. 186. Locomotive, Tender and two Passenger Cars. Three dozen in case. Gross weight of case. 114 lbs. 14 inches long. Measurement of case. 14 x 16 x 28 inches. Price per doz., **$4.00.**

Array of large cast-iron parlor trains featured in Ives 1892 catalog.

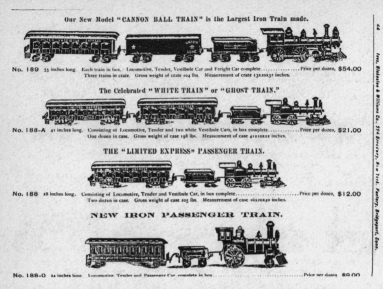

Array of large cast-iron parlor trains featured in Ives 1892 catalog.

embossed on black on tender, pair orange passenger cars with black trim and "Fast Express," orange animal cage freight car with sliding doors, 46½ in. l. overall.   *$650–$750*

No. 178 Nickel-Plated Locomotive and Lake Shore & Michigan Southern Passenger Train, maker unknown, 1880–1920, nickel-plated steam outline 4-4-0 locomotive with two arch-cut windows, nickel-plated tender with simulated rivets, four nickel-plated parlor cars with railroad name in relief, 55¾ in. l. overall.   *$800–$900*

Pair of late 19th-century cast-iron locomotives: (left) *Wilkins, and* (right) *Kenton; both black with red trim, 14 in. and 10 in. l., $600–$650 each.*

Pull-Along Black Locomotive and Tender, Wallworks, Manchester, England, ca. 1890, 4-2-2 locomotive with "1893" embossed, six-wheel tender with cast designation "Express," pair of carriages with "Wallworks Patent" in relief, tan finish, flanged wheels.

$600–$700

"Rosita" New York Central Train Set, cast iron, engine, tender, three passenger cars, 50 in. l. $650–$750

"Single-Track Elevated Railway," Hubley, 1893, 8-ft., 4-in. circular track, 2-2-0 cast-iron locomotive, steel rails, black finish, clockwork.   *Value Indeterminate*

"Single-Track Elevated Railway," same as above but steam powered.   *Value Indeterminate*

"Single-Track Elevated Railway," same as above with trolley, wire and poles, electric street car, added guard rail, 7 in. l.

Value Indeterminate

Steam Outline 4-4-0 Locomotive, Dent, ca. 1905, black with gilt trim and molded ribbing, black tender with orange and gilt molded trim, "New York Central & Hudson River" in gilt relief and eight arch-cut windows in passenger cars. $700–$800

Steam Outline Locomotive 2-4-0 and "C.P.R.R." Gondola Train With Parlor Cars, Carpenter, ca. 1890, locomotive black with gilt ribbing, cowcatcher, headlamp, and steam valve, gilt hubs, black tender plus black gondola cars with "C.P.R.R." in gilt, three porters 3 in. h. in pale blue uniforms, set on disks with hooks to attach to holes in gondolas, 29 in. l. overall. $900–$1,000

Steam Outline 4-4-0 Locomotive and "M.C.R.R." Gondola Train, Harris, ca. 1903, black with gilt cowcatcher, bell, whistle, and steam valve, two arch-cut windows, black tender with "976" in gilt relief, two yellow gondola cars with "M.C.R.R." in gilt relief, also caboose with initials again in relief, 40 in. l. overall.

$800–$900

Steam Outline 2-2-0 Locomotive and Gondola Train, Carpenter, ca. 1882, black locomotive and smokestack, two square-cut windows on rose-colored cab, rose-colored cowcatcher, gilt steam valve, orange tender plus two rose-colored gondola cars, "Patented May 25, 1880. Reissued March 14, 1882" in relief, 19 in. l. overall.   *$1,000–$1,100*

Steam Outline Locomotive With No. 189 Tender, Ives, ca. 1895, 4-4-0 wheel configuration, black locomotive with red stack, pressure and sand domes, wheels and cab trim, gilt ribbing on boiler and headlamp, black tender with No. "189" embossed in gilt over red inset, eight wheels, 23½ in. l. overall.   *$900–$1,000*

Steam Outline Locomotive, Tender, Gondola Cars, Carpenter, patented 1880, 2-2-0, black boiler and smokestack, gilt-topped pressure dome, red cab, frame, and cowcatcher, spoked wheels, open front tender, red, pair red gondolas, "Patented May 4, 1880. Reissued March 14, 1882" embossed on floor of tender and gondola undersides, 19 in. l. overall.   *$600–$700*

Steam Outline Locomotive and "Lulu" Tender, maker unknown, 1890s, black 2-2-0 locomotive with gilt trim and ribbing, rectangular-cut window at cab front, black tender with "Lulu" in gilt relief, two orange parlor cars with gilt-embossed trim, 12¼ in. l. overall.   *$650–$750*

Steam Outline Locomotive and Tender, Wilkins, ca. 1890, 4-4-0 wheel alignment, black locomotive with red smokestack, wheels, red and gilt trim, large eight-wheel tender, black, with elaborate rivet detail, pair trucks with embossed stars, patented floating action, also sold with a box car, tank car, and caboose, engine and tender: 21 in. l. overall.   *$800–$900*

Train, Locomotive, manufacturer unknown, 1890s, tender, flat car, P. & L. R.R., painted cast iron and pressed steel.   *$375–$475*

Train, Locomotive No. 152, Ideal, 1910, tender, two passenger cars, cast iron, 24 in. l.   *$400–$500*

Train, Locomotive No. 49, manufacturer unknown, 1910, tender, painted cast iron, 25 in. l.   *$300–$350*

"Wilkins' Largest Train Set," Wilkins, early 1900s, locomotive, tender, two coaches, 55 in. l. overall.   *$800–$1,000*

Pressed Steel Oversize Friction and Ride-Em Pedal Trains

Sheet Steel Trains

All-steel train engines and tenders, either of the push-pull or friction type, became widely produced in the early 1900s. In the 1920s and 1930s, Buddy "L," Keystone, Sturditoy, Dayton, Cor-Cor, Dopke, Structo, and others manufactured heavy gauge steel engines and parlor and freight cars that were oversized and often ridable.

Buddy "L"

Box Car, 1930s, painted pressed steel, 19 in. l., red.

$1,000–$1,200

Caboose, 1930s, painted pressed steel, 16 in. l., red.

$1,200–$1,500

Dredge for Railway, 1930s, painted pressed steel, 22 in.

$3,000–$3,500

Flat Car, painted pressed steel, 19 in. l., black.   *$1,500–$2,000*

Freight Car, 1930s, painted pressed steel, 19 in. l., black.
$1,000–$1,200

Gondola, painted pressed steel, 22 in. l.   *$1,200–$1,500*

Hand Car, 1929–1931, 2-in. gauge, orange.   *$900–$1,000*

Hopper, 1930s, painted pressed steel with couplers, 22 in. l., red.
$1,200–$1,500

"Improved Steam Shovel," 1930s, pressed steel, piston action on crane, on railroad flat car.   *$3,000–$4,000*

"Industrial Train Set," 1929–1931, 2-in. gauge, locomotive, rack car, rocker dump car, coal car, stake car, and ballast car, locomotive: 10¼ in. l., cars: 8 in. l., black.   *$1,000–$1,500*

Locomotive Wrecking Crane, 1930s, pressed steel, includes crane and bucket, 22 in. l.   *$2,500–$3,000*

"No. 51 Locomotive," 1929–1931, with various decals: "BL 12," "BL 14," and "BL 16," dark green, 2-in. gauge.   *$400–$450*

"New York Central" Locomotive and Tender, 1930s, pressed steel and cast iron, approx. 18 in. l.   *$1,500–$2,000*

Riding Yard Train, 1930s, engine, tender, and "35407" red box car, 63 in. l., black engine/tender.   *$1,000–$1,500*

Side-Door Hopper, 1930s, painted pressed steel, 19 in. l., green.
$1,500–$2,000

Stock Car, 1930s, painted pressed steel, 19 in. l., yellow.
$1,200–$1,500

Tank Car, 1930s, painted pressed steel, 16 in. l., yellow.
$1,000–$1,200

Buddy "L" 12-wheel locomotive riding toy, early 1930s, $900–$1,000.

Accessories

Crossing, 90 degrees, dark green.   *$30–$35*

Crossing, 60 degrees, dark green.   *$35–$40*

No. 80 Three-Stall Roundhouse and Turntable, dark green.
                                                        $325–$350

"Casey Jones" locomotive with tender, Garton Mfg. Steel with pneumatic tires: black and white; 1961 locomotive, 37 in. l.; tender: 32 in. l., $300–$400.

No. 81 One-Stall Roundhouse and Turntable, dark green.

$225–$250

R Switch No. 72, dark green. $25–$30

L Switch No. 73, dark green. $25–$30

Note: Track runs $5–$10 per section.

Other Oversize Train Manufacturers

"Cannonball Express" Pedal Car, Marx, No. 9, 1940s, steel, plastic, yellow and red. $75–$150

"Casey Jones, The Cannonball Express No. 9," 1920s, sheet metal pedal locomotive, cowcatcher and rubber wheels, bell, 22 in. h. × 15¼ in. l., red with white lettering. $500–$600

"Hill Climber" Tram, Dayton, 1920, sheet steel, friction power with large iron flywheel, with passengers, red, yellow, blue.

$125–$150

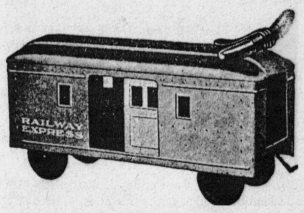

"156 Railway Express Car," maker unknown, 1937; 18 in. l., steel body, wheels, riding toy with handlebars on top; red, black, green, $400–$500.

Keystone Ride 'Em No. 6400 locomotive; red, black, $500–$600.

"Hill Climber," Dayton, 1920, 2-4-2 engine with tender, sheet steel, friction power, black, red. $250–$300

"Keystone R.R." No. 6400 Ride-Em Locomotive, Keystone, 1930s, sheet metal, steel, black boiler and frame, red cab, wheels, and trim, yellow lettering, saddle seat atop cab, wooden handlebars atop boiler. $600–$700

Marlines Ride-Em Gondola, Marx No. LM-22000, 19½ in. l., gray. ("Marlines" is Marx trade name.) $150–$200

"Rapid Transit" Trolley, maker unknown, 1920s, eight wheels, pressed steel, 20½ in. l., red with gold lettering. $300–$400

Ride-Em "Lightning Express," Marx No. 3000, 1939–1941, stamped-steel locomotive, torpedo style, Canadian Pacific-type, red or gray. $150–$300

Riding Engine/Two Cars, Cor-Cor Toys, 1930s, engine with integral tender and two Pullman coaches, 72 in. l. overall, red and black. $500–$700

Steam-Operated Floor and Track Trains

Earliest examples in this genre were simply toy steam engines designed in train form with wheels under them. In gleaming brass or chrome, their great appeal lay in the similarity to real steam trains. Steam toys and trains were produced as early as the 1860s and 1870s. In the United States, Weeden, Buckman, Garlick, and Beggs all produced superb steam-powered trains. In Europe, Bing, Carette, Märklin, Clyde Model Dockyard, Basset-Lowke, Hess, J. Bateman, Newton & Co., Rossignol, and Radiguet et Massiot all produced realistic examples. Steam trains often proved dangerous and difficult to operate. They were produced up through the 1920s, but were by then completely outmoded by the electric versions.

"Dart," Weeden, U.S., steam locomotive with tender and passenger car, tin, copper, embossed with "Dart" nameplate and rivet detail, ca. 1888.   *$1,000–$1,200*

"Dragon," maker unknown, probably English, ca. 1870, live steam, 2-2-0, II gauge, copper boiler, flaring smokestack, spoked cast-brass wheels, 9⅞ in. l.   *$450–$500*

Bing steam-powered locomotive with tender and coach, ca. 1912, $850–$900.

"1181-D" Locomotive and Tender, Bing, German, ca. 1928, live steam, blue sheet-steel boiler, cone-shaped front, front-projecting bumpers, black chassis with red trim, spoked wheels, tender with solid wheels, black with red striping. $450–$550

"Express" 2-2-2 Locomotive, Stevens Model Dockyard, Great Britain, 1880s, spirit-fired, rear-mounted oscillating cylinders, wide open cab, name embossed on boiler, brass, black, 14¾ in. l. floor train. $650–$700

"Flying Dutchman" Locomotive, Clyde Model Dockyard, Scotland, ca. 1885, live steam locomotive with 2-2-2 wheel configuration, III gauge, cast- and sheet-brass, name embossed on boiler side, 13 in. l. $500–$600

Early 1900s steam-powered locomotive, brass, probably German, $300–$350.

Garlick Live Steam Locomotive, U.S., 1888, 2-2-2, I gauge, large open tinplate cab, square front headlight, nickel-plated brass boiler, black cab, frame, red trim, 12 in. l.   *$700–$800*

"London & North-Western" Locomotive and Tender, Bateman, Great Britain, ca. 1880, 3¾ gauge, spirit-fired, steel and brass, brass safety valve, handrails, funnel, nameplate, locomotive and tender are black, red trim.   *$750–$800*

Newton 2-2-2, Newton & Co., London, 1890, steamer or "dribbler," brass, engine with tender, engraved plate on boiler.
$3,500–$4,000

"RO" Steam Locomotive, Märklin, German, 1902, gauge O, large boiler with unique fire tube running from center of boiler from cab to chimney, eccentrically driven valve gear, green, gilt, nickeled bell, valves, nameplate ("RO") on cab door, red cowcatcher, wheels, tender frame.   *$2,500–$3,000*

"Rocket 1829," Märklin, German, 1907, gauge I, locomotive, tender, three wagons, engine is red with tall smokestack, name in yellow on boiler, nickeled brass valves, black, red tender, yellow, blue, red coaches. (Sold at Sotheby's for $39,000 in 1984.)
Value Indeterminate

Steam Floor Locomotive, Schönner, German, 1892, flanged wheels but strictly floor runner, high stack, working steam pipes from steam dome to cylinder.   *$800–$1,000*

Storkleg Train Set, Carette, German, 1898, gauge I, steamer locomotive, tender, three wagons.   *$3,500–$4,000*

Tank Locomotive, Basset-Lowke, North Hampton, England, ca. 1925, live steam tank with 0-6-0 wheel configuration, hinged boiler front, cutout windows, entranceway, pair of spring-tension bumpers (operating) on front, rear, dark green with red trim, spoked wheels, heavy-gauge sheet brass, 15 in. l. (outdoor operating locomotive).   *$450–$500*

Painted tin, live steam locomotive, maker unknown, possibly English, 1890s, No. "248" on paper labels on both sides of cab, gold-colored boiler, black tender with red striping, wheels, several parts missing, some paint loss, $550 at Skinner's June Toys & Dolls Auction.

"Vulcan" Plank, German, 1895, spidery upright locomotive, swivel front wheels, brass with green painted cab and headlamps, red stripe.   *$1,200–$1,500*

Tin Clockwork
Trackless Trains

Painted tin, clockwork model trains were produced in the 1840s in Germany and France and as early as 1856 in the United States (by the firm of George W. Brown). Other major U.S. makers included Ives, Stevens & Brown, Merriam, and Hull & Stafford (all from Connecticut), and Fallows and Francis, Field & Francis (of Philadelphia). There are examples in which the clockwork mechanism was omitted and the train was sold as a simpler, less expensive pull toy. Both versions are absolutely legitimate. English, French, and German tin mechanical trains were imported to this country from the 1870s to the turn of the century. The advent of cast-iron trains spelled the end of popularity for these whimsical, highly decorated trackless gems. See ''Market Overview'' chapter for further details on tin clockwork trains.

''America'' Locomotive and Coaches, possibly Ives, U.S., black boiler, high orange cab with pair of arched windows, blue cylinders, four cast-iron wheels, clockwork, coaches (two): one orange with blue flanged roof, one blue with orange flanged roof, 22 in. l. overall. *$3,500–$4,000*

''America,'' James Fallows, U.S., ca. 1883, locomotive with black boiler, gilt stencilled, orange cab, arch-cut windows, blue roof, brass/steel clockwork movement, 12 in. l. *$3,000 plus*

20   Ives, Blakeslee & Williams Co., 294 Broadway, New York. Factory, Bridgeport, Conn.

MECHANICAL LOCOMOTIVES.

The "World's Fair."

Good
Models.
Strongly
Made.
Finely
Painted.

No. 19-000 8 inches long..Price per doz., **$6.00**

The "VULCAN."

No. 19-0 10½ inches long..Price per doz., **$9.00**

The "AMERICA."

The "VENUS."

No. 19-1 12 inches long. Per doz., **$16.50**
"   19-a 12 in. long, with gong "   **18.00**

No. 19-00 12 inches long. A good article. Price per doz., **$12.00**

The "ADONIS."

These are the best toy
Locomotives that can be
made.

   Every Locomotive
guaranteed to work per-
fectly.

Our Locomotives, with
gong attachment, are
very attractive.
   All our Locomotives
can be run in a straight
line, or a small or large
circle, by adjusting the
front axle and wheels.

No. 19-3 15 inches long...................... Per doz., **$24.00**
"   19-b 15 "   " with gong......................... "   **27.00**

*Ives 1892 catalog with lineup of some of the most coveted of all painted tin
clockwork trains. Any locomotive pictured commands prices at $2,000 and
up if offered in prime condition.*

Blue Locomotive, Hull & Stafford, U.S., ca. 1865, embossed scrollwork on boiler, turquoise windowless cab, brass belly, 8½ in. l. *$2,500–$3,000*

"Boss" Locomotive and Train, possibly Ives, U.S., 1880s, orange cab, with ornate punched-out windows, black smokestack, orange cowcatcher, gilt smokestack, green coal car, orange and gray passenger cars (two) stencilled "Union Pacific R.R.," oval-cut windows, 26 in. l. overall. ($2,500 at 1988 Perelman Museum Sale.) *$2,500–$3,000*

"Eclipse" Locomotive, George W. Brown, U.S., 1856, painted tin with green boiler, gilt-stencilled, yellow cab, orange ribbed roof, black stencilled windows, gilt bell, black, yellow striped cowcatcher, 9½ in. l. *$2,500–$3,000*

"Electric Railway" Tram, Carlisle & Finch, U.S., 1899, copper and nickel, green stained wood frame, track measurement similar to II gauge. *$800–$1,000*

"Boss" painted tin clockwork locomotive, possibly Ives, $2,500–$3,000 (because of noticeable damage, this entry brought only $825 at Skinner's June 1989 Toys & Dolls Auction).

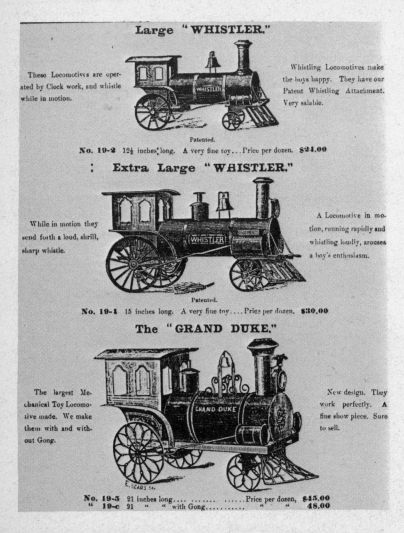

Large "WHISTLER."

These Locomotives are operated by Clock work, and whistle while in motion.

Whistling Locomotives make the boys happy. They have our Patent Whistling Attachment. Very salable.

Patented.

No. 19-2 12¼ inches long. A very fine toy...Price per dozen, $24.00

Extra Large "WHISTLER."

While in motion they send forth a loud, shrill, sharp whistle.

A Locomotive in motion, running rapidly and whistling loudly, arouses a boy's enthusiasm.

Patented.

No. 19-4 15 inches long. A very fine toy....Price per dozen, $30.00

The "GRAND DUKE."

The largest Mechanical Toy Locomotive made. We make them with and without Gong.

New design. They work perfectly. A fine show piece. Sure to sell.

No. 19-5 21 inches long.... ....Price per dozen, $45.00
"   19-c 21   "   " with Gong...........   "   "   48.00

Ives 1892 catalog shows the majestic "Grand Duke," one of the largest painted tin locomotives made. Note that catalog message is directed solely to the retailer.

"Excelsior" Locomotive, George W. Brown, U.S., tin, with high stack, wire cowcatcher, brass bell, orange, red, black stencilling and wheels, 14 in. l.   *$3,000–$3,500*

"Firefly" Locomotive, maker unknown, 1870s, black, red, with high stack, gilt-stencilled name, trim. ($1,750 at 1988 Perelman Sale.)   *$1,500–$2,000*

"Flash" Passenger Train, Fallows, U.S., ca. 1883, black, red locomotive with gilt stencil lettering, tender and two Lake Shore R.R. coaches, red, green, 33 in. l. overall, engine: 8¼ in. l.
                                                   $2,500–$3,000

Floor Train, F.V. (Emile Favre), France, 1865, open locomotive, tender, three wagons, simulated wooden boiler, painted and decaled tin, multicolor, clockwork mechanism.   *$2,000–$2,500*

Floor Train, Lutz, German, ca. 1860, open cabless locomotive with high stack, firebox with opening door, die-cast wheels, tender, flat car, passenger coach, cattle truck, deep green, black, 2:25 in. gauge.   *$3,000 plus*

Floor Train, Lutz, Germany, 1875, no-cab locomotive with high stack, tender, two wagons, painted tin, black, red, yellow.
                                                   $1,500–$2,000

Hall's Patent Floor Train, British, 1885, locomotive (only) with high stack and bell, black with gilt stripes.   *$650–$750*

"Jumbo" Locomotive, Ives, U.S., 1885, name stencilled in gilt on green cab with red roof, blue boiler, red trim and wheels, 18½ in. l.   *$1,500–$2,000*

"L'Eclair" Tinplate Floor Train, French, 1880, high flange roof on locomotive cab, tender, passenger wagon and caboose.
                                                   $3,500–$4,000

Althof Bergmann "Mars" locomotive, 1870s, blue, yellow cab, black roof, red tender, copper asphaltum passenger coach, blue "U.S. Mail" car, $2,200 at Skinner's June 1988 Toys & Dolls Auction.

Locomotive, Hull & Stafford, U.S., 1870, large, sold with cars, larger heart-shaped cast-metal wheels in rear of locomotive, 9¼ in. l.   *$2,500–$3,000*

"Mercury" ("Merkur") Floor Train, Hess, German, ca. 1875, gilt-pressed tin with rivet detail, embossed name, oversized wide-spoked wheels, lithographed paper sides on tender, red, yellow, also on coaches (two).   *$1,500–$2,000*

"Pacific Express" Train Set, Issmayer, German, 1895, gauge 1, probably the first toy train with sectional tinplate track, clockwork, locomotive with box car and two passenger cars.   *$3,000 plus*

"Paris-Lyon-Marseille," Favre, France, set, 1895, axles set on radius, high stacked engine with two wagons, clockwork.
$1,000–$1,500

"Pegasus," Stevens & Brown, U.S., 1874, stencilled and painted tinplate clockwork locomotive, red, black, gilt, brass bell, flat tin engineer who holds wire connecting turning wheels, E.C. Phelps patent, 12 in. l.   *$4,000 plus*

Platform Train Set, Favre, France, ca. 1883, nine shells on three six-wheel platforms, engine is gilt, cars are red, blue, yellow, green, each platform is 9 in. l.   *$1,100–$1,300*

"Progress," possibly Merriam, 1880s, painted and stencilled tin, blue, red, black with yellow interior, four cast-iron wheels, 15 in. l.   *$1,750–$2,000*

"Progress" pull toy locomotive, possibly Merriam, 1880s, $1,750–$2,000.

"Red Bird" Locomotive, attributed to George W. Brown, U.S., 1856–1970, tin with black wooden base, orange tin stencilled boiler, pink, white cab with yellow, black stencilled windows, gilt cylinders, 8½ in. l.   *$2,500–$3,000*

"Rotary Railway Express," maker unknown, British, 1860s, steam-type locomotive, 2-2-2, green lead body with gilt smokestack, tender with green and gilt body, two parlor cars: one red, silver, one brown, silver.   *$600–$700*

"Toy" Locomotive, George Brown, U.S., 1870, three-wheeled, small wheel centered on wooden base pivots so train can move in circles, red, black, yellow, 3½ in. l.   *$2,000–$3,000*

"Union" Locomotive, Ives, U.S., 1880s, yellow cab with painted black windows.   *$500–$600*

"Union," Ives, U.S., 1880s, yellow cab with black boiler, painted black windows, sold separately or with two passenger cars. (An example in average condition sold for $1,000 at Perelman Sale in 1988.)   *$1,000–$1,500*

"Union Pacific" Train Set, Ives, U.S., 1870s, painted and lacquered tin locomotive, elaborately punched-out windows, orange cab, smokestack and cowcatcher, double-tiered whistle, red cast-iron wheels, coal car is green with white stripes, lion decal on each side, orange passenger car gilt stencilled, 32 in. l. overall.
$3,500–$4,000

"U.S. Grant" Locomotive, George W. Brown, U.S., 1870, pull-toy very similar to "Excelsior" design except the latter was clockwork-powered.
$4,000–$5,000

"Venus," possibly Althof Bergman, U.S., ca. 1870s, painted punch pattern is a Bergman hallmark, red, black; 6 in. l.
$2,000–$2,500

"Queen Victoria's Royal Train," German, possibly Lutz, made specifically for British royal family, modeled after first royal saloon and train of early 1840s, engine, tender, three coach cars, deep green, maroon, gilt with figural crown and royal crest, glass windows.
Value Indeterminate

"Victory," Ives Blakesly, U.S., 1870s, swivel front wheels, clockwork, 9 in. l., ornate punched-out windows.
$2,500–$3,000

"Vulcan," Ives, U.S., 1880s, painted tin with name stencilled in gilt on boiler, brass bell, red cab, black boiler, 10¾ in. l.
$1,500–$2,000

"World's Fair," Ives, U.S., 1870, locomotive 1892–1893, black boiler, red cab and smokestack, gilt lettering, high cab, large rear wheels, small front wheels, 8 in. l., honors World Columbian Exposition of '93.
$2,500–$3,000

"Zephyr" Locomotive and Coal Car, maker unknown, U.S., 1880–1890, locomotive is green and black, gilt-stencilled, pair of ornate cast-iron back wheels, tin front wheels, green coal car, 12½ in. overall.
$2,500–$3,000

Wooden Lithographed and Painted Floor Trains

The earliest wooden trains hark back to the 1840s, when wood-carvers in the German region of Erz Gebirge created crude but fanciful examples with wheel action. In the United States, the Tower Guild of South Hingham, Massachusetts, and Joel Ellis of Springfield, Vermont, led the way with wooden toys and trains.

Many of the early versions were of plain pine; later they were handpainted or stained. Stencilling was introduced before 1850 and lithographed paper glued on wood in the 1870s. Another interesting variation is the toy train with ink applied directly to the plain surface, with printed decorations impressed directly into the wood, leaving indentations.

Leading wooden train practitioners included Charles M. Crandall Co., Montrose, Pennsylvania; Milton Bradley Co., Springfield, Massachusetts; W.S. Reed Toy Co., Leominster, Massachusetts; and R. Bliss Manufacturing, Pawtucket, Rhode Island. Interest in lithographed wooden toys seems to have waned in the early 1900s, although Gibbs Manufacturing of Canton, Ohio, and Fisher-Price of East Aurora, New York, market cartoon novelty toys up to the present day.

Adirondack Railroad train set; R. Bliss, 1889–1895, 28 in. l. (each car filled with flat alphabet blocks), $1,000–$1,400.

"Adirondack Railroad" Wooden Floor Train, Bliss, 1890s, lithographed paper-on-wood, engine with number "61," baggage, express car, and "Saratoga" passenger coach, 28 in. l.

$1,000–$1,400

"Barnum Circus Train," R. Bliss, 1895, two sizes: 19 in. and 28 in. l. (complete with die-cut animals). $950–$1,050

"Brownie Picnic Train," R. Bliss, 1895, locomotive with two gondolas (open) containing 21 Brownie cutout figures, lithograph paper-on-wood. $1,200–$1,500

"Central Park" Lilliputian Railway Coach, W.S. Reed, ca. 1877, "Central Park," "Broadway," and "Reed's Lilliputian Coach" destinations appear along side of coach; silver-striped double-tiered roof with 10 passengers in coach, two horses pull coach, 14½ in. l. $1,700–$2,200

"Chicago Limited" Wooden Floor Train, Bliss, 1891, lithograph paper-on-wood, locomotive, tender, two passenger coaches, 48 in. l. $1,200–$1,500

Clark Locomotive and Tender, D.P. Clark & Co., 1900s, wooden steam-type friction, 4-4-0, cast-iron wheels, 17¼ in. l., black with red trim, white and gilt striping. $1,000–$1,300

Clark Locomotive, D.P. Clark & Co., 1900s, wooden steam-type friction, 4-4-0, headlamp with tin center, iron wheels, 12¾ in. l., orange, black, and gold trim.   *$1,000–$1,300*

"Empire State Express," R. Bliss, 1895, 4-4-0 locomotive with one 12-wheel passenger car.   *$850–$900*

Erz Gebirge Wooden Train Set, German, 1870, engine, two flat cars and caboose.   *$150–$200*

"Fairy" Railroad Wooden Floor Train, Bliss, 1890s, locomotive, tender, and two cars, lithographed paper-on-wood, 26 in. l.
                                                                $900–$1,000

"Golden Gate Special" Wooden Floor Train, Bliss, 1890s, lithographed paper-on-wood, locomotive, tender, and passenger coach, 36 in. l.   *$1,200–$1,500*

"Gravel" Train, R. Bliss, 1895, locomotive with three gravel cars with detachable standing brakeman, 24 in. l.   *$650–$700*

"Hercules" Wooden Floor Train, Milton Bradley, 1895, lithographed paper-on-wood "Hercules" appears on engine cab, "Atlantic & Pacific R.R." across top of coach.   *$800–$1,200*

"Jackson Park" Chicago Trolley Car, W.S. Reed, ca. 1893, double-tiered roof with antennae, "World Columbian Exposition," "Prarie Av.," "Lincoln Park," and "State St." destinations appear along upper tier, driver and brakeman (litho paper-on-wood), 17½ in. l.   *$1,500–$2,000*

"Lincoln Park Railroad" Wooden Floor Train, Bliss, 1893, lithographed paper-on-wood, eight-wheel engine, mail/express car, passenger car, 18 in. l., contained set of flat blocks and two picture puzzles.   *$1,200–$1,500*

"Menagerie Train," R. Bliss, 1895, with locomotive and two cage wagons with animals, 33 in. l.   *$850–$950*

"New York Central Railroad" Train, R. Bliss, 1889, 1895, locomotive with baggage/express car and passenger coach, 28 in. l.
$900–$1,000

"Nickel Plate Line R.R. Train," Nos. 295 and 296, R. Bliss, 1891, 12-wheel, high-stack locomotive with "N. Plate" just under cab window, number appears on tender, set includes a U.S. mail car and passenger car, 27½ in. l. and 40 in. l. *$750–$800*

"Reed's Palace Car" and *"America" Locomotive,* W.S. Reed, 1877, printed wood, 2-2-0 wheel alignment, paper label under coach roof, ". . . Every Boy His Own Engineer," black stencilling on natural wood finish, 32 in. l. *$900–$1,200*

"Reindeer Train" Wood Train Set, Milton Bradley, 1890, engine, tender, four cage cars, litho paper-on-wood plus stencilled wood, made to be assembled in puzzle fashion, cage cars have names of various animals: tiger, monkey, bison, bear, etc., 45 in. l.
$800–$1,000

"Stock and Lumber" Train, R. Bliss, 1889, 18 in. l. *$550–$650*

Wooden Floor Train, probably R. Bliss, 1880, lithographed paper-on-wood, engine, mail car, and coach (removable roofs to store blocks and other toys). *$850–$1,200*

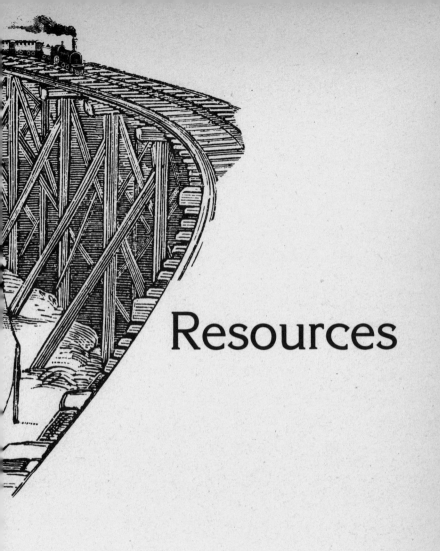

Resources

Toy and Model Train Auctioneers

United States

Noel Barrett Auctions & Appraisals
Carversville, PA 18913
(215) 297-5109
Barrett and his then partner, Bill Bertoia, managed the historic Atlanta Toy Museum Sale in 1986.

Butterfield & Butterfield
1244 Sutter St.
San Francisco, CA 94109
(415) 673-1362

Christie's East
219 East 67th St.
New York, NY 10021
(212) 570-4141

Continental Auctions
447 Stratford Rd.
P.O. Box 193
Sheboygan, WI 53081
Contact: Heinz A. Mueller

Gabriel's Auctioneers/ Appraisers
P.O. Box 390
Westwood, MA 02090
(617) 329-7484

Greenberg's Auctions
Timonium Fairgrounds Auction Arena
Timonium, MD
Mailing Address:
Bruce Greenberg
Greenberg Pub. Co.,
7566 Main St.
Sykesville, MD 21784
(301) 795-7447

*Hake's Americana &
   Collectibles*
P.O. Box 1444
York, PA 17405
(717) 848-1333
Mail Order: Ted Hake

Gene Harris Antique Center
P.O. Box 476
203 South 18th Ave.
Marshalltown, IA 50158
(515) 752-0600

Kruse Auctioneers
Kruse Building
Auburn, IN 46706
(219) 925-5401

Mapes Auctioneers
1600 Vestal Pky. West
Vestal, NY 13850
(607) 754-1193

Ted Maurer Auctions
1931 North Charlotte St.
Pottstown, PA 19464
(215) 323-1573

Mid-Hudson Galleries
2 Idlewild Ave.
Cornwall-on-Hudson, NY
   12520
(914) 534-7828
Auctioneer/Appraiser: Joanne
   C. Grant

New England Auction Gallery
P.O. Box 2273-T
West Peabody, MA 01960
Mail Order
(508) 535-3140
Contact: Debby and
   Marty Krim

Richard Opfer Auctions
1919 Greenspring Ave.
Timonium, MD 21093
(301) 252-5035
Contact: Rick Opfer

*Phillips Auctioning &
   Appraising*
Phillips Ltd.
406 East 79th St.
New York, NY 10021
(212) 570-4830
Contacts: Henry Kurtz and
   Eric Alberta
Toy Consultant: Jack Herbert

Lloyd Ralston Auctions
447 Stratfield Rd.
Fairfield, CT 06432
(203) 366-3399
Contact: Lloyd W. and Glenn
   S. Ralston

Robert W. Skinner Inc.
Route 117, 357 Main St.
Bolton, MA 01740
(508) 779-5144
Toy/Doll Consultant:
   Mildrid Ewing

Sotheby's
1334 York Ave. at 72nd St.
New York, NY 10021
(212) 606-7424
Collectibles Consultant:
  Dana Hawkes

Europe

Christie's South Kensington
85 Old Brompton Rd.
London SW7, 3LD, England
(441) 581-7611
Contact: Tom Rose

Galerie Andre
Place de Londres 13
B 1050 Bruxelles, Belgium
32/2/511.17.18 (Europe)
011/21/2/511.17.18 (From U.S.)

Hanseatisches Auctionhaus
Für Historica
Husken/Schafer OHG
Neur Wall 75-2000 Hamburg 36
West Germany
40/363137-38

Phillips Blenstock House
7 Blenheim St.
New Bond St.
London, England WIY OAS
01-629 6602

Weinheimer Auktionhaus
  Rolf Richter
Karlsruher Strasse 2/8
D 6940 Weinheim
West Germany
06201/15997

Collecting Organizations

American Flyer Collectors
    Club
P.O. 13269
Pittsburgh, PA 15243

Lehmann Gross Bahn
Model Railroad Club
3329 White Castle Way
Decatur, GA 30030
(404) 987-2773

Lionel Collectors Club of
    America
P.O. Box 479 (Business Office)
La Salle, IL 61301

Lionel Collectors Club of
    America
P.O. Box 11851
Lexington, KY 40511

Lionel Operating Train Society
7408 138 Place N.E.
Redmond, WA 98052-4008
(206) 885-6636 (evenings and
    weekends)
Contact: Geoffrey Swan

Märklin Enthusiasts of America
P.O. Box 189
Beverly, NJ 08010

National Association of
    S Gaugers
280 Gordon Rd.
Matawan, NJ 07747
Contact: Mike Ferraro

National Model Railroad
    Association
4121 Cromwell Rd.
Chattanooga, TN 37421
(615) 892-2846

Toy Train Collectors Society
109 Howedale Dr.
Rochester, NY 14616
Contact: Louis A. Bohn

*Toy Train Museum of the Train
    Collectors Association*
Stroudsburg, PA 18360

*Toy Train Operating Society
    (T.T.O.S)*
25 West Walnut St.
Suite 408
West Pasadena, CA 91103
(818) 578-0673

*Train Collectors Association
    (T.C.A.)*
P.O. Box 248
Stroudsburg, PA 18360
(717) 687-8623

Virginia Train Collectors, Inc.
P.O. Box 7114
Richmond, VA 23221

Toy Train Museums

United States

Lincoln Train Museum
Gettysburg, PA 17325

Lionel Train & Seashell
Museum
Sarasota, FL 33580

Nashville Toy Museum
2613 McGavock Pike
Nashville, TN 37214
Edward and Pamela Lannon
Collection of Transportation
Toys.

Toy Train Museum of the Train
Collectors Association
Stroudsburg, PA 18360
(717) 687-8976

Washington Dolls House & Toy
Museum
5236 44th St. N.W.
Washington, DC 20015
(202) 244-0024

Europe

London Toy & Model Museum
23 Craven Hill
London, W2, 01-262
262 7905/9450

Toy Museum/Matlock Bath
18 A North Parade
Matlock Bath
Derbyshire, England
Telephone: Matlock 56380
Large collection of trains.

Vintage Toy & Train Museum
Field's Dept. Store in the Marketplace
Gidmouth, England
David Salisbury Collection.

Model Railroad Shows
and Meets

*Atlanta Antique Toy, Doll, &
   Train Show*
Sheraton Century Center Hotel
Atlanta, GA
February and Fall shows.
Information: Anthea Knowles,
   Jack's Wall, Littlehempston,
   Nr. Totnes, Devon, England
   TQ9 6LY

*Greenberg's Great Train, Doll-
   house, & Toy Shows*
Held at least six times a year
   at various locations across
   the United States. Information: Greenburg Publishing
   Co., 7566 Main St., Sykesville, MD 21784, (301) 795-
   7447

*Lionel Collectors Club of
   America International
   Convention*
Held in July.
Information: Ray F. Long,
   University of South Carolina
   Coliseum, 3702 Greenbriar
   Dr., Columbia, SC, 29206,
   (803) 782-1087

Railroad Mania Show
Grand View Farm Auction
   Hall
Derry, NH
Annual show held last Satur-
   day in September.
Information: P.O. Box 1662,
Lewiston, ME 04241, (207)
   783-6843

St. Vincent DePaul's Model Train, Toy, & Doll Show
1510 DePaul St.
Elmont, NY 11003
1990 show schedule: Jan. 14, April 1, June 3, Oct. 28, Dec. 2.
Dealer and General Information: (516) 352-2127 or (516) 486-6658

Train Collectors of America (T.C.A.)
State Fairgrounds Exhibit Hall
York, PA
Semiannual shows (Spring/ Fall)
Information: T.C.A., P.O. Box 248, Strasburg, PA 17579

Westchester Toy & Train Associates Show
Bergen-Passaic Palisades, Wayne, NJ
Held in September
Information: (914) 235-0893

Note: There are countless train shows which are not regularly scheduled throughout a given year. For advanced notice consult such publications as *Classic Toy Trains, Antique Toy World, Antiques & The Arts Weekly, Model Railroader,* and other trade publications (see "Train Collector Publications").

Train Collector Publications

United States

Antique Toy World
P.O. Box 34509
Chicago, IL 60634
(312) 725-0633

Classic Toy Trains
Kalmbach Publishing Co.
21027 Crossroads Circle
P.O. Box 1612
Waukesha, WI 53187
(414) 272-2060

In-Scale
Hundman Publishing
5115 Montecello Dr.
Edmonds, WA 98020
(206) 743-2607
Bi-monthly.

Live Steam
P.O. Box 629
Traverse City, MI 49684
(616) 946-3712
Monthly. For live steamers and large-scale railroaders. Incorporates *Steam Power Quarterly*.

Mainline Modeler
Hundman Publishing
5115 Monticello Dr.
Edmonds, WA 98020
(206) 743-2607
Monthly.

Model Railroader
Kalmbach Publishing Co.
21027 Crossroads Circle
P.O. Box 1612
Waukesha, WI 53187
(414) 272-2060

Railfan & Railroad
Carstons Publications, Inc.
Fredon-Springdale Rd.
P.O. Box 700
Newton, NJ 07860
(201) 383-3355

Railroad Model Craftsman
Carstons Publications, Inc.
Fredon-Springdale Rd.
P.O. Box 700
Newton, NJ 07860
(201) 383-3355

S. Gaugian
Heimburger
    House Publishing Co.
310 Lathrop Ave.
River Forest, IL 60305
Bi-monthly.

Trains Illustrated
Kalmbach Publishing Co.
21027 Crossroads Circle,
    P.O. Box 1612
Waukesha, WI 53187
(414) 796-8776
Quarterly.

The following weekly general antiques publications provide listings of forthcoming train auctions, shows, and meets.

Antiques & The Arts
Weekly (Newtown Bee)
Newtown, CT 06470
Weekly.

Antique Toy World
P.O. Box 34509
Chicago, IL 60634
Monthly.

Great Britain

Continental Modeller
Peco Publications & Publicity Ltd.
Beer, Seaton, Devon
EX12 3NA

Model Railways
Model & Allied Publications
P.O. Box 35
Wolsey House, Wolsey Road
Memel Hempstead, Herts
HP2 4SS

Australia

Australian Model Railway
    Magazine
P.O. Box 235
Matraville, NSW

Glossary

"American." Nickname for a 4-4-0 wheel configuration.

Articulated Locomotive. Engine with two sets of wheels and cylinders which pivot on separate frames.

"Atlantic." Nickname for a 4-4-2 wheel arrangement.

Bi-Polar. A type of electric locomotive innovated by Minneapolis & St. Paul Railroad in the 1920s, which served as prototype for virtually every major U.S. train model manufacturer.

"Bird Cage." Raised roof section for guard's look-out on certain vintage coaches or vans.

Bogie. British term for a low truck-swiveling assembly in front or behind a locomotive's driving wheels. American term is *Truck.*

Bunker. Container for coal on a tank engine.

Cab-Forward. American steam locomotive-type with cab at *Head End.*

Caboose. The rear car that often contains guards, workmen, and their equipment. British refer to it as a *Van.* In railroad slang, a.k.a. *Hack* or *Shanty.*

Camelback. Locomotive with the cab astride the boiler; the fireman rode under a hood at the rear; a.k.a. "Mother Hubbard."

Carpet Runners. Tin, cast-iron or sheet-steel toy trains with smooth wheel rims rather than grooved; did not run on tracks but was spring-activated or handpropelled; a.k.a. "Floor Runner."

Cast Iron. A typical material for toy engines and tenders in the 1880s and 1890s. An American phenomenon, led by J. & E. Stevens of Cromwell, Connecticut. Molten gray high-carbon iron is handpoured into sandcasting molds; usually cast in halves, which are then mated and bolted or riveted to form a complete toy.

Climax. Type of articulated locomotive.

Clockwork. One of the basic activating mechanisms for trains; interlocking toothed gears are driven by the spring uncoiling, animating the toy for as long as 30 minutes.

Co-Co. Diesel or electric locomotive with two six-wheeled trucks, all wheel-driven; a.k.a. "C.C."

Combine. Pairing of model baggage and club cars.

Consists. Another term for the rolling stock that accompanies the engine in a train set; a makeup usually associated with freight trains.

Cowcatcher. A projecting device in front of American locomotives to clear any obstacle that may lie ahead on the track; a.k.a. "pilot."

Crossover. Track and switches that facilitate trains crossing from one parallel track to another.

Decapod. Refers to a 10-wheeled clockwork model patterned after a British experimental locomotive that featured 10 driving wheels; ca. early 1900s.

Diamond-Stacker. American-type locomotive with a smokestack or chimney, coned both ways to cool off sparks.

Die-Casting. A technique for creating metal objects by forcing a molten alloy through a mold and sustaining pressure until the toy engine or other object has hardened.

Dome. A round projection on locomotive boilers which houses steam controls or sand.

Dome Car. U.S. passenger car with observation dome on top.

Dribbler. Nickname for British solid brass steam-powered engines made from 1840s to the turn of the century; so named because of the vapor or water trail it left from steam cylinder; a.k.a. "Piddler."

E-Unit. A reversing device in model locomotives.

Fallen Flags. A reference to the great, but now obsolete or defunct, railroad lines of yore (i.e., the New York, Ontario & Western; the Lehigh Valley).

Fish Plate. A bar joining ends of rails.

Flange. Portion of railway wheel that is "stepped" to keep the wheel running on track.

Frog. Term applying to model track; a junction between two arms of a turnout (originally known as points); grooved for the wheel flanges; so called because of its resemblance to a frog.

Gandy Dancer. American slang for laborer who lays track, grades roadbeds, etc.

Gauge. Width between outer rails of track, normally determined by the scale of a specific manufacturer's line. Lionel, in recent years, is typified by O gauge, or 1½ in. spanning outer rail; contemporary American Flyers are S gauge, or ⅞-in. span. Most model trains today are HO (Half O) or ⅝ in. between rails.

Gondola. Open freight car; American term.

Head End. Locomotive front (American term). HEP is acronym for Head-End Power.

Heralds. The insignias of the legendary lines which are an integral part of railroads' grand history.

Highball. To speed; a sign to proceed; so called because of old ball-shaped signals.

Hollow-Casting. A technique for creating light-weight objects whereby a lead alloy is poured into a mold, then quickly emptied to form a hollow shell.

Journal. Part of a train engine or car's shaft or axle that rests on its bearings.

Layout. A complete railroad system comprising engine, rolling stock, accessories; limited solely by the imagination of the collector.

Lineside Equipment. Telephone poles, small tanks, sandloaders, express trucks, unloading ramps—any material or equipment used along the right of way.

Lithographed Paper-on-Wood. Many of the wood-sawed toys, including trains, produced in the late 19th century were decorated with lithographed paper glued on the wood.

Model Train. An exact replica in scale of a full-size operating train; known for strict adherence to detail; usually produced in limited quantity of higher quality materials as opposed to most electric toy trains.

Narrow Gauge. Introduced in the late 1940s and early 1950s, largely in kit form to accommodate G-gauge, N-gauge, and HO-type model trains.

"Nuremberg Style." Tinplate trains by German makers Bing, Carette, Kraus, Bub, and later Märklin that were known for detailed solder construction and handpainted and varnished finish; ca. early 1900s.

Outline. The features or distinguishing characteristics of a locomotive. *American outline:* typically had a tall smokestack, a large headlamp, a bell, and no splashers. *British outline:* rather small cab; low smokestack (q.v.), funnel or chimney; whistle and splashers. *German outline:* most often a large cab; occasionally splashers. *Electric outline:* applies to a locomotive that deceptively appears to run on electricity, but in many cases is clockwork-activated. *Steam outline:* by the same token, it looks as if the engine is steam-propelled, but in actuality may be driven by electricity or clockwork.

Pantograph. Diamond-shaped device located atop a carriage or locomotive that collects electric current from overhead wires.

Point. Old term (British) for diverging track; Americans refer to it as *Turnout.*

Prototype. The name modelers apply to real full-size engines and trains.

Pullman. U.S. builder of coaches and other rolling stock; a generic term for luxury coaches.

Rail Fans. Traditionalists who enjoy watching real trains and may not necessarily be modelers or collectors.

RCS. Remote Control System acronym; a type of Lionel track for unloading and uncoupling cars later replaced by UCS.

Reefer. Railroad jargon for refrigerator car.

Rolling Stock. All of the remaining series of cars or coaches attached to the locomotive to form a complete train or *Rake* (British term).

Saddle-Tank. A locomotive which carries its own water in tanks supported on, or by, the boiler.

Scale. Size ratio between the real thing and the toy or model train, usually denoted in fractions. Model Lionels are approximately 1/48th the size of actual counterparts. Toy tinplate trains are rarely in scale and tend to run smaller than they should be.

Scratch-Built. Handmade models from start to finish.

Sheet Metal. A popular material for trains and other toys; metal is rolled into a thin plate; normally brass, steel or copper.

Shunting. Moving rack or rolling stock to form train; Americans refer to this as *Switching*.

Single. Type of locomotive with but one pair of driving wheels.

Six-Coupled. An engine with six driving wheels.

Smokestack. Chimney or funnel of a locomotive.

Spectacle Plate. Vertical metal plate found on vintage locomotives which provide protection from the elements. Two round windows give semblance of spectacles, hence the name.

Splasher. Mudguard for the engine that protects passengers and conductors at stations from being splashed.

Standard Gauge. A 2 1/8-in. gauge introduced by Lionel in 1906, which in reality was nonstandard or an orphan gauge, yet it was christened by Joshua Lionel Cowen in a brilliant bit of one-upmanship as "Standard gauge."

Steeple-Cab. A cab with a high arched central portion of its roof, resembling a steeple.

Stock Rail. Moving part of turnout (point/switch).

Storkleg. An engine's two small plus two large driving wheel configuration, so called because of its resemblance to a stork standing on one leg.

Teakettle. A reference to any old locomotive, particularly a leaky one.

Tender. Car carrying water and coal, normally pulled directly behind locomotive.

Tinplate. A term often used interchangeably with a toy train; vintage electric toy trains were made of tinplated iron to deter rusting and facilitate soldering parts together. Later lithographed tinplate toys and trains were assembled with tabs and slots so as not to damage the lithographed surface.

Toy Railroads. Trademark term used by Ives Co., Bridgeport, Connecticut, in 1907. Ives took the leadership by offering not only individual trains, but an entire system of stations, tunnels, and other accessories as well.

Toy Train. Intended primarily for child's play; mass produced in sizable numbers; intended to only approximate or capture the imagery of the genuine article.

Truck. A low truck operating on one or more pairs of wheels, attached before or aft the locomotive's driving wheels or to the ends of an extended railway carriage. Moves by a pivot on which it swivels freely on turns. British refer to it as a *Bogie.*

Turnout. A British term for switch, also often used by U.S. modelers.

2-2-Type. Any engine with a wheel arrangement of two front, two driving, and no trailing wheels.

Well Tank. A type of locomotive which carries its own water on its underside.

Whyte System. Method of describing locomotive wheel configuration; i.e., 4-6-2.

Wide Gauge. Ives' terminology for 2⅛-in. *Standard gauge,* which they adopted in 1921; Lionel had copyrighted the latter phrase in 1912.

Wildcat. A runaway locomotive.

Wind-Splitter. Early streamline-style locomotive associated with Germans and French; featured V-shaped chimneys, domes, cab and boiler front; a.k.a. "Coupe Vents."

Wye (or "Y"). Track system with three switches and three legs enabling train to turn around.

Bibliography

Baecker, Carlernst, Hass, Dieter, and Jeanmarie Claude: *Technical Toys in the Course of Time,* 10 Vols. on Märklin. Hobby Haas, Verlag, Frankfort am Main, Germany, 1975–1983.

Bradshaw, John: *Greenberg's Guide to Kusan Trains* (American Model Toys & Kris Model Trains). Greenberg Publishing, Sykesville, MD, 1988.

Carlson, Pierce: *Toy Trains/A History.* Justin Knowles Publishing Group, Exeter, Devon, England, 1986.

Coluzzi, Count Antonio Giansanti: *The Trains on Avenue de Rumine.* Crown Publishers, New York, 1984. (First published by New Cavendish Books/Editions, Serge Godin, 1982.)

Fernandez, Don: *Trains/Railroading for Grown-up Boys.* The Encyclopedia of Collectibles, Time-Life Books, Inc., New York, 1980.

Garrison: *Model Railroading in Small Spaces.* Blue Summit Books, Blue Ridge Summit, PA (Tab Books), 1982.

Greenberg, Bruce C.: *Greenberg's Guide to Ives Trains/1901–1932.* Greenberg Publishing, Sykesville, MD, 1987.

Herly, R.: *Advanced Model Railroading.* Simmons Boardman Publishing Co., New York, 1955.

Hertz, Louis H.: *Messrs. Ives of Bridgeport.* Mark Haber Co., Wethersfield, CT, 1950.

——: *New Roads to Adventure in Model Railroading.* Simmons Boardman Publishing Co., New York, 1952.

——: *Collecting Model Trains.* Mark Haber & Co., Wethersfield, CT, 1956.

——: *Riding the Tinplate Rails.* Model Craftsman Publishing Co., 1944.

——: *The Toy Collector.* Hawthorn Books/Thomas Y. Crowell Co., 1967; Funk & Wagnells, New York, 1969.

Hollander, Ron: *All Aboard/The Story of Joshua Lionel Cowen and His Lionel Train Company.* Workman Publishing, New York, 1981.

Hubbard, John: *Williams Trains.* Greenberg Publishing, Sykesville, MD, 1988.

Kimball, Steven (Editor): *Greenberg's Guide to American Flyer Prewar O Gauge.* Greenberg Publishing, Sykesville, MD, 1987.

La Voie, Ronald (Editor): *Greenberg's Guide to Lionel Trains/ 1945–1969, Vol. II.* Greenberg Publishing, Sykesville, MD, 1988.

Lines, Richard (Compiler): *The Art of Hornby/Sixty Years of Model Railway Literature.* Kaye & Ward Ltd., Kingswood, England, 1983.

Mallerich, Dallas J. III: *Greenberg's Guide to Athearn Trains.* Greenberg Publishing, Sykesville, MD, 1988.

Martin, Joseph: *World of Model Railways.* Percifal Marshall, London, 1960.

Matzke, Eric J.: *Greenberg's Guide to Marx Trains,* Vol. I. Greenberg Publishing, Sykesville, MD, 1985. Revised 1989.

McComas, Tom and Tuohy, James: *A Collector's Guide and History to Lionel Trains: Vol. I, Prewar O Gauge.* TM Productions, Wilmette, IL, 1975.

——: *Vol. III, Standard Gauge.* TM Productions, Wilmette, IL, 1978.

McHoy, Peter: *The World Guide to Model Trains.* Greenwich House (distributed by Crown), New York, 1983.

Minns, Jonathan: *Model Railway Engines*. Octopus Ltd., London, 1962 (reproduced in 1973).

Monaghan, Robert P.: *Greenberg's Guide to Märklin 00/HO*. Greenberg Publishing, Sykesville, MD, 1989.

O'Brien, Richard: *American Premium Guide to Electric Trains*. Books America, Inc., Florence, AL, 1986. (Price guide)

O'Neill, Richard: *The Collector's Encyclopedia of Metal Toys*. Crescent Books, New York, 1988.

Ottley, John R.: *Greenberg's Guide to LGB Trains*. Greenberg Publishing, Sykesville, MD, 1989.

Parry-Crooke, Charlotte: *Märklin 1895–1914*. Denys Ingram Publishers, London, 1983.

Paust, Gil: *Model Railroading: How to Plan, Build & Maintain Trains & Pikes*. Doubleday, New York, 1981.

Reder, Gustav: *Clockwork, Steam and Electric: A History of Model Railways Up to 1939*. Ian Allan, Shepperton, Middlesex, England, 1972.

Rohlfing, Christian F. (Editor): *Greenberg's Guide to Lionel Trains/1901–1942, Vol. I*. Greenberg Publishing, Sykesville, MD, 1988.

Schleicher, Robert: *Model Railroading With LGB*. Greenberg Publishing, Sykesville, MD, 1989.

Spong, Neldred and Raymond: *Flywheel-Powered Toys*. Antique Toy Collectors of America, 1979.

Sutton, David: *Complete Book of Model Railroading*. Castle Books, New York, 1964.

T.C.A. (Train Collectors of America) Lionel Book Committee: *Lionel Trains "Standard of the World" 1900–1943*, 2nd Ed. T.C.A., Stroudsburg, PA, 1989. (Expanded edition, 760 color photographs, hard bound, 250 pages; copies may be ordered through T.C.A. at P.O. Box 248, Stroudsburg, PA 18360; 1st Ed. printed 1976, edited by Donald S. Fraley.)

Williams, Guy: *The World of Model Trains*. Chartwell (Andre Deutsch Publishing), London, 1970.

Index

TOYS ARE *NOT* JUST FOR KIDS!

The Official® Identification and Price Guide to Collectible Toys is a *must* for the beginning and expert collector!

RICHARD FRIZ* explores the wide range of collectible toys, from Disneyana, military miniatures, and transportation vehicles to riding toys and world's fair toys.

● Over 100 photos...8 pages of dramatic color...fully indexed!

THIS USEFUL GUIDE PROVES TOYS ARE NOT ONLY FUN, THEY'RE BIG BU$INESS, TOO!

*Richard Friz is the author of *The Official® Price Guide to Political Memorabilia* and *The Official® Price Guide to World's Fair Memorabilia* (House of Collectibles: New York).

HOUSE OF COLLECTIBLES
201 East 50th Street
New York, New York 10022

Please send me *The Official® Identification and Price Guide to Collectible Toys*, 5th Ed.... 0-876-37803-3...$10.95. I am enclosing $_____ (add $2.00 for the first book and 50¢ for each additional book to cover postage and handling). Send check or money order—no cash or C.O.D.'s, please. Prices and numbers are subject to change without notice.

Name_____

Address_____

City_____ State_____ Zip Code_____

Allow at least 4 weeks for delivery.

DOLLS — ENCHANTING AND COLLECTIBLE!

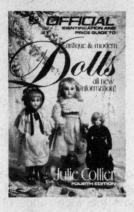

The Official® Identification and Price Guide to Antique and Modern Dolls explores the fascinating world of dolls, from Dresden china faces and porcelain figurines to Victorian fashion dolls and contemporary cuddly babies.

This invaluable sourcebook, in a unique format, offers the most comprehensive information on doll collectibles!

★ Over 500 photos...lavish eight-page color insert...fully indexed!

HOUSE OF COLLECTIBLES
201 East 50th Street
New York, New York 10022

Please send me *The Official® Identification and Price Guide to Antique and Modern Dolls,* 4th Ed. . . . 0-876-37091-1 . . . $12.95. I am enclosing $_____ (add $2 for the first book and 50¢ for each additional copy to cover postage and handling). Send check or money order—no cash or C.O.D.'s, please. Prices and numbers are subject to change without notice.

Name _____

Address _____

City _____ State _____ Zip Code _____

Allow at least 4 weeks for delivery.